Pennsylvania

Douglas Root
Photography by Jerry Irwi

COMPASS AMERICAN GUIDES
An Imprint of Fodor's Travel Publications, Inc.

Pennsylvania

First Edition

Copyright ©2000 Fodor's Travel Publications, Inc.
Maps Copyright © 2000 Fodor's Travel Publications, Inc.
Compass American Guides and colophon are trademarks of Random House, Inc.
Fodor's is a registered trademark of Random House, Inc.

Compass American Guides, Inc., 5332 College Ave., Suite 201, Oakland, CA 94618, USA
ISBN : 0-679-00182-4

Editors: Kit Duane, Jessica Fisher, Pennfield Jensen, Nancy Falk
Food & Lodging: Julia Dillon, Michael Oliver
Creative Director: Christopher Burt
Managing Editor: Kit Duane
Designers: Christopher Burt, Julia Dillon

Cover design: Siobhan O'Hare
Galley design: Kit Duane
Map design: Mark Stroud, Moon Cartography
Production House: Twin Age Ltd., Hong Kong
Manufactured in China

10 9 8 7 6 5 4 3 2 1

PUBLISHER'S ACKNOWLEDGMENTS

The publishers would like to express their gratitude to **Randall H. Cooley** and the **Allegheny Heritage Development Corporation** for making this project possible. Special thanks are also due to **Mark Biddle** and **Stephen Elkins** of the **Independence Hall Association** for their help in getting the project off the ground.

Abby Aldrich Rockefeller Folk Art Center, Williamsburg, Virginia p. 91; **Carnegie Library of Pittsburg** p. 38; **Cumberland County Historical Society**, Carlisle, PA p. 162; **Drake Well Museum**, Titusville, PA p. 268; **Heritage Center Museum**, Lancaster, PA pp. 116, 117, 120; **Historical Society of Pennsylvania, Library and Archives**, Pittsburgh, PA pp. 16 (#1833.1), 25 (#Bd61 B531.2 plate 15); **Historical Society of Western Pennsylvania Museum** pp. 208, 209, 242; Library of Congress pp. 33, 37, 79, 156 (both), 210, 211, 222, 254; **Metropolitan Museum of Art**, New York p. 95; **National Museum of American History Archives** p. 212; **Philadelphia Museum of Art** pp. 18, 48, 77, 119; **Shelburne Museum**, Shelburne, Vermont p. 23; **State Museum of Pennsylvania, Pennsylvania Historical and Museum Commission** pp. 100, 190; **Underwood Photo Archives**, San Francisco pp. 145, 155, 165, 225; **Valley Forge Historical Society** p. 32; **Washington and Jefferson College Historical Collection** p. 240; **Westmoreland Museum of American Art** pp. 232, 236, 241; **Yale University Art Gallery** p. 31 (Trumbull Collection #1832.3).

Thanks are due to **Judy Ross** of the **Westmoreland Museum of American Art**, Jessica Puma of the **Philadelphia Museum of Art**, and **Wendell Zercher** of the **Heritage Center Museum of Lancaster** for the gracious use of images from those museum collections.

Compass would also like to thank **Ellen Klages** for proofreading and **Cheryl Koehler** for map corrections and the essay on p. 245.

To my two grandmothers, Helen and Esther, who dearly loved their husbands and children but dreamed of traveling the world.

CONTENTS

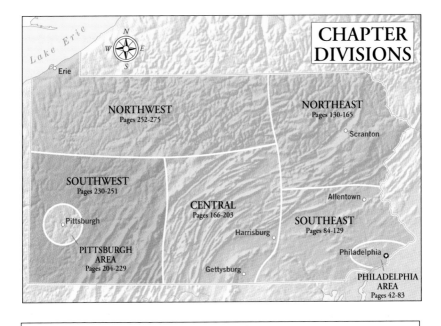

CHAPTER DIVISIONS

NORTHWEST
Pages 252-275

NORTHEAST
Pages 130-165

Erie

Scranton

SOUTHWEST
Pages 230-251

CENTRAL
Pages 166-203

Allentown

Pittsburgh

Harrisburg

SOUTHEAST
Pages 84-129

PITTSBURGH
AREA
Pages 204-229

Gettysburg

Philadelphia

PHILADELPHIA
AREA
Pages 42-83

Topical Essays and Literary Extracts

Maps

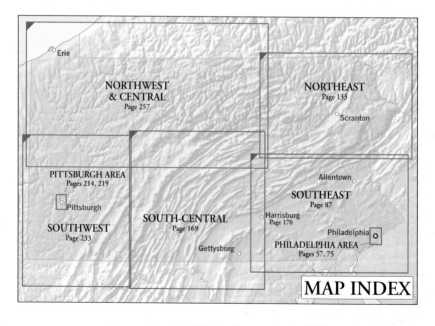

Enjoying the scenery in the Allegheny Mountains.

AVERAGE JANUARY TEMPERATURES

Celsius	Fahrenheit
-4.4	24
-3.3	26
-2.2	28
-1.1	30

AVERAGE JULY TEMPERATURES

Celsius	Fahrenhei
20.0	68
21.1	70
22.2	72
23.3	74

Lake Erie

North East

NEW YORK

Erie

Lake City   Avonia

Jamestown

Olean

Waterford

Albion

Union City

Bradford

Allegheny Reservoir

Cambridge Springs

Pittsfield

Warren

Smethport

Port Allegany

Couderspor

Pymatuning Reservoir

Conneaut Lake   Meadville   Titusville

Tidioute

Sheffield

Kane

Lantz Corners

Jamestown

Greenville

Oil City

Franklin

Tionesta

Ridgeway

St Marys

Emporium

Kettle Creek State Park

Driftwood

Shenango River Lake

Mercer

Shippenville

Clarion

Brockway

Du Bois

Slippery Rock

Brookville

OHIO

New Castle

Mayport

Reynoldsville

Clearfield

Bellefonte

Philipsburg

New Bethlehem

Punxsutawney

Port Matilda

State College

Butler

Kittanning

Rochester

Home

Barnesboro

Freeport
Tarentum

Indiana

Ambridge

Ohio

PITTSBURGH

Carnegie

Murrysville   Blairsville

Edensburg

Altoona

Huntingdon

Paris

Greensburg

Johnstown

Mt Ur

Washington

Ligonier

Shade

Scenery Hill

Jennerstown

Kanter

Brownsville

Waynesburg

Uniontown

Youghiogheny

Berlin

Garrett

Meyersdale

Bedford

Chamberst

Mt Davis 3,213
(highest point in Pennsylvania)

Mercersburg

WEST VIRGINIA

MARYLAND

WV

AVERAGE ANNUAL PRECIPITATION

Centimeters	Inches
101	40
106	42
111	44
116	46

AVERAGE ANNUAL SNOWFALL

Centimeters	Inches
101	30
127	40
152	50
177	70

PENNSYLVANIA

0   20   40 Miles
0   20   40   60 Kilometers

Elevation
in feet

3,213
2,200
1,800
1,400
1,000
600
100

NEW YORK

Elmira
Binghamton

Elkland
Sayre
Hallstead
Susquehanna
Delaware

Mansfield
Towanda
Montrose
Union Dale

Wellsboro
Wyalusing
Kingsley
Honesdale
White Mills

Grand Canyon
Pennsylvania

Liberty
Dushore
Tunkhannock
Carbondale
Hawley

Trout Run
Muncy Valley
Scranton
Dunmore

Williamsport
West Pittston
Wilkes-Barre
Milford

Jersey Shore
W Branch

Lock Haven
Berwick
Mt Pocono
Bushkill

Lewisburg
Milton
Hiskory Run
Hazleton
Stroudsburg
Delaware Water Gap

Potters Mills
Middleburg
Sunbury
Shenandoah
Kresgeville
Mt Bethel

Wagner
Shamokin
Palmerton
NEW JERSEY

Lewistown
Elizabethville
Millersburg
Pottsville
Allentown
Bethlehem
Easton
Kintnersville

Duncannon
Hamburg
Kutztown
Quakertown
Point Pleasant

HARRISBURG
Hershey
Lebanon
Reading
Pottstown
Doylestown
New Hope

Carlisle
Ephrata
Trenton

Shippensburg
Columbia
Lancaster
Paradise
Chatwood
Philadelphia

York
York
Quarryville
Chadds Ford

Gettysburg
Wilmington
DE
NEW JERSEY

MARYLAND
Conowingo

O V E R V I E W

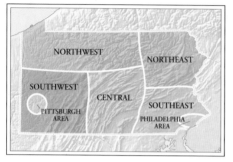

Mountainous, historic Pennsylvania, with its dense forests and well-plowed fields, its sophisticated urban centers and famous battlefields, is one of America's most fascinating states. Come here to relive the founding of the nation at Independence Hall. Visit Valley Forge, where George Washington's troops suffered through the cold winter of 1776–77 and the Gettysburg Battlefield, where North and South fought the bloodiest battle of the Civil War. Here you'll find variety, from the Amish farms of Lancaster County, to the Poconos resorts, the elegance of Philadelphia, and reborn Pittsburgh, one of America's most livable cities.

■ PHILADELPHIA

America's first capital, Philadelphia, was founded by British aristocrat and utopian William Penn, who hoped to found a government where the best of Christian virtues could flourish. Long home to Quakers, Mennonites, and other religious groups, its literate, hardworking, and civic-minded people hosted the rebirth of democratic ideals in government, absent since the days of Greece and republican Rome. Visit Independence Hall, where Benjamin Franklin sat with Thomas Jeffer-

son to sign the Declaration of Independence, see the Liberty Bell, and Philadelphia's fine museums. Visit Valley Forge and Chadd's Ford in nearby Brandywine Valley, birthplace of artist Andrew Wyeth and the site of Washington's early defeat by the British.

2 SOUTHEAST
This is Pennsylvania Dutch Country, with much of the land farmed without machinery, much as it was in the 1700s. Visit the Ephrata Cloister, home to a strict religious sect which sang through its hunger. Look for Pennsylvania Dutch crafts and quilts. Visit the

birthplace of Daniel Boone to see how woodsmen once lived. At the nearby town of Hershey, things are quite different: streetlights are shaped like chocolate kisses.

3 NORTHEAST AND POCONOS
The heavily forested Poconos have long been famous for both natural beauty and the rich coal deposits that lie beneath them. The spectacular autumn foliage is matched only by the vistas along the Delaware Water Gap. Come to Delaware Water Gap National Recreation Area to hike, fish, swim, and camp. Visit Bushkill Falls and wildlands blooming with wildflowers and mountain laurel. Travel Scenic Route 6 to see the charming towns of Hawley and White Mills, especially in the fall when the hills are ablaze with color.

Explore the state's coal-mining and railroad heritage around Scranton and Wilkes-Barre, visitng the Pennsylvania Anthracite Heritage Museum and the Lackawanna Coal Mine.

4 CENTRAL
PENNSYLVANIA
Follow the Civil War Trail to Gettysburg, scene of the Civil War's most brutal encounter, where Abraham Lincoln delivered his famous Gettysburg Address. Take a bike tour through

the rural landscape of Bedford County, known for its covered bridges. In Altoona, take in the rich history of railroading, including Horseshoe Curve, an engineering feat so important that Nazi saboteurs sought to destroy it during World War II.

5 PITTSBURGH

Formed where the Allegheny and Monongahela Rivers converge to create the great Ohio River, Pittsburgh has risen phoenix-like out of the (coal) ashes of the 19th century to become one of America's most livable cities. Visit the Carnegie Museums of Art and Natural History in historic Oakland, then take in a Pirates, Penguins, or Steelers game before visiting the site of old Fort Pitt, or dine at one of the city's excellent restaurants.

6 SOUTHWEST

The area surrounding Pittsburgh, once you leave the suburbs, is both "Rust Belt" and rural. Enjoy the beautiful ridges of the Laurel Highlands. Visit Fallingwater, the famous house designed by Frank Lloyd Wright near Ohiopyle State Park.

7 NORTHWEST

Visit lovely Presque Isle Park which curves out into Lake Erie, and see Commodore Perry's USS *Niagara*, his ship in a naval battle of 1813. Meander eastward into a grape-growing region, then "take the waters" 19th-century style at the picturesque towns of Waterford and Cambridge Springs.

INTRODUCTION

Home: the fields, red, with acid rows of corn and sandstone corner-markers.
The undertone of insect-hum, the birds too full to sing. A Sunday haze in
Pennsylvania.

—From *Leaving Church Early*, a poem by John Updike

As I write this, the birds in my patch of western Pennsylvania are too hungry to sing. It is early January and Pennsylvania is balled up in icy slumber under a blanket of fresh snow. Beyond the TV news videos of salt trucks and ditched cars, the wintery rural landscapes, the snow-covered city squares, are breathtaking.

The postcard-like scenes remind me of how I first came to Pennsylvania, for I was not born here. I was a teenager in Southern California when the captains of industry at Alcoa Aluminum decided my father would make a good labor relations executive at the company's headquarters in Pittsburgh.

Twenty-five years and 100 "real" seasons later, I am still discovering new ways in which to enjoy Pennsylvania. The face of Pennsylvania has an honest beauty—no makeup and few pretensions. History and age are not hidden here, they are worn with pride.

AUTHOR'S ACKNOWLEDGMENTS

Every book-writing journey begins in a wilderness where the author is lost and wandering. I am fortunate to have found a wise and patient editor in Kit Duane, who saw some promise in my Pennsylvania experience and set me on a sure path toward a worthwhile book. There are other guides and pathfinders who helped me along the way. The father of a dear friend, Ronald Tardio of Lansdale, is a Pittsburgher transplanted to Philadelphia. He knows the eastern part of this state in the same way he knows his family—with his heart.

Dozens of times in the researching of this book I found my bearings with the help of local librarians, university historians, and historical society volunteers. A few went out of their way to assist me in bringing tall tales down to truthful size. Among them: the staffs of the Easton and Lancaster libraries. I also gratefully acknowledge the assistance of the National Park Service rangers of Independence Hall National Historical Park, who allowed access to buildings undergoing renovation. I also want to recognize the assistance of workers in the Pennsylvania Department of Community and Economic Development and Barbara C. Chaffee, executive director of the Pennsylvania Center for Travel, Tourism, and Film.I am grateful to other Visitors and Convention Bureau workers across the state but especially to Lucinda Hampton of the Pennsylvania Dutch Convention and Visitors Bureau who brought a lifetime's experience living among the Amish to bear on my writing.

And many thinks to my father, my seven brothers and sisters and my friends, who graciously accepted my work on this book as a worthy excuse for missed phone calls and late arrivals.

*Pennsylvania's founder, idealist-aristocrat William Penn at the age of 22.
(Historical Society of Pennsylvania, Philadelphia)*

CULTURE & HISTORY

[Pennsylvania] is a clear and just thing, and my God that has given it me through many difficulties, will, I believe, bless and make it the seed of a nation. I shall have a tender care for the government, that it be well laid at first. . . . I purpose that which is extraordinary and to leave myself and successors no power of doing mischief, that the will of one man may not hinder the good of an whole country.

—*William Penn's letter to a friend in 1681*

■ LANDSCAPE AND EARLY HISTORY

Long before the good-hearted English aristocrat William Penn was bequeathed Pennsylvania by the King of England, its lands had long been home to tribal nations who enjoyed its forested mountains, great rushing rivers, and fine valleys. When the first European explorers arrived in Pennsylvania in the early 17th century, they found the peaceful Lenni Lenape tribe, the Susquehannocks, and the Eries. These tribes were by that time vassals to the powerful and warlike Five Nations of Iroquois, which had expanded from what is now New York during the previous century. Weakened by war, Pennsylvania's tribes had lost most of their population to measles and smallpox, diseases which had made their way inland from European coastal settlements during the previous half century. Despite these terrible difficulties, the Europeans found the Indians here a fine, well-built people living a settled life.

In *Pennsylvania, Birthplace of a Nation,* author Sylvester Stevens writes of the Pennsylvania native:

> *He* was living in an advanced Stone Age culture, which included settled life in villages and farming. He was making pottery vessels for his cooking and for the storage of food…even decorating his pottery in the later years of this era.…He was growing corn, along with tobacco. He lived in semipermanent bark houses and they were grouped into villages… [William] Penn described those he saw as "generally tall, straight, well built, and of singular proportion; they tread strong and clever, and mostly walk with a lofty chin." He also spoke of their "lofty" manner of speaking. In councils he found them very well able to conceal their true

feelings in a certain impassive attitude....He noted their "Liberality" and that "Nothing is too good for their friend."

Swedish and Finnish explorers began a fur and tobacco trade with the Indians and by the middle of the 17th century had established a few scattered forts—near New Castle in the southwest and around Wilmington, Chester, and Philadelphia in the southeast. However, the Dutch settlers in New Amsterdam (New York City), who feared their lucrative trade with the Iroquois would be siphoned off at the source, weren't pleased. Their soldiers marched on the settlements and easily won control.

The Dutch made a half-hearted effort to colonize the territory, changing the name of the Scandinavian fort near New Castle to New Amstel, and resettling other areas. But in 1664, the Dutch were driven out when the English dispatched hundreds of troops to claim the territory.

■ ENGLISH SETTLEMENT

By the 1680s, British control had thrown the territory wide open to European colonists—ragtaggers of every sort, some from Great Britain, some from Germany fleeing wars in the Rhineland. Most newcomers favored the

Portrait of a Native American Man of the Northeast Woodlands, *circa 1820. (Philadelphia Museum of Art, Collection of Edgar William and Bernice Chrysler Garbisch)*

This late 17th-century map was commissioned by the Catholic Church for missionaries. Note the portrait of converted Indians at top left.

lower Delaware River area and its nearby countryside, but there was no plan to the settlements and the territory was sorely in need of a strong governor.

Into this unsettled landscape came the aristocratic English idealist William Penn, granted title to Pennsylvania by Charles II of England. Penn was a Quaker, a follower of theologian and Society of Friends founder George Fox, who preached that individuals have a direct relationship with God and did not need the priests or ministers of religious institutions to mediate their faith. Civil hierarchies were similarly discredited: Fox's followers did not recognize titles, to the consternation of the titled British, nor would they take oaths. Religious persecution took the form of civil prosecution: William Penn himself was imprisoned four times, once for a refusal to swear allegiance to the crown.

Charles II's gift to William Penn can be seen as a brilliant solution to an intractable problem. Penn's beliefs, along with his status, eloquence and charm, made him a disruptive force in England. His father, Admiral William Penn, had been a distinguished naval officer, holder of various government posts, a wealthy landowner, and, most importantly, the king's friend and creditor. After Admiral Penn died, his son requested and accepted the land in payment of the king's debt.

The only land available to Penn was territory inland from the coveted North American seacoast, but what England's rulers considered undesirable hinterland would quickly turn out to be one of the richest—and the most strategically located —of all the new American colonies. But the difficult young aristocrat, who arrived in his new territory in 1682, stayed only two years before he sailed home again.

◆ TOLERANT, WELL-GOVERNED SOCIETY

Penn's Quaker faith informed his new passion, the planning of government and laying out of cities in the new colony. When Penn stepped in to enact his vision of a free and tolerant society, about a thousand Europeans were living near the Delaware River, many of whom had risked everything for an opportunity to make their fortunes unfettered by government interference. They awaited the first address of their new lord with apprehension. Penn's public proclamation to these people, written in Quaker style, began as follows:

> *D*ear Friends,
> You are now fixed at the mercy of no governor who comes to make his fortune great. You shall be governed by laws of your own making, and live a free, and if you will, a sober and industrious people.

For the populace, it was as if the King of England himself had removed his crown and thrown it into the crowd. Penn's beliefs pleased the people of his new colony—although it wouldn't be long before some of his "citizen friends" took advantage of their governor's allegedly haphazard way of surveying land.

What Penn lacked in business acumen (or in his understanding of human nature) he made up in promoting his colony to immigrants and investors and in "urban planning." He took advantage of some of the progressive thinking of the time, including the notion that cities and towns be located to serve as trading and supply centers for farming areas.

For Philadelphia, the capital of the new colony and, eventually, the de facto capital of all the colonies, Penn envisioned a "greene Countrie Towne" of straight, wide streets, with orchards and gardens interspersed with buildings. Although the vision only partly materialized, it served to inspire the planning of hundreds of other cities in the new nation.

By the time of his death in 1718, the most important legacy Penn had left to his province was a genuinely tolerant and self-governing democracy—an extraordinary legacy in a world ruled by autocrats.

Penn's sons, less idealistic than their father, hoped to profit from the sale of land their father had promised the Indians, and they promoted Philadelphia in European newspapers and journals as the best place to set up a business in the colonies. Penn's middle son, Thomas, even advertised in the *English Bristol Journal* that any craftsman willing to "go over to the most flourishing city of Philadelphia" would be given a new suit of clothes.

◆ PROSPERITY AND TAXES: RECIPE FOR A REVOLUTION

In 1700, Philadelphia's population was about 6,000 and that of the outlying territory totaled 20,000. By the beginning of the Revolutionary War, 75 years later, Pennsylvania's population was estimated at 300,000. Most of the new settlers came as indentured workers, obliged to work off their ship passage and supply costs to businessmen in Great Britain and other parts of Europe. Promotional advertising by the Penn family and letters from settlers back to family and friends were well timed. Opportunity abounded in the brisk trade with the West Indies, especially in the commodities of grain, meat, and lumber that Pennsylvania had in abundance. As Indian treaties were broken, and settlements spread inland, the city became a point of internal transshipment for produce and animal furs.

(ENGLISH SETTLEMENT *continues on page 24*)

WILLIAM PENN: THE FOUNDER
1644–1718

*W*illiam Penn had made every effort to correct England's ills before he decided to start from scratch in the New World. He had preached and protested. He had railed against excess and luxury in church and in the world. He had refused to take off his hat or swear allegiance to the crown, and he had defended himself so effectively that the jury found him innocent. He went to jail anyhow: one of the evils he denounced was the judges' habit of disregarding jury verdicts they didn't like. He had championed human rights. He had written tracts with titles like "No Cross, No Crown" and "The Great Case of Liberty of Conscience." He had defended not just his own Quaker faith but the right of all to follow their own beliefs. But in England, he had not been persuasive enough to bring the changes he sought.

Penn had another reason for founding his colony. His father died in 1670, leaving him an uncollectible debt from King Charles II. The crown was land rich and cash poor, a condition Penn himself would one day know all too well. He took Pennsylvania in payment.

The new colony was vast, making Penn the largest landholder in the kingdom aside from the king himself. Penn was proprietor, owning the lands outright with "free, full and absolute power" over them. His political power was somewhat limited. He and his Council proposed laws, but the Assembly had to approve them.

Remarkably, Penn did not take advantage of his power but instead wrote increasingly liberal charters, allowing more and more representative government. It is also remarkable that he did not grow rich. The people who ran the colony (Penn spent only a few years there) were far more conscientious about billing him for their salaries than they were about collecting rents for him. His land did not bring him wealth but cost him an estimated £75,000. His trusted Quaker agent in London defrauded him, and a debt owed to the agent's widow put Penn in prison for several months. Finally, in debt and despair he made plans to return the colony to the Crown, but he suffered a stroke before he could sign the transfer documents.

Penn wrote prolifically on religious and philosophical subjects. According to his later account, he first felt the presence of God at the age of 12. Soon afterward he heard a preacher named Thomas Loe, of the Society of Friends (Quakers). He was drawn to the Quaker faith, and neither expulsion from Oxford, his father's fury, nor four prison terms dissuaded him. In Pennsylvania he was able to put his ideas to the test. That they did not entirely succeed is not the fault of his plan of government. As he himself wrote, "Governments, like clocks, go from the motion men give them; and as governments are made and moved by men, so by them are they ruined too."

In the end, Penn made only two visits to his colony, one from 1682 to 1684, and again, from 1699 to 1701.

One of Penn's unrealized dreams was that colonists and Indians would live side by side in harmony. In the words of one historian, "He seems to have been one of the few genuine Christians Christianity has ever produced."

In the 1840s, sign painter Edward Hicks painted several idealized versions of Penn's treaty with the Indians, including the one shown here. (Shelburne Museum, Shelburne, VT)

A powerful, literate, and worldly merchant class—most of whom were Quaker —soon emerged in Philadelphia. Many business leaders in the colonies had come from prosperous mercantile families in Europe. One of these was Robert Morris. Born in Liverpool in 1734, he joined his father in Maryland in 1747, then entered a mercantile house in Philadelphia. It was Morris and many of his Pennsylvania colleagues whose taxes paid for the military adventures of the British Empire, such as the French and Indian War. The merchant class—many of whom served in elected positions in colonial governments—were furious at the new taxes levied upon them to support the campaigns. Eventually, they would use their wealth to finance the Continental Army in the War of Independence. Morris was slow and reluctant to accept the necessity of a break with England, but eventually it was he who raised the money necessary for George Washington to move his army to

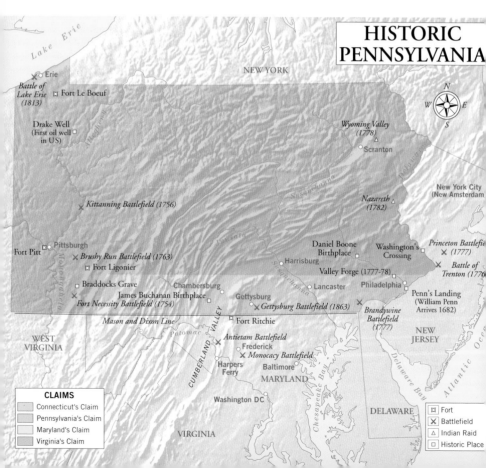

HISTORIC PENNSYLVANIA

Lake Erie

NEW YORK

Erie
Battle of Lake Erie (1813)   Fort Le Boeuf

Drake Well (First oil well in US)

Wyoming Valley (1778)
Scranton

New York City (New Amsterdam)

Kittanning Battlefield (1756)

Nazareth (1782)

Fort Pitt   Pittsburgh
Brushy Run Battlefield (1763)
Fort Ligonier

Daniel Boone Birthplace
Washington's Crossing
Princeton Battlefield (1777)
Battle of Trenton (1776)

Harrisburg
Valley Forge (1777-78)

Braddocks Grave
Chambersburg
James Buchanan Birthplace
Fort Necessity Battlefield (1754)
Lancaster
Philadelphia
Penn's Landing (William Penn Arrives 1682)

Gettysburg
Gettysburg Battlefield (1863)
Brandywine Battlefield (1777)

Mason and Dixon Line
Fort Ritchie
NEW JERSEY

WEST VIRGINIA
Potomac
Antietam Battlefield
Frederick
Monocacy Battlefield
Harpers Ferry
Baltimore
MARYLAND

Delaware Bay

Atlantic Ocean

Washington DC

DELAWARE

VIRGINIA

Chesapeake Bay

CLAIMS
Connecticut's Claim
Pennsylvania's Claim
Maryland's Claim
Virginia's Claim

Fort
Battlefield
Indian Raid
Historic Place

William Birch's Second Street North from Market, *circa 1799, depicts a bustling and orderly city. Christ Church is visible in the center of the painting.*
(Pennsylvania Historical Society, Philadelphia)

Yorktown in 1781, where the British general Cornwallis surrendered.

Another of Philadelphia's businessman-politicians was Benjamin Franklin, who at 17 had arrived from Boston and, at 23, established his own newspaper, *The Pennsylvania Gazette.* He pursued elective and appointive offices, including deputy postmaster general of Philadelphia, where he introduced the novel idea that the postal service pay for mail too long delayed. Like Morris, Franklin believed for some time that disagreements with England over taxes could be resolved, and as a colonial agent in London, he attempted to negotiate solutions.

◆ DISSENTERS, SEEKERS, AND PLAIN PEOPLE

The liberal and tolerant principles of William Penn's government attracted a steady flow of immigrants to Pennsylvania. Some were dissenters desiring religious freedom; some were from the lower classes wanting economic opportunity. In Pennsylvania, they had heard, a person might easily accumulate enough land to be able to vote and even become an elected official. There was no compulsory military service, and civil liberties were guaranteed even to Indians.

Between 1680 and 1710, most settlers who followed William Penn were, like him, Quakers from England, Wales, and Germany. Their numbers and wealth made them the dominant force in the Pennsylvania Assembly until 1756, when their pacifism lost them the support of frontier settlers who wanted armed protection against Indians.

Along with the Quakers came the first of the Germans from the Rhineland, beginning with the Mennonite Francis Daniel Pastorius, the founder of Germantown, now part of Philadelphia. The early German settlers were for the most part members of smaller religious sects who came and settled as groups—Mennonites, Amish, Dunkers (German Baptists), German Quakers, and Moravians.

After 1727, German immigrants were mostly members of the larger Lutheran and Reformed churches. Their farming skills made the region where they settled a rich agricultural area. By the time of the American Revolution they numbered about 100,000—more than a third of Pennsylvania's population. German farmers provided food for the Revolutionary Army and made excellent rifles (the legendary "Pennsylvania long rifle"). With the exception of the Amish, they loved music and decorative arts and added to the beauty of small settlements and homes in this area, now known as "Dutch" country, a derivation of the German word "Deutsch," (meaning "German.")

Between 1717 and 1776, about 250,000 Scotch-Irish emigrated from Ulster to America. These were Presbyterians whom the English had moved into northern Ireland in order to counteract the Catholic Irish in the 1600s, but the economic hardship they faced was so severe that many signed on as indentured servants to pay their way to Pennsylvania. At first they settled in the Dutch country, farming without much success. From 1730 on, they led the movement west and north, to the frontiers. The Scotch-Irish were a stern and self-sufficient group, too independent to settle into the agrarian communities envisioned by Penn but devoted to education and to the founding of schools. Eventually they became leaders in the revolutionary movement.

PATCHWORK OF FAITHS

William Penn's Quaker faith persuaded him to form a colony where all could worship freely, not just the Quakers. And he succeeded. A visitor to Penn's colony reported finding "Lutherans, Reformed, Catholics, Quakers, Menninists or Anabaptists, Herrnhuters of Moravian Brethren, Pietists, Seventh-Day Baptists, Dunkers.... In one house and one family, four, five and even six sects may be found...."

Quakers

It was the Quakers, or Friends, whose tolerance allowed other faiths to flourish. In England these followers of the theologian George Fox had been persecuted because they believe in neither churches nor creeds, but in the "inward light" by which they could sense God's presence. At meetings they meditate silently or testify to their faith. Outside the meetinghouse they practice tolerance and pacifism and, historically, have demonstrated their simplicity and honesty by adopting plain dress and manners.

Mennonites

Mennonites, who emerged in Europe well before the Society of Friends was founded by George Fox in 1650, first reached Pennsylvania in 1683. Mennonites were Anabaptists, believers in baptism only for those who have chosen the faith. They sought to live separately from—and be left alone by—the rest of society, but in time they showed a willingness to mingle with the non-Mennonite world where their social concerns have led them into the helping professions and even politics.

Amish

Jakob Ammann was a strict Mennonite leader who preached that church members who had left the fold should be shunned. His followers became known as the Amish, members of the Old Order Amish Mennonite Church. Like the Mennonites, the Amish are Anabaptists and pacifists, but they have remained stricter in remaining apart from the outside world. Whether to enforce the separation or to demonstrate it, they maintain an archaic style of dress and speech, and they avoid use of such modern contrivances as automobiles, telephones, and electric lights.

Moravians

Pietists, of whom the Moravians are a sect, sought a faith more intimate and emotional than the dominant Protestant churches of 17th-century Germany. Together with the Mennonites, the Amish, and the "Dunkers," or German Baptists, they became known collectively as the Pennsylvania Dutch.

This 1757 engraving depicts Bethlehem, a communal religious settlement about 50 miles north-west of Philadelphia that eventually became an industrial city. (New York Public Library)

■ WESTWARD EXPANSION

William Penn had envisioned a settled land of orderly townships of about 5,000 acres each, consisting of farms grouped around a central village. Lands were offered to "first purchasers" in England at a uniform price, to be resold as farms, with 10 percent retained by the proprietors as manors. That plan was undermined after a decade or two by speculation on the part of the proprietors, by additional purchases from Indian tribes, and by the refusal of settlers to live in villages. Settlement was far from orderly.

Until 1730, most expansion beyond Philadelphia followed the Schuylkill and Delaware Rivers and their tributaries. But the landlocked farm region to the west of Penn's original three counties had a population sufficient to justify the creation of Lancaster County in 1729. By the middle of the 18th century, new waves of immigrants, border disputes with other colonies, and the colonial government's consequent encouragement of settlers pushed the boundaries of settlement beyond the Susquehanna and into southwestern Pennsylvania.

The first stage in the growth of the farming frontier was the true wilderness of the typical frontiersman. He usually merely squatted upon the land for a time and lived in a very crude cabin or lean-to. He was the man with the leather jacket and breeches, the fur cap, and the long Pennsylvania rifle with which he shot game, or Indians, if occasion made it necessary. He came on foot, or at best with a pack horse or mule. He was not apt to own any livestock and lived from hunting, fishing, and crude cultivation of the soil in a small clearing where he raised some corn and vegetables. This type of pioneer was restless and did not wish to be crowded. When a few others penetrated his wilderness...he sought a new wilderness home.

—Sylvester K. Stevens, *Pennsylvania,*
Birthplace of a Nation, 1967

As settlement continued, towns were laid out, and some emerged as cities in the wilderness. Between 1768-1788, two thirds of the total area of Pennsylvania was wrested from Native Americans.

Settlers built log cabins as they moved into the state's wilderness frontier.

■ REVOLUTIONARY ERA

In Boston in 1773, a group of anti-tax demonstrators transparently disguised as "Indians" threw a shipload of tea into Boston Harbor. In Philadelphia, protesters invited the captain of a British tea ship to its own more polite protest. And in London, Benjamin Franklin put his finger up and detected the political ill winds blowing toward Britain from the colonies.

At the same time, new ideas were coursing through the colonies. Quakers and other Protestant sects had long stressed the importance of individual conscience, free of the dictates of traditional institutions and guided by a sense of civic responsibility. One aspect of this notion was the Protestant belief that all people should be able to read the Bible, and the high concentration of Protestants living in the northern colonies gave that region one of the highest literacy rates in the world. The spirit of freedom of individual expression encouraged the writing of ideas and opinions, especially in the fields of religion and politics. Pennsylvania in particular, because of its well-established Quaker beliefs, provided fertile ground for revolution. Philadelphia was the publishing center of the colonies, where books and pamphlets by political thinkers such as Thomas Paine were published and distributed.

These literate, prosperous people, moreover, were 4,000 miles from Great Britain, three-to-four weeks' sailing time, and they had escape routes to unsettled land in the west, circumstances sufficient to embolden dissent. Yet a democratic form of government was without precedence; models came from the ancient world, from Athens in Greece and early republican Rome. Most colonists were not willing to take such a step into the unknown.

America's democratic idealism was badly tarnished by the institution of slavery. At the time of the Revolution, this injustice seemed beyond remedy and at any rate secondary to maintaining a united front against Britain. Apologists for slavery were a source of frustration to Jefferson: although the original draft of the Declaration of Independence included a condemnation of the slave trade, Southerners and some New England politicians insisted it be deleted.

◆ GREAT MEN CORRESPOND

By 1774, the men who would become the patriots of the American Revolution and the founders of the United States were in correspondence. In Philadelphia, City Tavern (which you can visit today) was the center of social, business, and political activities. Informal debates held there laid the groundwork for the Declaration of Independence, and later for the Revolution.

The Philadelphia Committee of Observation, Inspection, and Correspondence, operating out of its tavern headquarters, proposed that a Congress of the Thirteen Colonies convene in September of 1774 to discuss grievances with Britain. This first meeting of the Congress in Philadelphia adjourned without a demand for independence, but after the British marched on Lexington and Concord the following April, the voices of those advocating rebellion grew louder. By May, Paul Revere was galloping his horse towards Philadelphia. When he arrived, he made straight for City Tavern seeking support for the city of Boston.

A second Continental Congress convened, and the few Pennsylvania conservatives in attendance were no match for the fiery oratory of fellow Philadelphians such as Thomas Paine.

Virginian Richard Henry Lee offered a resolution declaring, "That these United Colonies are, and of right ought to be, free and independent States," and that a plan of confederation be created. A committee, composed of Thomas Jefferson, John Adams, Benjamin Franklin, Roger Sherman, and Robert R. Livingston was formed to draft a declaration "setting forth the causes which impelled us to this

John Trumbull took 30 yeaers to finish his famous painting, The Declaration of Independence.
(Yale University Art Gallery)

mighty resolution." Working at a desk in the home of a young bricklayer and drawing on the political thought of the Enlightenment, Thomas Jefferson wrote the Declaration of Independence in two weeks. On July 2, 1776, Lee's resolution was adopted after a heated debate, and two days later the Congress formalized this act by adopting the Declaration of Independence.

The course of armed struggle for independence was consequently set and when the Congress met in July 1776, at what is now known as Independence Hall, to adopt the document, the few remaining Pennsylvania conservatives reluctantly added their signatures.

The English monarch, King George III, was not amused. From his point of view, the insurgents were traitors and deserved a traitor's punishment. The British army consulted with colonial representatives, and war was declared.

◆ REVOLUTIONARY WAR

The early years of the war did not go well for the Americans. The circumspect and soft-spoken general from Virginia, George Washington, led an inexperienced and poorly supplied army. The government that was to support him barely existed and had almost no money. Having lost several early campaigns in New York, he was forced to retreat across New Jersey to Pennsylvania.

In this 1883 painting by William B. T. Trego, Washington reviews his troops at Valley Forge in the winter of 1777–1778. (Courtesy of Valley Forge Historical Society)

In this painting, Benjamin Franklin reviews his company at Versailles in 1776. Specifically, Franklin was sent to Paris to seek aid for the Revolutionary cause from the French court. Marie Antoinette is shown seated, in a yellow gown. (Library of Congress)

Momentum turned and popular support for Washington rallied the day after Christmas, 1776, when he ordered a successful surprise attack on a garrison of German mercenaries camped on the east bank of the Delaware River in Trenton. A month later he captured another contingent of British soldiers at Princeton.

The British commander who had taken New York City, Major Gen. William Howe, struck back, defeating the forces of the Continental Army at Brandywine Creek in Pennsylvania in September of 1777. Howe then settled into Philadelphia, forcing the Congress into exile.

George Washington and his motley army of farmer-soldiers did not give up. Digging in at nearby Valley Forge through what turned out to be a brutal winter, they suffered disease, hunger, and cruel cold; and more than 2,000 of the 12,000 soldiers died. Nevertheless, Valley Forge has been credited with bringing these disparate people together and forging a more disciplined fighting force.

The Continental Congress, still on the run, took heart in Washington's stiff resistance, especially after the the Battle of Saratoga in October 1777, which resulted in the surrender of British forces in New York.

◆ FRENCH ASSISTANCE

The fledgling United States government, lacking funds and allies, looked to France for help against Britian, their common antagonist. In late 1776, Philadelphia's Benjamin Franklin sailed to France for a meeting with King Louis XVI. Self-interest had already prompted the king to offer help, but Franklin's enormous popularity in France may have increased his generosity. Louis immediately ordered secret assistance to the revolutionaries, and in 1778, after treaties had been signed promising favorable trade status, the French declared war on Britain and sent its fleet of war ships in open support. Howe raced out of Philadelphia to lend support to troops in New York.

In 1781, the highest ranking British commander, Lord Cornwallis, settled in the Virginia seaport town of Yorktown after failing to capture Thomas Jefferson in a chase through the Piedmont region of the colony. Washington saw another opportunity for surprise attack and forced his soldiers—16,000 strong—on a horrendous march from New York south. Reinforced with French soldiers, the army cornered the British, who waited in vain for reinforcements to come by sea. After a three-week standoff, the vastly outnumbered Cornwallis accepted the inevitable and surrendered.

While several battles continued in New York during the next 18 months, the stunning British defeat at Yorktown secured victory for American forces. The captured British colors were sent to Philadelphia by General Washington and presented to the Continental Congress in a formal ceremony in Independence Hall.

Philadelphia, and Pennsylvania with it, had been the staging ground for a revolution. When the Constitutional Convention met at Independence Hall after the war and a few years of an unsatisfactory confederation, Philadelphia further fulfilled William Penn's dream in "planting the seed of a nation." Pennsylvania was second, after Delaware, to ratify the U.S. Constitution in December of 1787.

■ PROGRESS IN PENNSYLVANIA

Pennsylvania was in the vanguard of states that took advantage of the economic freedoms guaranteed by the new central government. In the decade after independence, both Philadelphia and Pittsburgh began developing the infrastructure required for an economy with the capacity to trade with the world.

From the 1780s through the 1820s, there was a flurry of expansion—regional roads, bridges, a series of canals, and more financial institutions able to bankroll public works projects and business start-ups. The federal government was moved to Washington but Philadelphia still held special status: because of its financial commitment in the war, the city enjoyed a brief period as the financial center of the new United States. The state was primed to lead the way in a second economic expansion—from the mid-1820s through the 1850s—that would bring the state to the level of many of Europe's economic powerhouses.

The key was the state's abundant natural resources—among them, the largest anthracite coal deposits in the world, lumber to meet the building demands of an ever-expanding nation, and waterways to transport these products.

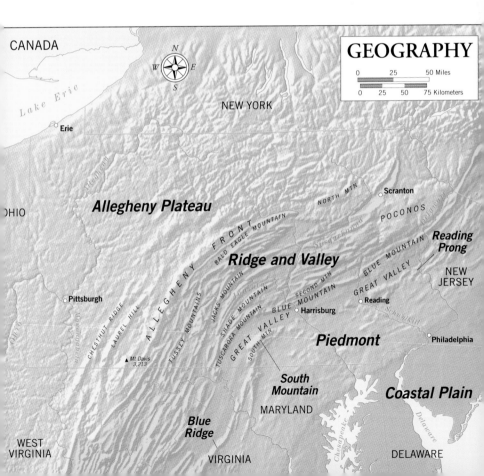

GEOGRAPHY

0   25   50 Miles

0   25   50   75 Kilometers

CANADA

Lake Erie

NEW YORK

Erie

Allegheny Plateau

OHIO

NORTH MTN

Scranton

POCONOS

FRONT

BALD EAGLE MOUNTAIN

Ridge and Valley

BLUE MOUNTAIN

Reading Prong

NEW JERSEY

Pittsburgh

A L L E G H E N Y

CHESTNUT RIDGE

LAUREL HILL

Mt Davis
3,213

TUSSEY MOUNTAINS

JACKS MOUNTAIN

SHADE MOUNTAIN

TUSCARORA MOUNTAIN

GREAT VALLEY

SECOND MTN

BLUE MOUNTAIN

Harrisburg

SOUTH MTN

GREAT VALLEY

Reading

Piedmont

Philadelphia

South Mountain

MARYLAND

Coastal Plain

Blue Ridge

WEST VIRGINIA

VIRGINIA

Chesapeake

Delaware

DELAWARE

CULTURE &
HISTORY

A memorial to General Robert E. Lee at Gettysburg National Military Park.

■ CAN SUCH A UNION LONG ENDURE?

If Pennsylvania was central to the founding of the nation, it was also intensely involved in the moral and emotional debates that preceded the Civil War. Quaker-dominated Pennsylvania had abolished slavery in 1780, the first state to do so, and it had long been a way-station on the Underground Railroad, which directed escaped slaves north. Its people were sympathetic to the abolitionist cause. And, as a state where the union of the states had first begun, it wasn't one to take national dissolution lightly.

Pennsylvanians reacted angrily to the U.S. Supreme Court's infamous Dred Scott decision of 1856, invalidating an act of Congress—the Missouri Compromise—and permitting the spread of slavery into American territories. In 1860, Pennsylvania's vote was pivotal to the election of Abraham Lincoln to the Presidency. Powerful Southerners had declared they would secede from the Union if Lincoln were elected, and when he was, Southern states began to carry out that threat.

When Lincoln called for troops to support the Union in 1861, no other state was as ready as Pennsylvania to go to arms. The President requested 14 regiments; volunteers filled 25 regiments almost immediately.

It fell to Pennsylvania to be the site of the war's most devastating battle, as Confederates led by Gen. Robert E. Lee crossed Pennsylvania's southern border (separated from Virginia by the narrow border of the Maryland panhandle) and brought the war to the sleepy farming community of Gettysburg. The ferocious Battle of Gettysburg from July 1–3, 1863, caused more than 50,000 Confederate and Union casualties, almost all under the age of 21.

■ CAPITALISTS AND UNION MEN

The Civil War had stimulated Pennsylvania's industrial might. With the end of the war came an era of industrial expansion led by entrepreneurs who built the mills, mines, and factories of the late 19th century. Shrewd young businessmen like Pittsburgh's Andrew Carnegie, Henry Clay Frick, and Robert Hunt, and Philadelphia's Joseph Wharton and William Scranton, saw fortunes to be made in steel production and coal mining and they set about building enormous empires. Along with them came some of the country's most innovative financiers—the Mellons of Pittsburgh and the Cookes of Philadelphia.

In these "beehive ovens," coal was baked into coke—which burns at the high heat necessary to produce steel. Henry Clay Frick, who controlled Pittsburgh's coke supply, later joined forces with steel magnate Andrew Carnegie to form a powerful industrial empire. (Library of Congress)

Ironworkers at a Sharon, Pennsylvania, factory. (Carnegie Library of Pittsburgh)

Factories need laborers, and they came to Pennsylvania by the thousands, not only the East's poor and the South's blacks but the Irish Catholics who settled in Scranton, the Welsh and the Scotch-Irish who went to the towns of the west, the Russian Jews in the southeast and the Eastern Europeans in the southwest. To a great degree, Pennsylvania owes its cultural wealth and economic success to those ethnic groups who did the heavy lifting. These immigrants gratefully accepted the dirty and dangerous jobs—mining coal and laying track, stoking the coke furnaces and pouring the molten iron ore into ingots.

As the titans of industry were largely unfettered in their pursuit of full production in their plants, Pennsylvania became the prime testing ground for the American trade union movement. Several important labor struggles took place in the burgeoning semi-skilled labor forces of railroad, mining, and steel manufacture, most notably the Homestead Steel Strike of 1892.

■ 20TH CENTURY

Pennsylvania followed an almost predictable course for an industrial state in the first half of the century. Economic slumps were devastating, and wars were financially invigorating. The Great Depression brought unemployment as high as

80 percent in the steel and railroad industries. The Second World War eliminated unemployment with a vengeance: factories ran around the clock and even women were recruited into the labor force.

So much is said about the "Rust Belt" in the post-industrial age that it is slightly surprising to learn there are still steel mills and coal mines in Pennsylvania. But steelmaking and other heavy manufacturing have declined steeply in the past 30 years, and services now play a much larger role in a diversified economy. Government initiatives encourage growth in such high technology industries as electronics and biotechnology.

Postwar prosperity and the decline of heavy industry made it possible to undo some of the environmental damage wrought over the decades by mining and manufacture. Pennsylvania's two major industries, agriculture and tourism, benefit from improvements in air and water quality and repair of mined lands.

Pennsylvania still grapples with problems vexing every state—race relations, public safety, and educational opportunities among them—as well as a "brain drain," that has inspired a unique campaign in the last years of the 20th century to bring Pennsylvania emigrants home. Fred Rogers (Mister Rogers) and Bill Cowher, the current head coach of the Pittsburgh Steelers football team, remind errant natives that, wherever they go, "Pennsylvania is a part of you," and that opportunity awaits in the "New Pennsylvania."

A promotional piece for the Pennsylvania Railroad.

NOTABLE PENNSYLVANIANS

William Penn
1644-1718
English Quaker leader, founder of the American Commonwealth of Pennsylvania. In state 1682–1684 and 1699–1701.

Benjamin Franklin
1706-1790
Publisher, author, inventor, scientist, diplomat, leader in the American Revolution. Born in Boston, Franklin lived most of his life in Philadelphia. Best known for his role in helping to frame both the Declaration of Independence and the American Constitution.

Daniel Boone
1734-1820
Early American frontiersman, hero. Born in Berks County, PA. Helped blaze a trail through the Cumberland Gap and was a legend at the time of his death.

Betsy Ross
1752-1836
Seamstress and patriot in the Revolutionary War. Ross may have sewn the original American flag (adopted June 14, 1777 by the Continental Congress), but this has never been proven. She was a well known figure in Philadelphia who attended Patriot rallies.

Stephen Foster
1826-1864
Composer; born in Pittsburgh's Lawrenceville neighborhood; best known for his songs "Old Folks at Home" (also known as "Swannee River") and "Jeannie with the Light Brown Hair."

Andrew Carnegie
1835-1919
Industrialist and philanthropist. Born in Scotland, Carnegie moved with his family to Allegheny in 1848. Led the enormous expansion of the steel industry. Also one of the most important philanthropists of his era.

Mary Cassatt
1844-1926
Painter; born in Allegheny City, PA, though she spent much of her life in France. She exhibited with the impressionists. Best known for works featuring mothers with children.

Andrew Mellon
1855-1937
Financier, philanthropist; born in Pittsburgh. Mellon was U.S. Secretary of the Treasury from 1921 to 1932 and was largely responsible for tax reforms during those years. One of the nation's foremost art collectors, he made possible the building of the National Gallery of Art in Washington D.C.

Milton S. Hershey
1857-1945
Chocolatier and philanthropist. Born in Dauphine Co., PA, he set up shop in the town that bears his name and helped popularize chocolate throughout the world.

George C. Marshall
1880-1959
World War II general and post-war statesman, U.S. Secretary of State (1947-49); Secretary of Defense (1950-51). Born in Uniontown, PA. Famous for his 1947 European Recovery Program, better known as the Marshall Plan, for which he received the Nobel Prize for Peace in 1953.

Martha Graham
1894-1994
Choreographer. Born in Pittsburgh, one of the most influential modern dance choreographers, performers, and teachers of the 20th century.

Alexander Calder
1898-1976
Sculptor; born in Lawntown, PA. Best known as the originator of the mobile. See page 73 for his sculpture at the Philadelphia Art Museum.

Marian Anderson
1902-1993
Singer; born in Philadelphia. One of the most renowned musical voices in the 20th century.

Andrew Wyeth
1917-
Painter; born in Chadd's Ford, PA. Much of Wyeth's work depicts the Brandywine Valley. A realistic painter, he is well-known for his painting *Christina's World.*

Andy Warhol
1928-1987
Artist, filmmaker; born in Pittsburgh. An initiator and leading exponent of the Pop Art movement of the 1960s, Warhol was a well-known fixture in the fashion and avant garde art scene.

Grace Kelly
1929-1982
Actress, princess; born Philadelphia, PA. The star of 11 films, including *High Society* (based on the *Philadelphia Story)* and Hitchcock's *Rear Window.* Married Prince Rainier of Monoco in 1956.

John Updike
1932-
Novelist; born in Shillington, PA. Winner of the Pulitzer Prize. First acclaimed novel, *Rabbit Run* takes place in Pennsylvania.

Wilton "Wilt" Chamberlain
1932-1999
Born and grew up in west Philadelphia. Basketball player; set many professional basketball records. Spent much of his 14-year career playing in his native Philadelphia.

PHILADELPHIA
AMERICA'S FIRST CARITAL

■ HIGHLIGHTS

Food & Lodging
map 276; charts 277
listings by town, in alphabetical order 278

■ TRAVEL BASICS

America's first true capital was the city where Thomas Jefferson, Ben Franklin, John Adams, John Hancock, and the other Founding Fathers convened to sign the Declaration of Independence. Today a city of 1,600,000 people, Philadelphia contains everything from modern highrises and old-time ethnic neighborhoods to many of America's most revered historical sights. Here are two of the world's great art museums, a convivial urban scene, and one of country's great colleges, the University of Pennsylvania. Which is not to say all is rosy in Philadelphia. The city is losing population and in some neighborhoods housing is derelict. Yet in charming Chestnut Hill, you'll find a village within a city, where young families are moving in and staking a claim to the city's future.

South of Philadelphia lies the beautiful Brandywine Valley where George Washington suffered defeat at the hands of the British, and west of the city, Valley Forge, where he retreated and waited with his ailing army through the bitter winter of 1776-1777.

Getting Around: Laid out in a grid pattern by its founder William Penn, Philadelphia is relatively easy to navigate. However, on-street parking is virtually impossible, so if you're arriving by car, it's best to park at one of the many garages available and use buses, taxis, subways, or—better yet—your feet to get around. The streets are narrow, often one-way, and congested with traffic. There are many squares and circles such as Rittenhouse Square and Logan Circle that can confuse you by interrupting the grid pattern. Signage is bad, if it exists at all, and some surprises face the casual tourist— Interstate 95, for example, the major north-south highway along the Delaware, does not intersect with the Pennsylvania Turnpike, the major east-west toll road.

Arriving by train at the beautiful **30th Street Station** (the main terminal), puts you in downtown—an easy cab, bus, or subway ride to most hotels and attractions. The North Philadelphia station is about five miles from City Hall.

One caution: visitors should avoid neighborhoods that aren't recommended by this book or by friends, and plot driving routes with care.

Philadelphia International Airport lies 6.5 miles south of City Hall. The SEPTA (Southeastern Pennsylvania Transportation Authority) airport rail line runs every half hour from 6 a.m. to midnight to three destinations including 30th Street Station.

Philadelphia has excellent mass transit. For tourists and shoppers, there's "Phlash," purple vans that follow a route to all the main downtown attractions. An all-day pass costs $3; city buses, subways, and commuter trains travel the entire city and to nearby counties.

Climate: Summers can be hot and humid with temperatures in the 80s and 90s. Spring and fall are the nicest times to visit. Winter rarely brings heavy snows but weather is unpredictable and can run from zero to 40 degrees in the daytime.

Food & Lodging: Philadelphia is known for its excellent restaurants. A wide variety of lodgings can be found from highrise hotels downtown to comfortable inns and B&Bs in Center City and the Society Hill area. **Food & Lodging map** page 276; **charts** page 277; **listings** in alphabetical order by town begin on page 278.

(following pages) Sunset over Philadelphia. Built around the circles and squares of the city is an eclectic mix of architecture, from colonial-era homes to glass-and-concrete skyscrapers.

■ OVERVIEW

Philadelphia has appeared in many different guises over the past 300 years. Once as proper and upright as its English Quaker founders, it relaxed its ways under the influence of immigrants from all over Europe. A center of revolutionary fervor in the late 18th century, by the late 19th it was basking in the prosperity of the Gilded Age. In the 1920s, Philadelphia was known in movies and novels for its "Main Line" society of high-toned, well-bred aristocrats, but the city was down at the heels by the 1970s and '80s. Today it's improving and rebuilding its urban landscape, and buffing up its eclectic mix of fine buildings from many eras.

The thoroughly mixed population of this casual, energetic city has cultivated an eclectic blend of tastes. Citizens can be found patronizing fine art museums and dining in some of the country's best restaurants, or cheering on the Phillies and tucking into a cheesesteak sandwich—a highly caloric combination of thin-sliced steak topped with grilled onions and smothered with your choice of Cheez-Whiz (the authentic choice) or provolone, lettuce, tomato, and pizza sauce on a bun.

Elegant and grubby, high-minded and jive talkin', at once earthy and hoity-toity, Philly is full of pleasant surprises.

■ PHILADELPHIA'S HISTORY

◆ WILLIAM PENN'S VISION

When William Penn arrived aboard the *Welcome* at a quay along the Delaware River in 1682 he found 10 small houses along a wooded shore and a settlement that had foundered for 44 years, first as a Swedish trading post, then later as the Dutch outpost of New Amsterdam. Penn, then 38, a devoutly religious and idealistic aristocrat, stepped ashore possessed of a powerful humanitarian vision: he wished to build a society based on trust in man's better instincts.

> *I* purpose that which is extraordinary and leave to myself and successors no power of doing mischief, that the will of one man not hinder the good of the whole country.

That he did not falter in this purpose was remarkable given his aristocratic background and the natural inclination of people to abuse power. He held to a vision of mankind as essentially good and deserving of dignity, a vision which would sustain his spirits as he struggled to apply high principles to real life.

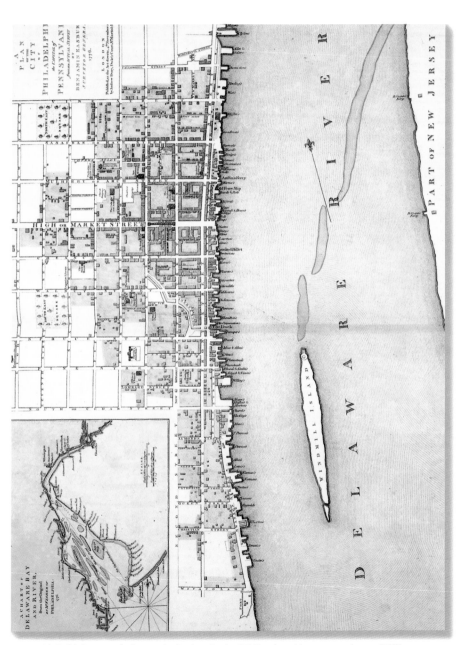

Philadelphia was the largest city in America in 1776, when this map was drawn. William Penn's original plan still can be seen in the right-angled streets and green spaces.

Penn laid out detailed plans for his town—one where commerce would prosper, all religions would be tolerated, and order and Christian rectitude would prevail. Philadelphia (Greek for "Brotherly Love") was also to be—if not fireproof—fire resistant. Heeding the advice of Sir Christopher Wren after the great London fire of 1666, Penn designed a city with straight streets intersecting at right angles—considered an improvement on the curving lanes of old European cities. Houses were to be placed at the center of their lots, with open space between them, for it was to be "a greene Country Towne, which will never be burnt, and always be wholesome." To that end he also proposed public parks for the commercial center, something unknown in English cities at the time.

◆ THE 1700s: PROSPERITY AND CIVIC IDEALISM

With its access to shipping routes through the Chesapeake Bay and its proximity to trappers, hunters, and wheat farmers in the surrounding countryside, Philadelphia soon prospered. The city exported lumber and furs from the western forests, wheat from what are now Lancaster and Bucks Counties, and cast iron and flour from city mills.

By 1700, Philadelphia's population had reached 6,000 and the pastor of Old Swedes' church was writing proudly: "All the houses are built of brick, three or four hundred of them, and in every house a shop, so that whatever one wants at any time he can have, for money."

If Quakers were the backbone of the early city, their tolerance brought in their wake Anglicans, Catholics, Jews, and "Plain People"—including Mennonites and Pennsylvania Germans, or "Deutsch." Newly prosperous merchants patronized equally successful craftsmen: silversmiths, cabinetmakers, coachmakers. (If the Quakers' philosophy of simplicity led them to eschew show, the Anglicans had no such scruples).

The large scale and ornate detail of this high chest, made in Philadelphia, circa 1770, is a fine example of the sophistication of both craftsman and merchant in the city at that time. (Philadelphia Museum of Art)

> ## NOT SO PLAIN PEOPLE
>
> *E*nglish and French visitors were amazed by the luxury displayed in the city: President Washington's splendid coach and four, his liveried footmen; staid Quakers carrying gold canes and gold snuffboxes, and wearing great silver buttons and buckles; ladies with sky-high coiffures, in costumes of the most costly brocades and velvets, silks, and satins; the grand wigs and queues, new buckles and silk stockings, worn by the men. "Ladies paid their French maids no less than two hundred pounds a year; and there were statesmen like Gouverneur Morris who had his two French valets and a man to buckle his hair in paillots." So long as the capital was in Philadelphia and the Federalists were in power, social life was luxurious and stately.
>
> —Clarence P. Hornung, *The Way It Was*

Literate and prosperous, Philadelphians were well abreast of the egalitarian and democratic ideas circulating during the mid-18th century. By the time of the Revolutionary War, theirs was the most prosperous city in the colonies, and with 24,000 residents, the most populous. These residents were by some accounts the most outspoken and opinionated on the continent. The Rev. Jacob Duche wrote in 1772:

> The poorest labourer upon the shore of the Delaware thinks himself entitled to deliver his sentiments in matters of religion and politics with as much freedom as the gentleman or the scholar. Indeed there is less distinction among the citizens of Philadelphia than among those of any civilized city in the world....For every man expects one day or another to be upon a footing with his wealthiest neighbor.

These self-confident people established libraries and discussion clubs; patronized societies studying science, painting, and music; undertook reform and civic improvement, and, as they drank their ale in pubs, talked politics. Why shouldn't they govern themselves, and establish a democracy?

So the character of the city—not just its location—helped to make it the birthplace of the American republic, beginning with the First Continental Congress in 1774. During the hot, sticky July of 1776, representatives from 12 of the 13 colonies—among them Franklin, Jefferson, Washington, Adams, and Hancock—composed and signed the document we know as the Declaration of Independence. On July 8, their declaration was read to an enthusiastic if not entirely representative group of citizens.

A year later, as General Howe led the British Army into Philadelphia, the active patriots had fled, and the city's thousands of loyalists welcomed the British with open arms. Howe's troops found warm comfortable quarters for the season, while Washington and his army settled in at Valley Forge for a miserable winter. Yet, the occupation of Philadelphia served no strategic purpose, and when Howe was dismissed from his command in May 1778 for "inactivity," it was widely said that Philadelphia had captured him rather than he capturing Philadelphia.

◆ EPIDEMICS AND POLITICAL GAMESMANSHIP

Centrally located among the 13 colonies, and the most prosperous city on the seaboard, Philadelphia became the new nation's capital. Its reputation was so positive that immigrants sailed in by the shipload. Hundreds of thousands disembarked at Water and Market Streets, many of them willing to indenture themselves for years in order to live in and around the city.

As businesses mushroomed and skilled workers were enticed to make their fortunes, the city struggled to keep pace. Housing was scarce, and crowding favored

The first federal bank in the United States opened in Philadelphia in 1791. Some questioned the need for such an institution. (New York Public Library)

*This 1850 lithograph shows the produce and seafood markets that once ran
the length of Market Street.*

the spread of disease and fire. Outbreaks of yellow fever occurred frequently,
killing thousands in each epidemic. Still, the city managed to move ahead.

In 1790, the new U.S. government decided to move the nation's capital to a
marshy site at the confluence of the Potomac and Anacostia Rivers, some 144
miles south of Philadelphia; by 1800, Philadelphia was no longer the capital of the
United States.

By 1823, it was no longer the most populous city either. New York had edged
out Philadelphia in population but not in innovation. William Penn's town already was known as the City of Firsts—in public safety, in education, in the arts
and in business. Philadelphia became a leading manufacturing center for textiles,
apparel, shoes, machinery, tools, iron, steel locomotives, and shipbuilding.

Philadelphians formed the Anti-Slavery Society in 1838, and Philadelphia regiments answered the Union call to arms.

After the Civil War the city continued to flourish. The telephone was introduced here, as were the first automated building elevator and the first medical college for women. The Pennsylvania Academy of Fine Arts, the country's first art school, opened, and extraordinary artists were nurtured here, among them Benjamin West and Thomas Eakins.

✦ 20TH CENTURY PHILLY

As a major manufacturing area, Philadelphia drew thousands of immigrants, each group settling into its own neighborhood: Italians in South Philly, Chinese in part of Center City, blacks in North Philly, Irish in Olney, Jews in Northeast, and much later, the Vietnamese in West Philly. Old-time Philadelphians—those who traced their lineage directly to the city's founders and prominent early leaders—were already well established in Chestnut Hill.

Mayors Richardson Dilworth and Joseph Clark presided over a kind of golden age between 1951 and 1962, when the city was prosperous and citizens thought and behaved as if they belonged to the city Philadelphia, rather than just to their

Philadelphian youths cool off in Logan Circle. City Hall rises in the background.

own ethnic enclaves. The 1970s and 1980s proved a depressing contrast, as the politics of race and the reality of crime and poverty divided the city during the mayoralty of Frank Rizzo, a combative mayor known by all and loved by many for his tough-guy approach to politics and crime suppression.

Replacing him in the 1980s was Wilson Goode, a former city manager, who enjoyed the support of the city's black community. That support survived the disastrous engagement with the radical black MOVE organization in 1985, when police bombed the MOVE headquarters and accidentally destroyed an entire city block of 60 houses (earning Philadelphia a new sobriquet, "The City that Bombed Itself"). Yet by the end of the century the city had rebounded once more. Much of the credit is given to the administration of Ed Rendell, a Democrat known for an aggressive style and a knack for getting things done. Under Rendell, Philadelphia, which has been steadily losing population, began encouraging economic growth in fields that seemed a good fit for the city, such as warehousing and distribution, education, health care, and tourism. It was the Rendell administration that breathed new life into Center City, creating the Avenue of the Arts along North and South Broad Streets to support an emerging arts district of theaters and performance centers. Hundreds of millions of dollars, both private and public funds, are being invested in sports stadiums and other building projects. Many residents, however, resent the five-percent wage tax levied by the city to help finance the expansion and seek to avoid the tax by relocating their business or residences beyond Philadelphia's city limits.

Philadelphians may be coming into a future that measures up to its past. For visitors, it is the city's past that draws them here.

■ INDEPENDENCE NATIONAL HISTORICAL PARK   *map page 57, E/F-3*

Perhaps no place in the country has more of an emotional grip on America's historical psyche than this national park just off the city's center. Here are the buildings in which Americans cast off colonial ties with England. From here was directed a long and uncertain war to secure their liberties, and here was instituted a democratic form of government which is to this day admired by many other nations around the world.

Half a century ago, the area around Independence Park was a dank industrial zone, cluttered with factories and abandoned warehouses. Today, the site has been reclaimed and turned over to the federal government for maintenance as a national treasure. While the friendly, green-uniformed rangers who patrol, maintain, and conduct tours at the site refer to their workplace as "the Mall," the national park actually spreads out over 42 acres and encompasses several city blocks of an area known as "Old City." It is the place where some of the greatest events in American history took place, and it is where any tour of Philadelphia should begin.

Most of the main mall is closed to traffic and protected by a combination of eight-foot-high brick walls and colonial-era buildings. Inside this area, the noise and bustle of modern life are left behind, and the ghosts of the colonial city seem to come to life.

DECLARATION OF INDEPENDENCE

*W*hen, in the course of human events, it becomes necessary for one people to dissolve the political bands which have connected them with another, and to assume, among the powers of the earth, the separate and equal station to which the laws of nature and of nature's God entitle them, a decent respect to the opinions of mankind requires that they should declare the causes which impel them to the separation.

We hold these truths to be self-evident, that all men are created equal, that they are endowed by their Creator with certain unalienable rights, that among these are life, liberty, and the pursuit of happiness. That, to secure these rights, governments are instituted among men, deriving their just powers from the consent of the governed. That, whenever any form of government becomes destructive of these ends, it is the right of the people to alter or to abolish it, and to institute new government, laying its foundation on such principles, and organizing its powers in such form, as to them shall seem most likely to effect their safety and happiness.

—Thomas Jefferson, 1776

Considering the historic importance of Independence Hall as the place where democracy was reborn after a several-thousand-year hiatus, its architecture seems surprisingly simple.

◆ INDEPENDENCE NATIONAL HISTORICAL PARK SIGHTS

Visitors Center *map page 57, F-3*

The best way to orient yourself is at the Visitors Center. A 28-minute film, *Independence*, runs through the day. The film is somewhat battered from zillions of showings but it is an excellent overview and wonderfully entertaining.

Maps provided at the Visitors Center include historical tidbits and easy-to-follow directions. The staff at the information booth are welcoming and knowledgeable about the park and sites beyond. There's also a well-stocked bookstore. *Information numbers provide current hours and a calendar of events; Open daily 9–5; Third and Chestnut Sts.; 215-597-8974.*

Independence Hall *map page 57, E-3*

In the center of the park is Independence Hall, a two-story redbrick building with white wood trim and gable roof, startling in its simplicity. Originally built as the Pennsylvania State House (circa 1732–48), it was planned and designed by Andrew Hamilton, a speaker of the assembly, and is considered a fine example of Georgian architecture. A square tower and octagonal steeple at one end (not the original) were added in 1753 to hold the Liberty Bell.

It was in the assembly room of this building that the Declaration of Independence was adopted on July 4, 1776, declaring that the colonies would no longer abide by the laws of England. It was here that George Washington received formal command of the Continental Army, and that the Articles of Confederation were ratified in 1781.

It was here as well, between May and September of 1787, that delegates from 12 states (Rhode Island did not send a representative) assembled to frame a thoroughly original instrument of government: the Constitution of the United States of America. In closed sessions, during long, hot days, delegates argued over and agreed upon the basic tenets of government, the balance of powers between branches of the government, and the civil protections accorded citizens.

The 55 men who met here included Alexander Hamilton of New York, Bostonian John Adams, Virginians Thomas Jefferson and James Madison, and Pennsylvania delegates James Wilson, Robert Morris, and Benjamin Franklin, then 70 years old. They constituted an intellectual elite astonishing even at the time. Louis Otto, the French *charge d'affairs*, commented to his superiors at home:

> *If all the delegates named for this Convention at Philadelphia are present, we will never have seen, even in Europe, an assembly more respectable for the talents, knowledge, disinterestedness, and patriotism of those who compose it.*

On my visit one January morning, there were few visitors. A pair of park rangers had time enough to recount for a group of foreign college students the significance of the main Assembly Room. The nicks and warping in the floor helped us to visualize the likes of Thomas Jefferson and Benjamin Franklin pacing back and forth

CENTRAL
PHILADELPHIA

1,000 Feet

300 Meters

0

0

between their desks and conferring with supporters while James Madison, seated at the main table, tried to move delegates toward consensus. *Open 9–5 every day; line up outside east entrance. Groups admitted every 15 minutes, no tickets required. Chestnut St. between Fifth and Sixth Sts.; information: 215-597-8974.*

Independence Hall connects with **Congress Hall**, the meeting place of the country's fledgling legislative body between 1790-1800. Two Presidents were inaugurated here: George Washington (for his second term) and his successor, John Adams.

Outside Independence Hall, close to the statue of George Washington, are **two bronze plaques** set in the brick sidewalk. One is where President Abraham Lincoln stood when he visited Independence Hall and raised a flag here in February of 1861. The other is where John F. Kennedy delivered an address on July 4, 1956.

Liberty Bell *map page 57, E-3*

North of Independence Hall, one block up the mall, the Liberty Bell sits in well-protected splendor. The bell's history is now a nearly impenetrable blend of fact and fiction. Originally called the State House Bell, the name Liberty Bell was coined by 19th century anti-slavery groups inspired by the engraved inscription on it: "Proclaim liberty throughout all the land, unto all the inhabitants thereof." (Leviticus 25:10).

The bell was cast in England in 1752 to commemorate the 50th anniversary of the Charter of Privileges, the democratic constitution that William Penn granted his colony in 1701. The first time it was rung, the bell cracked beyond repair. Local craftsmen Pass and Stow recast the bell and etched the famous inscription upon it.

The recast bell was hung in the tower of the State House and rang on July 8, 1776, to call the citizens of Philadelphia. Shortly after noon, a crowd having gathered, Col. John Nixon climbed up onto a wooden platform and read "The unanimous declaration of the 13 United States of America." Later that afternoon, at the green covered tables in the Assembly Room, the parchment copy of the Declaration of Independence was signed by delegates.

During the Revolutionary War, the bell was moved to Allentown and hidden in a cellar until the British evacuated Philadelphia. By the 1830s, when abolitionists began calling it the Liberty Bell, it had begun to crack again. According to tradition, the crack occurred while the bell tolled during the funeral of Chief Justice John Marshall in 1835. It rang for the last time in 1846 in celebration of George Washington's birthday. In 1852, the bell was put on display in Independence Hall, where it remained until 1976, when it was moved to the glass Liberty Bell Pavilion for the U.S. Bicentennial. *Visitors admitted at intervals, free; Market St. between Fifth and Sixth Sts.*

Franklin Court *map page 57, F-3*

East of the Liberty Bell Pavilion on Market Street is Franklin Court, the site of Benjamin Franklin's home. The original building was lost long before the park was

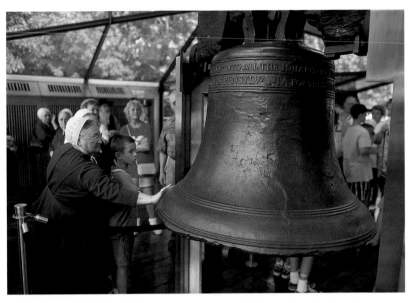

In 1776, the Liberty Bell was rung to announce the Declaration of Independence.

created, and architect Robert Venturi designed a steel-framed replica. The white-painted structure stands in the middle of a garden and is fronted by several row houses that are original to the property and were once rented out by Franklin.

Franklin lived in (the original of) this 10-room, three-story house and print shop with his wife, Deborah, and their two children. Franklin was often absent, most notably in London, where he spent a good deal of time during his 15 years as representative of Pennsylvania and several other colonies. However, he corresponded with his wife concerning the furnishing and maintenance of the house. Deborah put up with Franklin's philandering and was considered a good homemaker. Biographers describe their relationship as convivial. After Deborah's death in 1774, Franklin continued to live in the house with his daughter Sally and her family.

A basement museum houses examples of the many achievements of this inventive man. They include a glass armonica (a musical instrument composed of glass bowls that make music when tapped); a four-sided music stand; and the famous Franklin stove.

A 20-minute film sketches out Franklin's life, and there is also a replica of a typical Colonial-era print shop, the type Franklin would have worked in as a young apprentice. *Nos. 314-322 Market St. between Third and Fourth Sts. Also an entrance by way of Chestnut St. walkway; information: 215-597-8974.*

CHARMING BEN FRANKLIN

1706-1790

Benjamin Franklin arrived in Philadelphia from Boston in 1723, stopped at a baker's shop, and bought "three great Puffy Rolls." With a roll under each arm and munching on the third, he made his way up Market Street, where he passed his future wife Deborah Read at the door of her family's home. She watched him "& thought I made as I certainly did a most awkward ridiculous Appearance."

Franklin moved into Deborah's father's house and courted the young woman, but when he left for London, she married a man named John Rogers, who, as it turned out, already had a wife. Eventually Rogers deserted Deborah and Franklin took her her as his common law wife. Their marriage lasted until her death in 1774, although they were frequently apart.

Franklin's versatility and long life defy summary. He did everything it is possible to do on the printed page, as writer, editor, publisher, and printer. He served his city, colony, and new nation as postmaster, assembly delegate, and foreign envoy. He founded a library and a fire insurance company. He was as versatile and accomplished as a scientist as he was as a writer and statesman. He was also the life of the party, to judge from all accounts, as well as from this lyric he wrote:

> There's but one Reason I can Think
> Why People ever cease to Drink
> Sobriety the Cause is not
> Nor Fear of being deam'd a Sot,
> But if Liquor can't be got.

> If on my Theme I rightly think
> There are Five Reasons why Men drink:
> Good Wine, a Friend, because I'm dry,
> Or least I should be by and by
> Or any other Reason why.

The list of Franklin's inventions might include not just bifocals and the Franklin stove, but also shuttle diplomacy and international superstardom. He commuted between England and the colonies during the decade before the Revolution. Once that conflict was under way he spent his time in France, seeking aid for the war effort. That the French gave generously testifies both to their animosity toward the British and their infatuation with the American envoy. As the historian Page Smith writes in his history of the American Revolution, *A New Age Now Begins*:

> *F*ranklin, a man as subtle and devious as a French diplomat, as sophisticated in his tastes as the most decadent aristocrat, was nonetheless cast by the French in the role of a simple American agriculturalist. And Franklin —editor, author, courtier, scientist, inventor, sensualist, and roué —played the role with zest. He even wore a beaver cap, which was more enchanting to his admirers than the most bejeweled crown could have been. Everywhere in Paris he was feted, admired, and acclaimed. His picture was reproduced on snuffboxes, plates, vases, and commodes and sold by the thousands. Enterprising businessmen sold seats at places where the people of Paris could watch him ride by in his coach. Elegant ladies vied for his favors."

At Franklin's death in 1790, the French National Assembly took time out from its own tumultuous affairs to observe three days of mourning for a man they praised for "the simplicity and sweetness of his manners...the purity of his principles, the extent of his knowledge, and the charms of his mind."

—Jessica Fisher

Benjamin Franklin, whose accomplishments included being named the first Postmaster General of the United States, was honored by having his portrait adorn the nation's first official postage stamp, in 1847. Less official likenesses of Franklin appeared on more pedestrian objects abroad.

■ OTHER HISTORIC BUILDINGS AND NEIGHBORHOODS

Many interesting and historic buildings are adjacent to Independence National Historical Park, or set within the larger area it administers. The city of Philadelphia extended only as far as Old City and Society Hill in the 18th century. The natural relationship of these neighborhoods to the city's port on the Delaware River was evident until the 20th century, when they were cut off from each other by Interstate 95.

Betsy Ross House   *map page 57, F-2*

Historians can neither confirm nor deny that Betsy Ross sewed America's first flag, and they are equally unsure whether George Washington came secretly to her house just before he went to war and asked her to make a flag based on his roughly sketched design. Whatever the truth about Ross's flag-making, she was well known to 18th-century Philadelphians as a tough-minded draper's widow who appeared regularly at Patriot rallies.

We do know that on June 14, 1777, members of the Continental Congress, sitting in Philadelphia, decided that "the flag of the thirteen United States be thirteen stripes, alternate red and white; that the union be thirteen stars, white, in a blue field representing a new constellation."

In the Ross house furnishings and comforts are few, and the contrast between this house and the fine homes of the local gentry is startling. *239 Arch St. between Third and Bread Sts.; 215-627-5343.*

Elfreth's Alley and Old City
map page 57, F-2

Old City and Society Hill are two Colonial-era neighborhoods that are part of Independence Park. Elfreth's Alley in Old City is the oldest continuously occupied residential street in America—and at least one of the homes dates back to 1702. The cobblestone street is original. (From a distance cobblestone lanes are quaint and inviting, but a long walk over them—especially on a rainy day—will give pedestrians a unique understanding of why the first paved roads were such a godsend.)

In Old City (north of Chestnut between Front and Fifth Streets) the two- and three-story brick houses are typical of homes where the skilled craftsmen resided.

In recent years, the interiors of old factories and warehouses here have been converted into spacious lofts that have attracted a younger set, especially artists and architects.

Two of the homes on Elfreth's Alley are open continuously year-round for tours, but if you're visiting over the first weekend of June, make plans to tour when most of the 30 homes are open for guided tours during Fête Days. A smaller number are open for holiday tours during the Christmas months. *Admission fee; Front and Second Sts. between Arch and Race Sts.; 215-574-0560.*

Christ Church   *map page 57, F-2/3*

Christ Church was built between 1724 and 1744 to replace a rickety wooden structure,

Elfreth's Alley is the oldest continuously occupied residential street in the United States.

modeled after the post-Baroque style of English architect Sir Christopher Wren. George Washington attended services regularly here. Benjamin Franklin, a professed deist, was an active member of the church, and a series of lotteries he ran helped pay for the 196-foot steeple and its bells.

On my last visit, workers were polishing the brass plaques that identified the pews occupied by former well-known parishioners. Look for George and Martha, Benjamin and Deborah, and Betsy Ross. *Second St. one block north of Market.*

Christ Church Cemetery: Although visitors are now prohibited from walking through the cemetery, it's still worth a look through the gates to observe the grave markers of seven signers of the Declaration of Independence. Also here is the final resting place of the Franklins, buried alongside a son who died at age four. Look for pennies on Ben Franklin's grave marker, a local tradition: "A penny saved is a penny earned." *Fifth and Arch Sts.*

Bishop White House   *map page 57, F-3*
Built in the Georgian style for the first Episcopal bishop of Pennsylvania, this home was typical of this city's upper-class residences in the late 1700s. The bishop played host to many of the era's most famous statesmen and kept a tight reign on his priests. It was not unusual to see several of them fidgeting in hardback chairs in the second-floor hallway outside his library, waiting to be received.

Tickets to tour the house may be purchased at the visitor center for one-hour tours that include the Todd house, a more modest home which once was the residence of Dolley Madison, wife of James, the nation's fourth president. *Open daily 9:30-4:30; 309 Walnut St. between Third and Fourth Sts.*

City Tavern *map page 57, F-3*

Built in 1773 by the "principal gentlemen" of the city, for three decades City Tavern was a social, political, and economic center, boasting several large meeting rooms, lodging rooms, two kitchens, and a bar. John Adams called it "The most genteel tavern in America."

Paul Revere rode here with news of Boston in 1774, and at a famous meeting here in May of the same year, radicals pushed the heretofore moderate colony into the forefront of a dispute with England. It was the site in 1775 of George Washington's farewell dinner before leaving as the newly elected commander of the Continental Army. The tavern was a watering hole and gathering place for members of the Continental Congresses, the Constitutional Convention, and officials of the Federal Government from 1790-1800. The present structure is a faithful reproduction of the original. It is furnished with period reproductions and serves lunch and dinner. *Northwest corner; Second and Walnut Sts.; no fee; 11:30 –10 P.M.; 215-413-1443.*

Society Hill *map page 57, F-4*

If there is one city neighborhood that has endured in station and purpose, it is Society Hill, the wealthy enclave of early 19th-century Philadelphians and an exclusive, meticulously preserved neighborhood today. It begins at the Delaware River and stretches up to Sixth Street, near Independence National Historical Park. More a rise in the road than a hill, within its streets are several historic churches and the Society Hill Synagogue.

At 321 South Fourth Street is **Physick House,** the only freestanding Federal mansion left in Society Hill and an excellent place to get a sense of how the wealthy lived in the early part of the 19th century.

Be sure to stroll along Delancey Street, a side street with an eclectic array of colonial structures and contemporary houses. Other good streets to amble are American, Cypress, and Philip. Observe the subtle architectural details—roofs with copper of a nice patina, chimney pots, and courtyards with breathtaking gardens.

This is a neighborhood that is so frequently photographed for travel feature stories that several homeowners have posted signs requesting copies of articles that feature neighborhood photographs.

Penn's Landing *map page 57, F-3*

Society Hill's waterfront on the Delaware River is known as Penn's Landing, a 37-acre river park which marks the place where William Penn stepped ashore from the *Welcome* in 1682 and took possession of Pennsylvania. Today its attractions are a little less dramatic and tend toward the touristy and sometimes even schlocky, but it's still an appealing place to while away a sunny afternoon.

Looking across the granite-blue Delaware River you can see New Jersey about a half-mile away. The park has been reclaimed from the working waterfront, and if you look north toward the Ben Franklin Bridge, you'll see cargo ships and tankers

William Birch's sketch of the Bingham Mansion, which once stood on the corner of Spruce and Third on Society Hill. The Binghams were pillars—if scandalous pillars—of Philadelphia society.

loading and unloading. Farther north along the waterfront is an area of run-down industrial buildings.

Masts of the sailing ship *Moshulu* (now a restaurant) are visible downstream. Several tourist ships depart from Penn's Landing including the *Liberty Belle* paddle wheeler, the *Spirit of Philadelphia* cruises, and the smaller *Holiday* and *Captain Lucky.*

The **Independence Seaport Museum** exhibits Admiral George Dewey's 1892 cruiser *Olympia* and the World War II *Becuna*, a guppy-class submarine commissioned in 1943 to serve in the Pacific Fleet. *Open daily 9–5; admission; Columbus Blvd. at Walnut St.; 215-925-5439.*

The grassy waterfront park hosts more than 70 different family events from May through September, including multicultural festivals, children's theater, concerts, and Philadelphia's Fourth of July celebrations. During good weather, it's a popular spot for strolling or picnicking.

Several nightclubs and more than a dozen restaurants can be found along this three-mile stretch. Construction is underway for an office building and two hotels, which hopefully won't dwarf their surroundings. *On the Delaware River east of Christopher Columbus Blvd. between Market and Lombard Sts.*

■ WASHINGTON SQUARE DISTRICT   *map page 57, C,D,&E-3,4*

Antique Row, the Reading Terminal, Washington Square, and the stately Bellevue Hotel make up the four sides of this center-city area. Washington Square itself—one of Philadelphia's original five squares—is a large park at Walnut and Sixth Streets. In the park is the Tomb of the Unknown Soldier, the only such monument to Revolutionary War soldiers.

Within this district can be found **Thomas Jefferson University, Jefferson Hospital,** several historic homes (now bed and breakfasts), the **Historical Society of Pennsylvania**, and several theaters. **Antique Row** is along Pine Street between Ninth and 13th. *The district's boundaries are Market, Sixth, Lombard, and Broad Sts.*

■ SOUTH STREET   *map page 57, A,B,C,D,E,&F-4*

It's jarring, to say the least, to walk from the colonial-era enclaves of Independence Park and Old City into the antic gyrations of the surrounding trendy neighborhoods. Along these streets, grunge meets antique chic; businessman meets bohemian; gay bar meets cigar bar; and boozy corner cafes meet fabulous restaurants.

In the **South Street** neighborhood, the closest thing Philly has to New York's Greenwich Village or San Francisco's North Beach, there are far-out fashion

(above) The Mummers Parade, held in Philadelphia every New Year's Day, might best be described as the city's version of Mardi Gras. (opposite) A colorful emporium on South Street.

boutiques, a mainstream Gap store, tattoo parlors, new-age book shops, a supply store for witches, fringe-art galleries, and scores of ethnic restaurants. In the early 1980s, property was going at fire-sale prices after city officials let it be known they planned to raze the neighborhood to make room for an expressway overpass. The fly-over never happened but the low land prices remained, and the funky but financially challenged moved in. *South St. is southwest of Washington Square, bounded east-west from about 10th St. to Front St. and north-south from Lombard to Catherine Sts.*

■ CENTER CITY

New York may be the city that never sleeps but Philadelphia's **Center City** district catches only a few winks. Highrise office buildings, trendy restaurants, shops, and mega stores line the streets. Stand between 14th and 15th Streets along Market Street and strain to take full measure of the Art Deco–styled twin office towers at Liberty Place, which, at 63 stories, are the tallest buildings in the city.

City Hall *map page 57, C-3*
Until 1987, City Hall was the most prominent feature of the Philadelphia skyline, its pre-eminence protected by a gentlemen's agreement among architects and builders that no structure should dampen the dramatic impact of the William Penn statue crowning its dome. (Designed by sculptor Alexander Milne Calder, this 37-foot bronze statue is the largest single piece of sculpture on any building in the world. Penn's nose alone is 18 inches long!) From the outside the building seems grand, but walk into the courtyard entrances and you'll realize this is a working building which has suffered from wear and tear. Above the compass rose in the center rise dingy walls stained from the drips of the rusted air conditioners hanging out of every window.

Though dwarfed by office towers, City Hall is still very much worth a tour. A grand granite and white marble edifice decorated with an eclectic and not entirely coherent mix of columns, pilasters, pediments, dormers, and sculptures, it remains the keystone of downtown Philadelphia. Free tours are offered every 15 minutes on weekdays, and a fine view of the city may be had from the observation deck on the 40th floor. *Broad and Market Sts. Tour information: 215-686-2840.*

Masonic Temple *map page 57, C-2*
Membership in the Philadelphia Free and Accepted Masons, a fraternal society founded in the Middle Ages, was coveted in colonial times. Many statesmen of the Revolution, including George Washington, belonged to the Philadelphia Guild and supported building of the temple as a state-wide meeting place. The temple is divided into seven lodge halls, each ornately decorated in the styles of various cultures,

A view of City Hall down Benjamin Franklin Parkway.

A lion dance in the Chinese New Year's parade, held in Chinatown each year.

including Egyptian, Asian, Gothic. On display in the building's museum is a Masonic apron embroidered for Washington by the wife of the Marquis de Lafayette. *Guided tours; One N. Broad St.; 215-988-1917.*

Pennsylvania Academy of Fine Arts
map page 57, C-2
America's first art museum, this building is a national historic landmark—an architectural jewel by the noted Philadelphia architects Frank Furness and George Hewitt that incorporates both Victorian and Gothic styles. The stone and brick entranceway and the carefully laid grand staircase inside make it a worthy showcase for the works of three centuries of American master painters, such as Benjamin West, Winslow Homer, Andrew Wyeth, and Red Grooms.

Open Mon–Sat; 10–5; Sun at 11; 118 N. Broad Street at Cherry; 215-972-7600.

Reading Terminal Market
at City Center *map page 57, C/D-2/3*
The predecessor to this indoor market began in 1893 by the Delaware riverfront. (In fact, High Street was renamed Market Street in its honor.) The market eventually moved indoors to a train terminal shed and was then renovated as part of the convention center development. Some of the city's best produce, pretzels, prepared foods, and crafts can be found in the 80 food stalls, artists' booths, and craft kiosks. Foods range from local favorites like the classic Philly cheese steak and Pennsylvania Dutch comfort dishes to Vietnamese-French and Ethiopian delicacies. Crafts range from

country cute to urban edgy. Amish families have a section where they sell their produce Wednesday through Sunday.

All in all one will find the products here to be of superior quality. Aside from the crafts and good food, it's worth touring this building that was once owned by the Reading Railroad—now a national historic landmark, and visit the old train shed, one floor above the market. *Mon–Sat; 8–6; 12th and Filbert Sts.; 215-922-2317.*

Chinatown *map page 57, D-2*

Adjacent to the Reading Terminal and the convention center, this eight-block area offers a wide selection of inexpensive Vietnamese, Thai, vegetarian, and of course, Chinese restaurants. The multi-colored Chinese Friendship Gate (at 10th Street between Arch and Cherry) was built in

1984 as a joint project with Philadelphia's sister city, Tianjin in China. *N. Eighth and 11th Sts. between Vine and Arch Sts.*

Civil War Library and Museum

map page 57, B-4

Founded in 1888, this museum preserves thousands of historical documents related to the War Between the States. What makes the place fascinating is the collection of personal weapons and possessions held by the war's most famous soldiers, and plaster life casts of Abraham Lincoln's hands and face. *Tues–Sat; 11–4; 1805 Pine St.; 215-735-8196.*

Fairmount Park *map page 75, A-2,3,4*

At 14 square miles, Fairmount Park provides Philadelphians with plenty of space to run, stroll, bicycle, or picnic. The park has 100 miles of bridle and walking paths, and

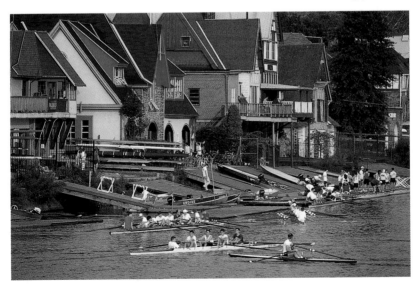

Boathouse Row, at the southern end of Fairmount Park.

an eight-mile paved path for jogging, cycling, and walking, and a five-mile gravel path on the west bank of the creek that has spectacular scenery. **Wissahickon Gorge**, in the northernmost part of the park, is a particularly beautiful hiking area. The **Philadelphia Zoo**, the country's first, is part of the park, as is the **Philadelphia Museum of Art** *(see page 73)*. In the warm weather months, the **Mann Center for the Performing Arts** holds open-air concerts. Ten Victorian homes, known as **Boathouse Row,** front Kelly Drive and have backyards that run into the Schuylkill River. These are the headquarters of the city's popular rowing clubs, whose members can be seen slicing through the glass-like river water on early-morning practice runs.

Along Kelly and West River Drives are splendid 18th- and early 19th-century houses, once "rural" retreats for well-to-do Philadelphia families only a horseback ride from the city's commercial center. Among the 90 historic homes, most are open for tours and a few are rented out for private events. Well back from the prime river views, you'll find the far more modest homes of 17th-century Swedish and German settlers.

Typical of the upper-class homes is **Sweetbriar**, the retreat built on the west bank of the Schuylkill in 1797 by Samuel Breck, a wealthy merchant who served in the state legislature and wrote the bill calling for the emancipation of all slaves in the state. The elegant, federal-style house was

A solitary sculler on the Schuylkill River below the elegant facade of the Philadelphia Museum of Art.

*A Calder mobile graces the airy interior of the Philadelphia Museum of Art—appropriate,
because Alexander Calder was a Philadelphia native.*

the scene of much entertaining when the city served as the nation's capital. Many of the rooms were decorated in 18th-century French style, probably due to Breck's friendship with such French notables as Lafayette and Talleyrand. The grounds included ornate, English-style gardens and a landscaping design that draws the eye to an island Breck owned in the Schuylkill River. *Open July–Dec; Wed–Sun, 10–4; on Sweetbriar Hill off Lansdowne Dr.; 215-222-1333.*

Philadelphia Museum of Art

map page 75, A/B-4

This is Philadelphia's great museum, with impressive collections of impressionist works, American and Pennsylvania Dutch decorative arts, even a full-scale medieval cloister and fountain. Also on display is the work of Thomas Eakins, considered one of America's greatest 19th-century painters. His portraits of Philadelphians say more about the quality of life in the city during that era than all the words in this book.

A few years ago the statue of Rocky Balboa stood at the bottom of the front steps —immortalized in the Hollywood blockbuster movie *Rocky.* (This also says more about Philadelphia in the modern era than all the words in this book.) It has since been moved to the sports complex in South Philly, where its presence is perhaps more appropriate. *At the top of Faire Mount, the plateau at the end of the Benjamin Franklin Parkway, joining the southern tip of Fairmount Park; 215-763-8100.*

■ SOUTH PHILADELPHIA *map opposite*

Little Italy *map opposite, B-5*
South Philadelphia is best known for its Little Italy district and the "momma e pappa" eateries that seem to be on every street corner. While there are expensive restaurants featuring sophisticated wine lists and romantic ambiance, the smaller establishments prepare equally wonderful dishes.

Mario Lanza Museum *map opposite, B-5*
World-famous tenor and actor Mario Lanza (1921–1959) was born in this neighborhood. He was discovered when, while working as a piano mover, he belted out a song on the stage of the Academy of Music. The Mario Lanza Museum is a veritable shrine to Lanza, with photographs, video-cassettes of Lanza's films, and souvenirs. *Third floor, Settlement Music School; 416 Queen St.; 215-468-3623.*

Ninth Street Market *map opposite, B-5*
A tour of South Philly would not be complete without a stop at the Ninth Street Italian Market, dating back 125 years to the Italian immigrant founders. Here farmers and food vendors haggle over prices with demanding Italian homemakers as well as other locals who travel miles to shop here. A large selection of excellent, low-priced produce is displayed on plywood tables. Nearby are food, specialty, cookware, and cheese shops. *Ninth St. between Washington Ave. and Christian St.; Tues–Sat, 9:30–4; Sun 9:30–12:30.*

Rowhouses of South Philadelphia.

■ CHESTNUT HILL   *map page 75, A-2*

Pleasant Chestnut Hill was created when Germantown's railroad extended here in 1884. This village within a city is graced by unique restaurants, boutiques, and art galleries that line 12 blocks of Germantown Avenue, the cobblestoned main thoroughfare. Many of the residential houses are architectural gems. One of them, **Stenton,** was Lord Howe's headquarters before the Battle of Germantown. Chestnut Hill remains one of the city's best communities, where a 50-year-old dry cleaning shop may thrive next to a hip restaurant, and young families keep moving in. *Historical and architectural tours: 215-247-6696.*

■ MANAYUNK   *map page 75, A-3*

Taken from a Lenni Lenape phrase for "where we go to drink," Manayunk, on the Schuylkill River, was once connected by canal to the rest of the Pennsylvania canal system that was built in 1819 and which established the infrastructure for a strong industrial base. Today, Manayunk's industries are all closed, but the town has become a lively, hip neighborhood, with boutiques, restaurants, nightclubs and intimate bars, all of which are spotted in and around the remains of the mills and other 19th century industries. In fact, Main Street in Manayunk has become so popular that parking is almost impossible on weekends.

The community hosts a superb arts festival on the last weekend in June of each year, offering food from area restaurants and showcasing local artists.

A separate village when it was settled in 1683, Germantown's citizens were a mix of German Quakers and Mennonite farmers who proved to be even more progressive and welcoming than many mainstream Philadelphians. European immigrants with differing religious beliefs and cultural mores were surprised to find not only a tolerant community but a receptive one. Residents of Germantown were quietly supportive of the Revolution (although as Quakers they were pacifists) but much more subdued than the great revolutionary leaders and activists residing in the city center.

Because of its industrial facilities, the British army made a bee-line for Germantown after routing Gen. George Washington's army and occupying Philadelphia in 1777. The Battle of Germantown, actually a series of attacks on the British troops by Washington, was a bitter early defeat for the revolutionaries.

(opposite) Fairman Rogers' Four-in-Hand, *a Thomas Eakins painting depicting a Main Line Sunday drive, circa 1879. (Philadelphia Museum of Art: gift of Mr. William Alexander Dick)*

MAIN LINE FAMILY

The old families of Philadelphia, aristocrats of the Main Line, are described in this extract, which contains information (one might say gossip) upon which social status turns.

Take Philadelphia's assets, the Grand Gestures, the public monuments. Each one bears, like a thumbprint, the impress, usually, of some one prominent Old Philadelphia family: [for instance] ...Philadelphia's museum of science of which one of the proudest exhibits has been the Bible of the Duane family, descended so casually from Benjamin Franklin....The Duanes were originally far more controversial than the Bradfords ever thought of being. "We consider Mr. Franklin to have been of a somewhat shady family"... ❖

William Duane ...[became a newspaper editor] The *Aurora* was obviously Duane's niche. He...carried mudslinging to such a length that even some Democrats blanched. He "exposed" all sort of Federalist misdoing, and did more than any other journalist to elect Thomas Jefferson. The Duanes headed for Law, and in the fourth generation...a Russell Duane did well to become one of Philadelphia's most prosperous lawyers....The final offshoot of all this has been Morris Duane, son of Russell. With the exception that he went to Harvard ('23) instead of the University, he has followed the Old Philadelphian pattern....His taste in boards has been excellent; he's been on the Finance Committee of the Philosophical Society, concerned with the American Lawn Tennis Association, and needless to say, member of the Philadelphia Club. He married a Harrison. When Philadelphians refer to Franklin's "somewhat shady family" they certainly do not mean to include his most conspicuous descendant in Philadelphia today.

—Nathaniel Burt, adapted from *The Perennial Philadelphians,*
The Anatomy of an American Aristocracy, 1963

■ BARNES FOUNDATION   *map page 75, A-3/4*

Residents and shopkeepers in the comfortable Philadelphia bedroom community of Merion (about 10 miles west of Center City) know that most outsiders wandering around lost are looking for the quirky, world-famous art museum known as the Barnes Foundation. Housed in the French Renaissance–style mansion that was his home, the art collection of Albert C. Barnes, a physician and chemist, contains some of the most significant French impressionist and postimpressionist paintings in the world, as well as an extensive collection of African and American Indian art, some 900 paintings, and 2,000 additional artworks spanning 3,000 years.

For much of his adult life, Barnes was a man with a mission. He had made his fortune developing Argyrol, an antiseptic widely used prior to the development of antibiotics, and used his wealth to finance his passions: collecting art and educating people about art. He bought early and bought well, spending millions of dollars to acquire some of the finest works by such masters as Van Gogh, Degas, Matisse, Monet, Modigliani, Picasso, Cezanne, Rousseau, Seurat, and Renoir. There are more works by Cezanne here than in all of France.

A populist who believed that art was self evident if presented properly, Barnes prepared "ensembles" of elements–an ax and an ax handle, for example, next to a Moreau to compliment the composition on the canvas–primarily for working-class audiences, especially people who worked with their hands. "It's not really a museum in the traditional sense," explained the foundation's director, Kimberly Camp. "It's really a school."

Barnes achieved notoriety for openly scorning art historians and refusing them access to his collection. Art historian Clement Greenberg supposedly disguised himself as a worker to gain entrance, but was ultimately discovered and summarily thrown out. When asked to confirm this famous incident the foundation director replied: "Probably. There were a great many instances of that nature."

Art historians were desperate to see the collection because so many of the paintings in it reflect critical moments in the development of artists and of modernism itself. The 1905 Matisse painting, *The Joy of Life,* for example, marks the transition of Matisse from a talented young painter to the artist whose themes and style we revere today.

Barnes's antipathy toward art historians and art critics was in part the result of an exhibition he created in 1923 for his alma mater, the University of Pennsylvania. Critics and historians panned the exhibit and the University added insult to injury by rejecting his offer to bequeath his collection to it, a gift easily worth a billion dollars today. In 1961, a lawsuit brought by the Pennsylvania attorney general opened the collection to everyone.

The Barnes is a must for any lover of art. *Advance reservations required; admission $5, parking $10. Open Sept–June: Fri–Sun, 9:30–5; July-Aug: Wed–Fri, 9:30–5; 300 North Latches Lane, Merion; 610-667-0290.*

If you make the trek to Merion to see the Barnes collection, be sure to take in the **Joseph Lapsley Wilson Arboretum** on the grounds of the Barnes Foundation. The personal passion of Mrs. Barnes, the arboretum covers 12 acres with a tea house, a spring-set pond, over 200 varieties of lilacs, a greenhouse and more, and is the reason the Barnes Foundation is located in Merion. *Admission to the arboretum is included with admission to the museum.*

■ BRANDYWINE VALLEY *map page 87, D-3&4*

Twenty-five miles southwest of Philadelphia, the city gives way to verdant farm and horse country. In the spring, when the ponies are taking the first measure of their privileged lives, and the air is thick with the fragrance of honeysuckle and mowed grass, it is difficult to imagine that this was also the ground upon which so many men in the American War of Independence fought and died.

Country roads stretch into rolling honey-colored hills past heavy green spruce trees and, in springtime, pastel wildflowers. To find rural beauty, turn north off US 1 onto Route 100 at Chadd's Ford and drive along Creek Road toward West Chester. This is also the exit for the Brandywine Battlefield State Park, and if you go south, the Brandywine Valley Museum.

Just about any turn off US 1 west of I-476 will take you onto rural roads. Exit at Route 82, for example, six miles from the Brandywine Valley Museum, and you will find yourself in the the heart of a mushroom-growing region.

John Rubens Smith's Mill on the Brandywine, circa 1830. (Library of Congress)

Brandywine River Museum
map page 87, D-4

In 1967, a group of residents, many of whom could trace their family history in the valley back to colonial times, succeeded in putting a cap on development and worked to clean up pollution in the Brandywine River. To defray costs of the work, they enlisted the considerable talents of valley artists and opened the Brandywine River Museum in a converted 1880s gristmill. The glass-walled lobby brings in views of the river and surrounding woods. Included here are many of the breathtaking paintings of Andrew Wyeth and his son Jamie, which depict the rural beauty of this area. *US 1 and Rte. 100, Chadd's Ford; 610-388-2700.*

Brandywine Battlefield Park
map page 87, D-4

On this battlefield the British dealt George Washington one of the worst setbacks of the American War of Independence. On September 11, 1777, with half of his army gone to defend Manhattan, Washington faced a well-equipped British force and lost, forcing his retreat to Lancaster and then to Valley Forge. Without Washington's army to protect it, the British captured Philadelphia, dealing the Revolutionary cause both a physical and a psychological blow. At the 50-acre battlefield park are a reproduction of the farmhouse used by Washington as headquarters and a preserved farmhouse used as quarters by the French soldier-adventurer, the Marquis de Lafayette. *Admission fee; open all year except Christmas; closed Mon; US 1, Chadd's Ford; 610-459-3342.*

Chadd's Ford Winery   *map page 87, D-4*

Operating out of a renovated 18th-century barn, this winery produces small lots of varietal wines using grapes grown in its vineyards and the nearby area. *Tastings daily; US 1, five miles south of Rte. 202; 610-388-6221.*

Longwood Gardens *map page 87, D-4*
Once the country estate of industrialist
Pierre S. du Pont, Longwood Gardens was
designed to include elaborate fountains,
two lakes, large heated conservatories of exotic tropical flowers, and formal outdoor
gardens. About 11,000 kinds of plants, (especially roses, and orchids) bloom within
the 1,050-acre garden estate. In spring, the
azaleas and rhodedendrons are especially
beautiful; in fall, the chrysanthemums and
changing leaves. Water lillies with huge up-
turned leaves and large beautiful flowers
flourish in the lakes. In the formal gardens
there are artistically sculpted topiaries such
as one might find in an English garden. As
you wander the paths you'll pass sculptures
that blend in beautifully with the plantings.
*Open daily, 9–5; US 1, Kennett Square;
610-388-1000.*

Winterthur *map page 87, D-4*
Just a few miles from US 1 across the Pennsylvania border in Delaware is the Brandywine Valley's most famous attraction, the
Winterthur garden and museum, once the
country estate of Henry Francis du Pont.

Du Pont expected fresh flowers from his
own gardens to bedeck his dinner tables,
and dictated that the china must match the
flowers and the food complement the
plates. An inveterate collector, he owned
hundreds of sets of china. Of the two
buildings on the property, one has 175
rooms. Winterthur holds the world's finest
collection of early American decorative arts.
*Tours; admission $13; open daily; Delaware
Ave., Rte. 52; 800-448-3883.*

The interior of the tropical plants conservatory at Longwood Gardens.

■ VALLEY FORGE NATIONAL HISTORIC PARK *map page 87, D/E-3*

After his stinging defeat in September of 1777 by the British at Brandywine, George Washington re-grouped his forces briefly at Lancaster, then set up headquarters with 16 of his brigades across the Schuylkill River from the city of Philadelphia at Valley Forge. An arch sculpture at one end of Valley Forge National Historic Park, the National Memorial Arch, honors the soldiers who endured the terrible winter encampment of 1777–78. Conditions were so debilitating that many soldiers deserted camp and more than 2,000 soldiers died from malnutrition and disease. One officer who spent the winter with them and trained them in the cold, helped many find the will to survive. He was not an American, but a Prussian drillmaster, Friedrich von Steuben, and much of the tour material on the park is devoted to the critical role that foreign officers and soldiers played at this crucial point in the the War of Independence.

Seeing the Park: Today Valley Forge is part of suburban Philadelphia, and it looks like a wooded, grassy county park. The site is impressive if you absorb its history and walk along its paths, using your imagination to recall the courage and endurance of the men who suffered here.

Among the sites in the park open for touring are several simple, colonial-era homes that were used by Washington and his officers during that winter. Valley Forge Park also has a six-mile hike-bike trail, a 10-mile horse trail, and several picnic areas. If you plan to drive a loop tour through the park, pick up an audio tour for your car at the visitors center. *Eighteen miles west of downtown Philadelphia off I-76 at exit 26B, then Rte. 422 west one mile to Rte. 23 west; 610-783-1077.*

PHILADELPHIA
VALLEY FORGE

(opposite) Snow covers a cannon in Valley Forge.

(right) Washington's headquarters at Valley Forge.

SOUTHEAST

SOUTHEAST BASICS

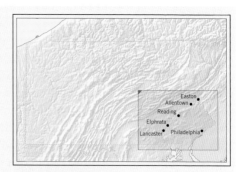

Food & Lodging
map 276; charts 277
listings by town, in alphabetical order 278

■ TRAVEL BASICS

The rolling hills and long stretches of farm country in southeastern Pennsylvania are only a short drive from the greater Philadelphia area. Come here to pass lazy afternoons poking about craft shops and cluttered antique stores, to hike or bike along the park-like trail of the old Delaware Canal tow path, or to float a canoe down the wide Delaware River.

West of Philadelphia, you may catch a glimpse of the fascinating world of Old Order Amish farmers and other Pennsylvania Dutch religious communities. Explore interesting museums such as the Moravian Pottery and Tile Works in Doylestown or the Cornwall Iron Furnace near Reading, then retire in the evening to one of many warm and inviting bed-and-breakfast inns.

Getting Around: Since the real allure of the region lies on the backroads, and since Pennsylvania Dutch Country and Bucks County are hardly touched by mass transit, a car is a necessity. A good, detailed map will help you navigate the well-marked backroads that snake throughout the countryside.

Climate: Summer is T-shirt and shorts weather with temperatures averaging in the 80s. Humidity is unpredictable, but in general, July and August are the most oppressively hot. Spring and fall are the most comfortable for traveling and hiking, with temperatures ranging from nighttime lows in the 50s to daytime highs in the upper 60s to low 70s. Winters are milder here than in any other part of Pennsylvania, with temperatures in the upper 30s to below freezing for most of December and January. Snowfall is not particularly heavy, averaging about 25 inches per season. Pack an umbrella as rainy days are common year round.

Food & Lodging: Some of the best restaurants in the east are here. The best lodging is often off the beaten paths. Often for the same nightly rate as higher end chain hotels, rooms can be had in charming, informal inns in the communities most worth visiting. For families and travelers on a budget, there are a variety of chain hotels at interstate exits throughout the region. **Food & Lodging map** page 276; **charts** page 277; **listings** in alphabetical order by town begin on page 278.

■ INTRODUCTION

In Pennsylvania Dutch Country, about an hour's drive from Philadelphia, a modern couple in a convertible BMW fleeing the city for a posh country inn breezes by an Amish family in horse and buggy as it clings to the berm. In Bucks County, also about an hour's drive from the city, stone farmhouses older than the Declaration of Independence stand near pricey, new, gated housing developments. Near Reading, the town founded by William Penn's sons, the Hopewell Furnace which produced iron cannons and shot for the Continental Army sits peacefully just a mile away from one of the most monstrous and bustling discount outlet malls in the country.

Throughout this bucolic region of rolling hills, farmland, and quaint little towns that work hard to stay that way, rich pockets of early American history co-exist with the trappings of modern life. In some places, the pairings are antipodelian, but in many others, the conjoining of American past and present provide the traveler with a harmonious blend of creature comforts and fascinating historical sites.

The understated beauty of southeastern Pennsylvania's landscape—the earthy browns and dark greens of the hills interrupted by huge swaths of neatly tilled farmland—has a mesmerizing effect on those who pass through. So mesmerizing, in fact, that some people do more than pass through, and the placid country towns of the southeast are seeing more and more urbanites from Philadelphia, New York, and New Jersey snatching up second homes and property.

■ LAND AND PEOPLE

This region lies within the fertile Piedmont Plateau between the Delaware River in the east and and the Susquehanna in the west. The immigrants who first settled here bought their land from William Penn's sons, whose advertisements promised rich harvests on tracts of land as far as the eye could see. The settlers arrived to find thick forests as far as the eye could see, but once the land was cleared, these rolling hills—lying on a nutrient-rich limestone substrata and watered by abundant streams—proved to be exceptionally fertile. Before the Midwest opened to settlement, the region was known as the breadbasket of the United States.

Today, about 5,000 farms cover the area and only small patches of the once thick woodland remain. Much of the land is worked by Amish and Mennonite farmers—known collectively as "Pennsylvania Dutch"—and many of their farms are less than 100 acres. Following a tradition that eschews modern inventions, these farmers use many of the same agricultural methods employed in colonial times.

Southeastern Pennsylvania communities have been favored places of refuge and rejuvenation for the rich and famous. In winter, many are drawn by the crisp country air and deep snows, or in summer, by the river-cooled breezes and tree-shaded streets of quaint towns. Bucks County, especially, has been attracting crowds of glitterati and literati since the 1930s. Nobel Prize–winning authors Pearl S. Buck and James Michener had homes here, as did the composer Oscar Hammerstein. Painters are drawn here by the magical way the light dances upon the Delaware River and weaves through the branches of the bankside trees.

■ HISTORY

The first colonists who took advantage of the Penn family's land offering were much like the Lenni Lenape Indians they displaced, "neither having much nor expecting much," as William Penn described the Indians. In treaties negotiated in William Penn's time, the Lenni Lenapes owned the land and "leased" it to settlers for a fee, usually traded goods. But by the time of Penn's death in 1718, there was a steady stream of settlers moving into the valleys, picking the forests clean of wildlife and clearing huge sections of it for farming. It wasn't long before the treaties were ignored and the Lenni Lenapes were edged off their land and forced to move beyond the fertile valleys.

(HISTORY *continues on page 90*)

(following pages) Dairy farms form a green and beige quilt in this view over Lancaster County.

SOUTHEAST PENNSYLVANIA

Among the settlers who poured into the region in the decade after Penn's death were the wave of Quaker, Mennonite, Amish, and other religious sects that found room for their communities to grow and a tolerance that allowed them to practice their beliefs in the open. Today's Pennsylvania Dutch farm communities of the southeast are the remnants of these early sects.

During the French and Indian War, and later, the Revolutionary War, some Quakers and other sects with pacifist beliefs refused to join the war effort but did supply food and clothing to the Continental Army. Other religious communities openly supported the British.

The southeast figured prominently in several key military encounters during the Revolutionary War, supplying fresh frontiersmen-soldiers and supplies to hold off British gains in New York and New England. The only significant inroad into Pennsylvania territory during the war occurred just two months after the signing of the Declaration of Independence when British forces landed on upper Chesapeake Bay and marched 57 miles north to capture Philadelphia. Washington's attempt to stave off the invasion failed after hours of fighting at Brandywine Creek; he withdrew to Valley Forge and the Continental Congress fled to York.

The re-grouping and retraining of troops at Valley Forge and France's decision to side with the Americans led to several key American victories and forced the British to negotiate peace, the Treaty of Paris, in 1783.

After the war, southeastern Pennsylvania farmers and craftsmen returned to their homes to enjoy relative prosperity. In the 1820s, a wave of immigration pushed the Pennsylvania frontier farther west, and a new railroad system spurred economic growth.

While the region's economy grew steadily through the 1850s, so, too, did political and religious movements that aimed to set a moral compass for the country. In the years leading up to the Civil War, the Quakers and other Pennsylvania Dutch Country pacifist sects were leaders in the abolitionist movement and instrumental in keeping Pennsylvania an anti-slavery state.

Many farm communities and small towns along the Delaware River established networks of safe houses known as the Underground Railroad to help slaves from Southern states make their way to freedom in New England and Canada. During the war years, Quaker and Amish farms once again supplied food, this time for the Union Army.

After the Civil War, southeastern Pennsylvania again played a leading role in the industrialization of the nation. While farming continued to dominate the economy, steel mills, iron works, and mining operations were built here because of the area's proximity to coal fields and to the Delaware River (and later railroads) which provided efficient means to transport goods.

While residential and commercial areas have grown significantly along the "Main Line," the collective name for a series of communities that sprouted up along the country's first toll road, Route 30, between Philadelphia and Lancaster, the rural-agrarian nature of the southeast remains. Two-thirds of the land is still farmed. That's much less than there was 10 years ago, but people can still drive for miles across wide open spaces and take in the sights and smells of growing vegetables and grazing dairy cows. In recent years, urban planners and public officials have tried to address the dual problem inherent in loss of farmland. Not only is beautiful countryside being destroyed, but the city of Philadelphia is losing some of its most energetic and creative people. As Maxwell King, former editor of the *Philadelphia Inquirer* said recently of Philadelphia and its outlying areas: "The

Edward Hicks's depiction of David Twining's farm in 1787 (painted circa 1845–47) idealized the farmers of Bucks County, where Hicks grew up. (Abby Aldrich Rockefeller Folk Art Center)

hole is quickly emptying into the doughnut; all the action is in the suburbs."

There are signs that communities are heeding these warnings, understanding that the unique, back-country character of the region—from the Amish roadside food markets to national historic treasures—is the soul of Pennsylvania's southeast.

■ BUCKS COUNTY *maps pages 87, D, E, &F-1, 2&3; and 94 west of river*

Bucks County is perhaps best known for its idyllic scenes of farm life and quaint little towns which on weekends are filled with urbanites escaping city life. The stretch of Route 32 that follows the Delaware River from Washington Crossing State Park north to Erwinna winds through one of the most beautiful and historic sections of the state.

The two-lane road hugs the tow path of the old Delaware Canal, and just a few hundred yards beyond that, often hidden in spring and summer by birch, oak, and hickory trees in full leaf, the shallow, slate-blue Delaware River rolls slowly toward its outlet into Delaware Bay.

In the early morning, deer gather along the tow path of the canal to graze or sneak into the organic gardens of the local B&Bs. In summer, hummingbirds flit through wildflower patches near the riverbank; in late fall, Canada geese use the river as a stopover on their migration south.

In fall and winter, the river views are unobstructed. The soft afternoon light reflecting off the river is so unique that painters have flocked to these Delaware banks hoping to capture it on canvas, and many have ended up settling here. Mixed in with views of trees, water, and light are glimpses of riverfront homes, some dating back to the early 1700s. Some have been restored to perfection, while others have been long abandoned.

The hour-long drive from Washington's Crossing National Historic Park to Easton is best taken as a leisurely day trip. You can stop along the way at roadside produce stands, antique stores, and several wineries open for tastings and tours. Many of these attractions are located in tiny, picturesque villages—most of them former mill towns that have aged rather gracefully.

◆ ANTIQUES

Antique stores abound, in village squares, by way of mom-and-pop stands along highways, even in giant warehouses. All are stuffed with the gems and junk of Revolutionary War–era Pennsylvania. In fact, there are more registered dealers (several

Summer idyll on a raft.

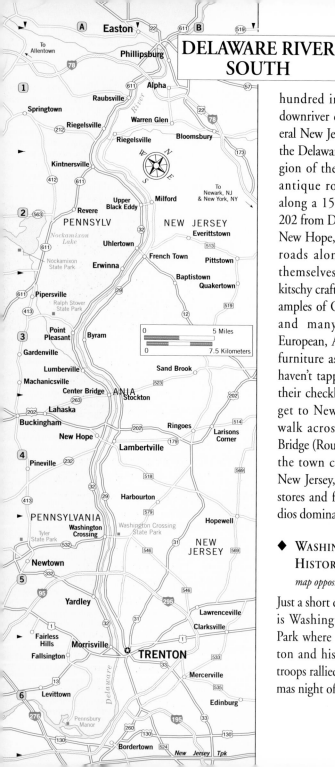

hundred in Philadelphia and its downriver counties, including several New Jersey communities across the Delaware) than in any other region of the country. The premier antique row in the region runs along a 15-mile stretch of Route 202 from Doylestown to Lahaska to New Hope, spilling onto a few side roads along the way. Antiques themselves, of course, run from kitschy crafts to museum quality examples of Colonial-era furniture—and many dealers here offer European, Asian, and Scandinavian furniture as well. For buyers who haven't tapped out their energy or their checkbooks by the time they get to New Hope, a five-minute walk across the Delaware River Bridge (Route 202 East) puts you in the town center of Lambertville, New Jersey, where upscale antique stores and furniture designers' studios dominate a four-block area.

◆ WASHINGTON CROSSING HISTORIC PARK

map opposite, A-5

Just a short drive out of Philadelphia is Washington Crossing Historic Park where Gen. George Washington and his demoralized, haggard troops rallied on the freezing Christmas night of 1776 to fight a decisive

Emanuel Gottlieb Leutze's Washington Crossing the Delaware, *painted in 1851, depicts Washington's 1776 Christmas night crossing of the icy river. He and his troops surprised Hessian soldiers encamped in Trenton as they celebrated the holiday, resulting in Washington's first clear-cut military victory. (Metropolitan Museum of Art, Gift of John Stewart Kennedy, 1897. Photograph © 1992, Metropolitan Museum of Art, New York)*

battle. Climbing into cargo boats, 2,400 soldiers set out across the water in a snowstorm, using poles to bash their way through a river choked with chunks of ice. After surprising the garrison of Hessian soldiers celebrating the holiday in Trenton on the other side, the one ragtag Patriot division managed to capture the base in less than an hour.

The battle was Washington's first clear-cut victory, and it was a crucial one, giving the Revolutionary cause much-needed momentum—both physically and emotionally. Following the victory, the colonial forces were bolstered by an influx of new recruits, and eventually it helped influence the French government to back the American army in its fight against the British.

The park is split between an upper and a lower section, which are about five miles apart. Heading north on Route 32 you'll come first to the lower park—McConkey's Ferry section—which is the best place to start a tour. The rangers are informative, and a 30-minute film recounts the surprise attack in docu-drama style. From the visitors center, walk to the Memorial Building to see a reproduction of the famous painting of Washington's Crossing by Emanuel Leutze, then proceed down to the Durham Boat House to view reproductions of the cargo boats that carried the troops to battle.

Five miles farther north on Route 32 is the upper part of the park, the Thompson's Mill section, which includes an 80-acre wildflower preserve and the 18th-century Thompson-Neely House, which looks much as it did the night that Washington and his officers sat in the kitchen hashing out the details of their attack plan. *Lower Park: 7 miles south of New Hope on Rte. 32 near junction of Rte. 532; Upper Park: 2 miles south of New Hope on Rte. 32; 215-493-4076.*

◆ **NEW HOPE** *map page 94, A-4*

Seven miles north of Washington Crossing you'll enter the town of New Hope, where white clapboard and brick houses spread out along the banks of the slow-rolling Delaware River and its canal. Once known for its mills, which processed goods ranging from grain to metals, New Hope's present incarnation is part artist colony, part history center, and part resort town. The main street following Route 32 through town is lined with art galleries and classy boutiques interspersed with tacky T-shirt shops and hamburger joints. In summer, the streets are clogged with art lovers, souvenir hunters, history buffs, and city-weary wanderers, and the scene on warm weekend days is something akin to downtown Santa Fe meets Disneyland's Main Street USA.

The cosmopolitan village has been attracting off-beat characters for decades, and locals like to think of themselves as a people tolerant of unconventional lifestyles. Townspeople did figure prominently in several key national controversies. In the late 1700s, the town's most prominent citizens hid Aaron Burr from authorities when a warrant was issued for his arrest after a fateful (and illegal) duel in which Burr mortally wounded Alexander Hamilton. In the Civil War years, many of the town's homes were used as safe houses along the Underground Railroad, which aided slaves escaping to freedom in the northern states and Canada.

In the early 1900s, New Hope became a favored destination for artists and actors fleeing New York for the summer. Both the famous and the out-of-work settled here, giving the village a bohemian air. The area has also become a popular travel destination for gay and lesbian tourists, and there are several bed-and-breakfasts, restaurants, and bars that have taken advantage of this trend.

◆ VISITING NEW HOPE

By Barge

At one time New Hope was an important transportation center along the Delaware Canal—handling between 2,500 and 3,000 barges a month at its peak in 1862. The **New Hope Mule & Barge Co.** brings this aspect of the town's past to life, with the old coal barges now carrying tourists down the Delaware Canal on an old-fashioned mule-drawn barge, complete with folksinger tour guides. *215-862-2842.*

By Rail

Although the canal system met its demise with the advent of rail transport, the town continued to prosper with the arrival of the **New Hope and Ivyland Railroad.** Today you can take a nine-mile ride along the river in restored 1920s passenger cars pulled by a steam locomotive. *215-862-2332.*

By Foot

Perhaps the best way to see New Hope is to slip down any alley or side road off the main street where you'll encounter 18th-century stone houses with intriguing courtyards, alleys lined with cozy row houses, and cobblestone walkways that lead to the wooded trails that workers once followed out of town to get to various mill sites. The entire town is listed on the National Register of Historic Places; the New Hope Historical Association hands out free walking tour maps with the town's important sights

One of the pleasures of visiting Bucks County is taking a mule-drawn barge on the Delaware Canal.

highlighted. It is also well worth the walk across the bridge to Lambertville, New Jersey, to poke about the many antique stores clustered in the well-preserved downtown area. *New Hope Information Center, at S. Main and W. Mechanic Sts.; 215-862-5880.*

Parry Mansion
This stone house was built in 1784 for a wealthy lumbermill owner whose family occupied it for five generations. You can look around the house for $3. *S. Main at Ferry St.; 215-862-5652.*

Bucks County Regional Playhouse
In the 1920s, an old grist mill was converted into this nationally recognized theater which continues to stage Broadway-caliber musicals and dramas to packed houses year-round.

Gerenser's Exotic Ice Cream
Exotic is right! Polish plum brandy, African violet, and Indian loganberry are but three of the 40-odd flavors at this circa 1943 ice-cream shop. *22 S. Main St.; 215-862-2050.*

◆ LUMBERVILLE   *map page 94, A-3*

About a 10-minute drive north from the bustle of New Hope is the quiet village of Lumberville, where you can leave the car and tour the old homes crowded together on the main street of the village. Buy a picnic lunch at the Lumberville Store, in operation since 1770, and enjoy it on Bull's Island, accessible by way of a sturdy footbridge over the river.

◆ POINT PLEASANT   *map page 94, A-3*

If you grow tired of driving along the river, and want to get into it, the mellow reach of water near Point Pleasant, just north of Lumberville, is perfect for the decidedly non-adventure sport of "tubing." The folks at Bucks County River Country will set you up with truck inner-tubes, canoes, kayaks, or even guided raft trips. Reservations advised. *Byram Rd. just off Rte. 32; Point Pleasant; 215-297-8181.*

◆ ERWINNA   *map page 94, A-2*

A quaint town situated along the twists of the road as it follows the river's sharp curves, Erwinna has several inns that serve lunch and dinner to the general public. There are also antique stores, renowned **Tinicum Park** with its well-marked hiking trails, and the **Sand Castle Winery,** which offers regularly scheduled tours and a tasting room. *Tinicum Park: River Rd.; 215-757-0571. Sand Castle Winery: 755 River Rd.; 610-294-9181.*

■ EASTON   *map page 94, A/B-1*

Just over the Bucks County line in Northampton County, historic Easton was the site of the second public reading of the Declaration of Independence inside the colonies. In 1776 those fateful words, "We hold these truths to be self-evident…" were shouted from the steps of the Northampton County Courthouse on Centre Square. The land for this square had been presented to city founders in 1765 by William Penn's sons under a bill of sale that required the city to pay the Penn family an annual fee of one red rose.

By the early 1800s, thanks to its prime location at the confluence of the Lehigh and Delaware Rivers, Easton had become an important link on the Delaware River canal system. In the 1830s, railroad companies began constructing lines here, and by the mid-1860s, when the iron horses superceded the canals as the favored mode of shipping transport, Easton was already securely established as an interchange point for five separate railroads.

Today, after a solid century of industrialism, the town is in the early stages of an economic and cultural renaissance. New high-tech industries are setting up shop on old factory sites; tourism is on the rise, and city-funded renovations are slated for many of the town's historic buildings.

◆ DELAWARE AND LEHIGH NATIONAL HERITAGE
CORRIDOR VISITOR CENTER   *map page 87, E-1*

Whew, what a name, but if you can say it, why not drop by? The center consists of three unlikely parts: The visitor center; the Crayola Crayon Factory; and the National Canal Museum. *It is located at 30 Center Square in Easton.*

The first floor visitor center has exhibits and a short film about the history of Easton and the Lehigh Valley, including displays on the area's ethnic groups, historic canals, and main industries. The **Crayola Factory** on the second floor has everything you'd want to know and then some about how crayons and markers are made, as well as an outlet store.

The **National Canal Museum** charts the history of the country's extensive waterways transport system in the 19th century. The inland canal network is detailed in wall-sized panels and in displays of equipment used to build the canal. The museum offers mule-drawn canal barge rides on a section of the Lehigh River.

30 Center Square, Easton; 610-250-6700.

CANALS

Pennsylvania's canal system was actively utilized from 1826 to 1900, and in its heyday had 900 miles of state-owned and 300 miles of privately owned canals. Charles Dickens was 30 years old when he traveled on a Pennsylvania canal in 1842.

There was much in this mode of traveling which I heartily enjoyed at the time, and look back upon with great pleasure. Even the running up, bare-necked, at 5 o'clock in the morning from the tainted cabin to the dirty deck; scooping up the icy water, plunging one's head into it, and drawing it out, all fresh and glowing with the cold; was a good thing. The fast, brisk walk upon the towing-path, between that time and breakfast, when every vein and artery seemed to tingle with health; the exquisite beauty of the opening day, when light came gleaming off from everything; the lazy motion of the boat, when one lay idly on the deck, looking through, rather than at, the deep blue sky; the gliding on, at night, so noiselessly, past frowning hills, sullen with dark trees, and sometimes angry in one red burning spot high up, where unseen men lay crouching round a fire; the shining out of the bright stars, undisturbed by noise of wheels or steam, or any other sound than the liquid rippling of the water as the boat went on: all these were pure delights.

—Charles Dickens, *American Notes,* 1842

Canal Scene on the Juniata, *by George Storm.(State Museum of Pennsylvania)*

Red crayon liquid is poured on a belt at the Crayola factory in Easton.

◆ HUGH MOORE HISTORIC PARK   *map page 87, E/F-1*

Named after the Easton businessman who made his fortune selling Dixie Cups, and who also happened to have a fondness for canal history, this historic park spans six miles along the banks of the Lehigh River. Stand outside the 1890s lock-tender's house (now a museum) and watch canal boats entering Lock 47 rise eight feet in about five minutes as a hydrostatic valve is opened. The valve was invented by Lehigh Coal and Navigation Co. founders Josiah White and Erskine Hazard, and it helped give the Lehigh Canal the largest carrying capacity of any canal in the country. *Hugh Moore Historic Park: 2.5 miles north of I-78; 610-250-6700.*

■ DELAWARE LOOP DRIVE   *map page 94*

A popular day trip with New Yorkers, Philadelphians, and other travelers is the drive up the Pennsylvania side of the Delaware River through Bucks County along Route 32/ Route 611 to Easton, then crossing into New Jersey on I-78 and lazily following Route 29 back down the other side of the river, stopping to scout antique stores and crafts shops. Before you reach Trenton, New Jersey, you'll come to a bridge back over the Delaware leading to Washington Crossing. From there you can venture inland and absorb the rest that Bucks County has to offer.

■ BUCKS COUNTY WEST *map page 87, E-2*

While many argue that the most bucolic region in Bucks County is along the Delaware, some of the region's best museums and scenic sights are found well west of the river, and it is well worth a diversion off Route 32 to explore them.

■ DOYLESTOWN *map page 87, E-2*

Even though it's less than a 30-minute drive from the hustle and bustle of Philadelphia, the first thing you realize when driving into Doylestown's charming central business district is that the foot traffic moving about the tree-canopied streets eases along at a languid pace.

First settled in the 1730s, and once a stop on the stagecoach line between Philadelphia and Easton, Doylestown is steeped in early American history, and much of the town has been placed on the National Register of Historic Places. Take a stroll through the pleasant downtown to see the hundreds of preserved and carefully restored buildings, many of which now house boutiques, cozy cafes, and restaurants.

◆ MERCER MILE

Mercer Museum

Doylestown native Henry Mercer, a Harvard-educated millionaire, was a dedicated collector in the fields of anthropology, history, and ceramic art. Fascinated by objects used in everyday life, he began his collection of Americana in 1897 by visiting junk dealers and selecting pieces that would tell the story of work and leisure in the American experience. Today more than 60,000 objects reflecting that objective are housed in a large, 1913 brick and cement "castle"—one of three such castles constructed without the assistance of architects or blueprints. Some people find the architecture bizarre, others find it unique. *Mercer Museum, 84 S. Pine St.; 215-345-0210.*

Moravian Pottery and Tile Works

Truly, the art produced by craftsmen was Mercer's first love, and one of these arts, ceramic tile making, is celebrated in a second castle that houses the Moravian Pottery and Tile Works. The Works specializes in the preservation and production of distinctive decorative tiles, using traditional crafting and firing methods. (Prices range from $4 for basic pieces to $400 for hand-painted scenes copied from Indian and medieval motifs.) A slide show and lecture introduces visitors to Mercer's world, and tours include a walk through the factory where craftspeople are hard at work filling orders for unique tiles. *130 Swamp Rd.; 215-345-6722.*

Fonthill

Mercer's third concrete "castle," his residence, Fonthill, was inspired by whimsy rather than any architect's plans. Mercer hired local laborers to build Fonthill, none of whom had ever built a house before. The overall effect is one of a haphazard, multi-textured extravaganza. The basic structure is concrete but other building materials include sand, grass, his precious tiles, and wooden posts. With 18 fireplaces, 200 windows, and 32 stairwells, Fonthill is impressive in an odd sort of way, but exhausting to visit, and most people breathe a sigh of relief when they leave the place. *Guided tours only, $5; reservations required; E. Court St.; 215-348-9461.*

James A. Michener Art Museum

Author James Michener was raised in Doylestown, and this museum bearing his name (and built with his money) is housed in the former Bucks County Jail compound. Within the 23-foot-high walls of the 1884 facility are seven galleries and an outdoor sculpture garden that feature 19th- and 20th-century American art and often exhibit works from Bucks County artists. *Guided tours, reservations required; $5; 138 S. Pine St.; 215-340-9800.*

◆ **PEARL S. BUCK HOUSE** *map page 87, E-2*

Six miles north of Doylestown on Rte. 113, in the village of Perkasie, is Green Hills Farm, former residence of the Nobel laureate and Pulitzer Prize–winning author of *The Good Earth* and *My Several Worlds*. Born in 1892 to missionary parents, and raised in China from the age of four, Buck made her experiences with China and Chinese life the focus of much of her writing.

Buck and her second husband Richard Walsh purchased this 48-acre farm (dating from 1835) in 1934, as a home for themselves and their family (two natural daughters and seven adopted children). The house, fancifully filled with American and Asian antiques, remains much the same as when Buck lived and wrote here.

Buck died here in 1973, but her efforts on behalf of orphans is carried on by the Pearl S. Buck Foundation, the organization based on the property, that assists with international adoptions, especially those of Asian-American children. *Admission $5; 520 Dublin Rd.; 215-249-0100.*

■ **BERKS COUNTY DUTCH HEX SIGNS**

When the German Protestant groups who make up the Pennsylvania Dutch fled religious persecution and settled in Pennsylvania in the late 1600s, their old world customs, superstitions, foods, and dress came with them. The "fancy" Mennonite- and Lutheran-related sects decorated their barns with large, colorful geometric patterns. These hex signs, as they became known, had specific meanings or legends

HEX BARN TOUR *map page 87, C-1&2*

The following tour will take you through some wonderful country and past some of the better examples of hex signs in Berks County. *Maps for this drive are available from the Reading and Berks County Visitors Bureau; 352 Penn St. in Reading; 800-443-6610; or visit the Berks County website at www.berksweb.com/hextour.html.*

Continuing north from the western Bucks County area, take the Kutztown Road exit off of US 222, take a right and drive through town, cutting through the leafy campus of Kutztown State University, then continuing to the junction of Kutztown Road and Crystal Cave Road. Set your odometer to zero and take a right toward Crystal Cave park. You'll roll through wooded countryside interspersed with open farms and fields, and at 5.0 miles the **first barn**, on the Stutzman farm, will be tucked behind a clump of trees on the right. The winding road crests out on a open hilltop, offering views to all sides, then descends rather steeply and at 5.5 miles you'll see the monstrous, weathered white **barn of the Dreibelbis farm,** with its fading but intricate hexes, sitting quaintly in the middle of a luxuriantly green pasture.

At the 6-mile mark take a left onto Route 143 South, and after another half mile the **third barn** will be on the left, and the **fourth barn** is perched on a rise to the right at the 6.9-mile point. At 8.1 miles, keep your eyes peeled for easy-to-miss Route 662, and after turning right onto it proceed .3 miles, where just off the road on the right you'll find a **beautiful red barn** with four hexes painted on its broad side. There's a place to pull the car over and see the barn somewhat up close, without being overly invasive. The folk artists who create the signs are known as "hexologists," and this is a good opportunity to check out the craftsmanship of their work.

The next 3.5 miles are barn-free, so take in the quiet, hilly countryside, stealing glances skyward for hawks riding on thermals, or into roadside thickets to spy whitetail deer snacking on vegetation. At the 12-mile mark you'll pass the **Leiby farm barn** on the right, then swing immediately right onto Windsor Castle Road and past the **seventh barn,** which is on the Christman farm, at the 12.2-mark on the right. When you hit the 13.7-mile marker, turn right onto Virginville Road. On the left hand side of the road, between here and mile 14.0, are **barns eight, nine, and ten.** They're all huge dairy barns painted with hexes of horse heads (the Amish Carriage Horse hex protects horses and livestock) and rows of hexes with birds (the Double Distlefink hex, for double good luck), as well as the more standard star patterns. At the 14.9- and 15.0-mile points, the **two barns of the Miller farm** will be on your left.

At 16.4 miles turn north onto Route 143. The Sunday Farm barn is on the left at 16.7 miles and the **Leiby barn** is also on the left at 17.2 miles. Off to the right at 18.4 is the **Dreibelbis covered bridge,** which bears a colorful, star-shaped hex over the entrance. Mile 20 will bring you to Old Route 22, also known as the Hex Highway, where you'll go left and then right at the Old Duetsch Eck House Restaurant onto Route 143 North which will bring you to barn fifteen and the Pennsylvania Dutch Folk Museum. The hours are sporadic, but if you can catch someone there you might get a lesson on hexes as well as other Pennsylvania Dutch crafts.

Barn sixteen is just ahead on the left, and, after passing under Interstate 78, **barn seventeen** is also on the left at 22.9 miles. You'll wind past farms and scattered woods, then at mile 24.2 take a left onto Hawk Mountain Road (just past Raberts Garage on the right), and **barn eighteen** will be on the right at 24.5 miles.

The land starts to be a bit more steep and wooded now as you follow along Kittatinny Ridge to your left. Coming through here in the late evening, the fading sunlight covers the countryside with subtle bursts of color, and in the distance the spire of a church and a small, rounded hill studded with tombstones are illuminated in the glow.

Climbing slowly up the ridge, you'll come to mile 28.1 and **barn nineteen**, the shop of Robertson's Restorations, which is on the right and covered with a variety of hex designs. The final barn of the tour sits .3 miles farther on the right side of the road, and is adorned with a pair of freshly painted starburst-design hexes.

A farmer and his chickens in front of his barn in Berks County.

handed down from generation to generation within their religious communities.

While early hex signs appeared on every sort of building, supposedly to ward off the influence of the devil or those who would do his bidding, they were also painstakingly drawn, with more positive motives, on marriage certificates, family Bibles, and furniture. Some of the more popular symbols include the sun wheel for warmth and fertility, hearts for love, birds (known as *distelfinks*) for luck, stars for good fortune, and tulips for faith.

■ HAWK MOUNTAIN BIRD SANCTUARY   *map page 87, C-1*

The drive along Kittatinny Ridge, on Rte. 895 passes through open farm country until you reach the the 2,200-acre Hawk Mountain Sanctuary, where 16 species of raptors pass by on their annual fall migration to Central and South America. The preserve was founded by local conservationist Rosalie Edge in 1934 to save these magnificent creatures from hunters who slaughtered them wholesale for "sport" and under the guise of protecting their livestock. It was the first refuge for birds of prey in the world, and today more than 18,000 birds pass by every year.

The best time to spot ospreys, American kestrels, and broad-winged hawks is in

Birders on the North Overlook at Hawk Mountain Bird Sanctuary.

late August and September; peregrine falcons and merlins in October; red-winged hawks and golden eagles in November and early December. The best viewing points are from the South and North Lookouts. It's a short and easy five-minute stroll from the visitors center along a well-groomed path to the South Overlook where a panoramic vista reveals the rolling farm country below. The trail to the North Overlook is rockier and a more strenuous 45-minute climb, but worth every step when you arrive at the top and gaze out over a panoramic view encompassing sheer cliffs, rocky outcroppings, and dense forest in the valley below. *Off Rte. 895, 1700 Hawk Mountain Rd., Kempton; www.hawkmountain.org; 610-756-6000.*

■ READING AREA   *map page 87, C-2*

Reading is a struggling, post-industrial city reinventing itself by fitting into a new economic niche—in this case outlet shopping. Ten million consumption-crazed visitors flock to Reading every year to grab bargains at the 300 outlets packed in around the town. Among the most popular retail outlets are: VF Outlet Village, which, with some 90 outlets, offers some of the best selections and prices in town; the Reading Outlet Center, which consists of 70 shops housed in an old factory that once produced silk stockings; Reading Station, which has 30 upscale outlets set in a mall designed like a railroad town (inspired by the fact that in its former life the property was the headquarters for the Reading Railroad). The town itself hardly merits a stop, but there are a few worthwhile sites in the outlying area.

◆ DANIEL BOONE HOMESTEAD   *map page 87, C-2*

In Baumstown, 10 miles east of Reading, Daniel Boone Homestead offers a unique view of what rural life was like for Pennsylvania families in the mid-1700s. Dense woodlands make up most of the 600-acre park that surrounds the foundation of the cabin where Boone lived until the age of 16. The remote feel of the area—it's a three-mile drive from the entrance to the visitors center—makes it easier for the visitor to imagine how early settlers had to fend for themselves in remote sections of southeast Pennsylvania.

Boone gained the foundation of his legendary frontiersman skills while growing up here, mainly through the family's friendly relations with the Shawnees. In 1750, Boone's parents had a falling out with the Quaker church, which disapproved when one of their daughters and then a son married a "worldling." The Boones lit out for North Carolina, where 16-year-old Daniel quickly made a name for himself in the business of being a rugged individual (including dressing like an Indian when he went to church—Mohawk hairstyle, loin cloth, etc.).

There are 14 miles of wooded trails to wander around the historic site, which consists of the ruins of the original cabin, and a two-story stone house built in the late 1700s after the Boones had moved on. *Rte. 422 to Daniel Boone Rd.; Tues–Sat, 9–5; Sun, noon to 5; open national Monday holidays in the summer; winter weekdays by appointment. 610-582-4900.*

◆ HOPEWELL IRON FURNACE   *map page 87, C-2/3*

One of the earliest and now best-preserved iron manufacturing furnaces in the United States, the Hopewell Iron Furnace churned out cannons and shot for the Revolutionary War. During peaceful colonial times, it produced cooking stoves and farm tools.

The furnace was built in 1742 by British immigrant Peter Grubb who picked the location based on his survey of the area's rich iron ore deposits. Other natural resources such as timber and limestone were plentiful and ensured the success of the factory even through the period of intense competition from other furnaces that were sprouting up along the Delaware.

DANIEL BOONE 1734–1820

On woodland thoroughfares the hunters of many nations met, and over a smoke of tobacco or kinnikinnick, a pungent mixture of dried bark and leaves, they traded news and information. A pidgin tongue based on Algonquin but employing many English, French, Dutch and Scandinavian terms served as the lingua franca of the forest, and along the trails trees were often blazed, the bark pulled back and the trunks painted with pictographs that constituted a simple but common written language. There were camping places, sometimes with huts of small logs and bark, where hunters shared meat and sleeping quarters. It was in these circles that young Boone found his forest teachers. There were backwoods hunters descended from European colonists, many of them of Scandinavian background, whom the Delawares called *nittappi,* or friends. There were Indians of many ethnic varieties who also called friend this

James Otto Lewis engraved this image after Chester Harding's painting of Daniel Boone—the only one made from life. (Missouri Historical Society)

young hunter carrying the respected name of Boone. These men of the forest frontier instructed Daniel in a way of life that combined elements of both cultures and bridged many of the differences between Indian and European.

This way of life centered on hunting. Hunters from both cultures sought meat and hides to feed and clothe their families, as well as hides and furs for trade...Firearms were in wide use and included muskets, shotguns, pistols, and rifles....Most desired was the American long rifle....The tools of the trade were thus European, but its techniques—the calls, disguises, and decoys, the surrounds and fire hunts—were nearly all of Indian origin. Most emigrants to America came without any hunting traditions, for in most European countries hunting had been reserved for the nobility, so the hunting way of life that developed in the backwoods depended on Indian knowledge and skill.

Hunters from both cultures dressed in a composite of European and Indian styles....The frontier American was "proud of his Indian-like dress," wrote a preacher in western Pennsylvania. He had seen them in breechclout and leggings, their thighs and hips exposed naked to the world, strutting down village streets and even into churches, which, he added, "did not add much to the devotion of the young ladies." Boone adopted these styles as a youth in Pennsylvania, and they remained his through the whole of his long life.

—John Mack Faragher, *Daniel Boone,* 1992

"I doubt that elsewhere in the world is there a 19th-century iron-furnace complex with the degree of historical integrity to be found at Cornwall," writes Smithsonian Institution historian Robert Vogel, "where it has been estimated that fully 95 percent of the fabric is original." The entire physical plant for producing "pig" iron, a lower-grade product shipped to other forges for refining, is virtually the same as it was in 1857 when it was renovated by the Coleman family. The furnace was a money-maker until lower prices offered by larger and more efficient operations around Pittsburgh took away customers. By 1883, the Cornwall works had extinguished its flames for good, and is now managed as part of the National Park Service. *2 Mark Bird Lane, Elverson; 610-582-8773.*

◆ PAGODA   *map page 87, C-2*

Pagoda is a seven-story Japanese castle perched on top of Mount Penn on Skyline Drive, just south of Reading. It was built in 1908 by Reading businessman William Witman, who made his fortune as the owner of a rock quarry on the mountain. Concerns that the operation was turning the area's highest point into an eyesore got to Witman and he closed the quarry and built a resort modeled after a Shogun Dynasty castle. (And this years before Las Vegas was even on the map.)

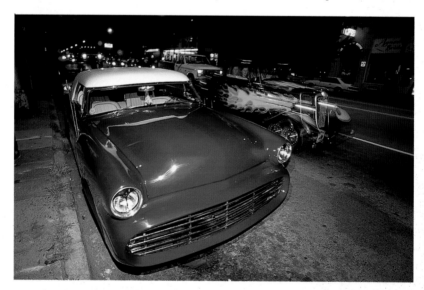

(above) Teenagers cruise hot rods in Pottstown.
(opposite) Pagoda, just south of Reading, was built in 1908 by William Witman.

Somehow, the mundane detail of creating a suitable access road got lost in the grand scheme and the resort failed. Neglected and abandoned by a series of owners, it was renovated by a local historic preservation group in 1969. The castle is now home to the Berks Arts Council. While the second-floor gallery offers fine exhibits, the real treats are the panoramic views of the Reading area and a peaceful Oriental garden. *Daily, 11–5; 98 Duryea Dr.; 610-655-6374.*

■ PENNSYLVANIA DUTCH COUNTRY   *map page 87, B&C–3&4*

Travelers from around the world flock to this region of southeast Pennsylvania to catch a glimpse of the quaint and simple life led by the "Plain People," the members of several different religious orders that have been quietly going about their business in this countryside for close to 300 years. Despite being known collectively as the Pennsylvania Dutch, the more than 35 Amish, Mennonite, and Brethren sects of this region have nothing really to do with the Netherlands. Most originated in Germany; "Dutch" in this case is a corruption of *Deutsch,* the German word for Germans.

The Mennonites rose out of the Anabaptist (adult baptism) movement of the Protestant Reformation that was swirling through Europe in the 16th century, and

A team of horses pulls a plow for this Amish farmer.

An Amish driver takes his buggy over the Jackson Mill covered bridge in Bart Township.

the Amish spun off from the Mennonites. Fleeing religious persecution in southern Germany and Switzerland, the first sizable groups of Amish and Mennonite settlers arrived in Lancaster County in the early 1700s. They were drawn by the promise of William Penn's "Holy Experiment" of religious tolerance, and, being farmers, to the region's fertile soil.

Today, about 18,000 Old Order Amish live in Lancaster County, especially in the countryside around the towns of Lancaster, Lititz, Ephrata, Bird-in-Hand, Intercourse, Paradise, and Strasburg, making this the second largest Old Order community in the country, next to Holmes County, Ohio. It's easy to spot them: men and boys wear dark suits topped with broad-brimmed hats of straw or black felt; women and girls wear modest, solid-color, mid-calf-length dresses covered with a superhero-housewife combo of a cape and an apron. Women never cut their hair, which they wear in a bun on the back of their head. If married, they wear a white prayer covering; if single, a black one. They do not wear jewelry, even wedding rings. The Amish feel these distinctive, simple clothes encourage humility and separation from the world—all considered expressions of their faith.

Old Order groups drive horses and buggies and do not have electricity in their homes. Their children attend school only through the eighth grade in private, one-room schoolhouses. After that they work on the family farm or in the family business until they marry.

Traveling in this region today, you'll witness the head-on collision of a religious people seeking to distance themselves from the modern world, while the inhabitants of that very same modern world clamber over one another to get a closer look. You'll see a host of incongruities and seeming contradictions: families in horse-drawn buggies clopping past the monstrous Wal-Mart store on Main Street in Ephrata; Madonna's "Papa Don't Preach" playing softly on the radio in the quilt and candle shop in Intercourse; a young girl—in a homemade dress with Laura Ingalls Wilder pigtails streaming behind her in the wind—schussing down a side road on a pair of Rollerblades with the grace of an Olympic athlete. Because many Amish driving in buggies have been injured by automobiles, some are considering taking buses (since they won't be operating the vehicle), a trend the local tourist bureaus hope to discourage.

If the local economy was once based on agriculture, tourism is now its star performer, with upwards of $400 million a year being brought into the county, most of it spent on food, lodging, and Amish-made goods and crafts.

■ LANCASTER   *map page 87, B-3*

Lancaster (LANK-uh-stir) was founded in 1710 by lieutenants of William Penn, and named affectionately by the town's chief magistrate, John Wright, for his home shire of Lancaster, England. By the middle of the century, Lancaster had become a center for gun production, and it was here that the highly accurate "Pennsylvania long rifle" was developed by Swiss and German weapons makers. Thanks to an abundance of craftsman and nearby iron ore furnaces, Lancaster became known as "the arsenal of the colonies" and it supplied the Continental Army during the Revolution with high-quality arms and ammunition. The town also became the colonies' capital for one day on September 27, 1777, after George Washington failed to defend Philadelphia at the Battle of Brandywine and the British took the city. Members of the Continental Congress paused here to hold a session in the courthouse on Penn Square before continuing their flight to York on the other side of the Susquehanna River, where they convened for nine months before returning to Philadelphia.

Martin's Pretzel Factory in Akron, outside Lancaster, is owned and run by Mennonites.

Today, Lancaster is an important center for agriculture and light manufacturing. The pleasant, historic city center is surrounded by a somewhat gritty outer ring, consisting of brick and wood-trimmed row houses standing in varying conditions of repair next to weathered industrial buildings, vacant storefronts, and rundown apartment buildings. But a few Amish-centered sites and a self-guided walking tour of majestic colonial- and Victorian-era homes that still stand near the square make it a good place to kick off a visit through the Pennsylvania Dutch country.

The easiest and most scenic way into the heart of the city is via Route 30 and Walnut Street. To get to Center Square from Walnut, turn left onto Prince Street, then left again onto King, which runs through a somewhat manic traffic circle at Center Square. **The Lancaster Visitors Center,** bursting with information on what to see and do, is just off the square. Here you'll find maps for a self-guided walking tour, or you can sign up for a guided tour that leaves from here. *South Queen and Vine Sts.; 717-392-1776.*

♦ LANCASTER SIGHTS

Heritage Center Museum
At the heart of downtown in the old city hall and a Masonic lodge dating back to the early 1790s, the museum displays the best of regional folk art and crafts. Pennsylvania Dutch crafts include painted furniture, quilts, and metalwork. Here you will find fine examples of all including floor clocks, quilts, silverware, copperware, homemade toys, weathervanes, and furniture of every sort. Children can visit a hands-on, interactive classroom that teaches aspects of early German immigrant life. *The Heritage Center: 13 W. King St. on Penn Square; Tues–Sat; 10–4; 717-299-6440.*

Central Market
Located around the corner from The Heritage Center, the country's oldest publicly owned farmer's market is a blend of upscale deli/pasta counters, gourmet coffee booths, and farm produce stands. A few of the latter are manned by Amish farmers. Primly dressed farm women offer organic farm produce and shoofly pie (molasses and chocolate pie). It seems more a morning meeting and gossip place for locals than a major or even minor tourist attraction. Best on a Saturday morning. *Tues–Fri, 6 A.M.–4:30 P.M.; Sat, 6–2; Central Market at Penn Square; 717-291-4723.*

This iron weathervane dates from the late 19th century.
(Courtesy of The Heritage Center Museum of Lancaster County)

This Pennsylvania Dutch "fraktur"—a form of illuminated manuscript—is a birth record of a Lancaster County boy. (Courtesy of The Heritage Center Museum of Lancaster County)

John Bachman A son of Jacob Bachman and wife Barbara A Daughter of Christian Kindig was born on the 10th Day of June in the year of our Lord 1832 In the Township of Lampeter in the County of Lancaster in the State of Pennsylvania in North AMERICA

Thou with thy counsel while I live wilt me conduct and guide And to thy Glory afterward receive me to abide

Whom have I in the heavens high but thee O Lord alone And in the earth whom I desire beside thee to love is none

Landis Valley Museum

Visitors can wander through a series of outdoor displays that depict daily life on a Pennsylvania farm. In authentically re-created buildings, costumed docents perform and explain the work of artisans and farmers.

A favorite display is the pottery shop where craftsmen create beautiful works of Pennsylvania redware. Parts of the movie *The Beloved* were filmed here, and two building constructed for the movie are still on site. Save time to browse through **The Weathervane,** the museum's shop, which houses an heirloom seed preservation project that has won Pennsylvania's coveted Historical Preservation Award. The project seeks to preserve plants and flowers lost to the effects of hybridization and mechanized agriculture. The museum offers a catalog of heirloom seeds for sale. *Admission fee; Mon–Sun 9–10 A.M. and 12–5 P.M.; Rte. 272, the Oregon Pike; 717-569-0401.*

Hans Herr House

The stone house built as a home for the Swiss Mennonite bishop and the first meeting place for Mennonite settlers in Pennsylvania was completed in 1719 and still stands as the oldest building in Lancaster County. It is considered one of the best examples of medieval German architecture in North America. Painter Andrew Wyeth, a descendent of Herr, included the stone house in several of his paintings. *Admission $5; open weekdays, 9–4; five miles south of Lancaster in the town of Willow Street [sic] at 1849 Hans Herr Dr.; 717-464-4438.*

JAMES BUCHANAN 1791–1868
U.S. President 1857–1861

One and a half miles west of Lancaster is the 1828 Federal-style mansion of Pennsylvania's only U.S. President, James Buchanan. The nation's only bachelor president, Buchanan often said publicly that he entered politics in his 30s as a diversion from grief after the death of his fiancee, a Lancaster woman. Elective office may have begun as distraction, but it soon became his calling; he made three attempts to win the Democratic Party nomination before finally succeeding, and gave his acceptance speech from the front porch of Wheatland, outside Lancaster, in 1856.

Buchanan also may have proved to be the ultimate politician—one who was able to put party loyalty before moral principle in the 1830s when the debate over slavery was raging across the country. Although he came from a state where abolitionist societies flourished and the Underground Railroad was active, Buchanan demonstrated no moral indignation on the issue of slavery and publicly blamed abolitionists for endangering national security and trampling over Southern states' rights.

As President, Buchanan was keenly aware that his power emanated from the South. Most members of his cabinet owned slaves and many of his administration's policies subtly promoted the practice. Northern Democrats were angered—especially Illinois Sen. Stephen Douglas who argued there could be no compromise on such human rights issues. In the 1860 Presidential election, a schism in the Democratic Party led to two different Democratic candidates running for president—Douglas, favored by the North, and John C. Breckinridge, favored by the South. The party's division was one of the factors in Republican candidate Abraham Lincoln winning the Presidency.

On March 4, 1861, with the secession of Southern states beginning and talk of war circulating, Buchanan was ready to retire to Wheatland. And when war did break out, he was quick to blame the South, in spite of widespread public criticism about his handling of secession and protecting federal forts in the South. In defense of his administration, Buchanan published his autobiography, which he wrote at Wheatland. Two years later, in June 1868, he died at age 77 from complications of pneumonia.

The estate still includes all the out-buildings and servants' quarters that made this rustic retreat more like a resort. The Victorian decor, furniture, and artwork reflects Buchanan's sophisticated sense of style gained from travels through Europe as a diplomat during the terms of three Presidents.

> ### Wheatlands
> *map page 87, B-3*
> President James Buchanan's home
> Open daily; Apr–Nov, 10–4;
> 1120 Marietta Ave., Lancaster
> 717-392-8721

■ INTO THE COUNTRYSIDE

Anyone interested in getting a taste of the authentic Amish experience must venture out to the smaller towns and gently rolling farm country where the Amish live and work. There's really no "best way" to tour the region, but the relative proximity of the towns, and the small area that contains them, tends to encourage you to follow your own impulses. Good places to start are any of the corridors heading out from Lancaster: East toward Bird-in-Hand and Intercourse along Route 340; toward Paradise situated on Route 30; and Strasburg, south of Paradise where Routes 869 and 741 meet.

◆ ARTISANS IN LANCASTER COUNTY

In Lancaster County, hand-made Amish quilts and Mennonite furniture— more like works of art than household goods—are sold from the makers' own homes and at retail outlets that come recommended by visitors bureaus. Primary locations include Lancaster, Intercourse—where the Amish conduct much of their regular business—and Bird-in-Hand. Other valued Pennsylvania Dutch crafts include needlework, such as tablecloths and napkins; gardening tools; leather goods; pottery; and toys.

Visitors centers throughout the region carry standard warnings that while there are reputable dealers who offer the best Pennsylvania Dutch craftwork, imitations are common, so the buyer must beware. Another reality check: much of the best work here passes by the local market and is handled through galleries in large cities such as Philadelphia and New York.

This magnificent hope chest, crafted about 1792 in Lehigh or Berks County, exemplifies the furniture built by German craftsmen from the late 18th to the early 19th century. (Philadelphia Museum of Art)

SOUTHEAST
ARTISANS

THE AMISH AND THEIR QUILTS

The story begins in Switzerland, where in 1525 a group called the Brethren separated from the state church. They eventually became known as Mennonites, after Menno Simons, one of their early leaders. The Mennonites believed in separation of church and state, saying that man couldn't swear an oath of allegiance to anyone but God. They also espoused adult rather than infant baptism, since a child didn't know enough about true faith to make a commitment. The state church banned the new religion and a long, bloody history commenced....

In 1693, Jacob Ammann, a Mennonite elder, formed his own splinter group. He felt that the Mennonites were too worldly. He also wanted to instigate the practice of shunning, whereby transgressors were ostracized. The Amish, as they became known...eventually migrated to America, seeking religious freedom....

The Amish goal is to be self-sufficient from the outside world. They don't want to be part of the government structure. They pay taxes, but build and maintain their own schools. They don't collect welfare, pensions, or social security. They won't hold public office, although some of them vote. The Amish are conscientious objectors, serving in hospitals if drafted. They won't go to court if sued, and won't file suit themselves if wronged.

Amish women often love to embroider and to quilt. As always, since there must be a utilitarian function, the embroidery is done on tea towels and bed linens. Quilts are used for warmth, and are made at times of birth or marriage, and when old ones wear out....The Diamond and Bars quilts are as unique as the Amish themselves. They are simple and unlike any other quilts in the mainstream of American quilting. Even

when the Amish work with familiar patterns, their version will be unusual because of their use of only solid colors. Prints are considered too worldly. No one knows for sure why the Amish have chosen to use color as they do. The end result is very strong and powerful. Perhaps that is reason enough.

—Roberta Horton, *An Amish Adventure,* second edition, 1996

A center diamond pattern quilt circa 1930. (Courtesy of The Heritage Center Museum of Lancaster)

Along these routes and in these towns you will find the craft shops, museums, restaurants, roadside stands, and other attractions. For an even more authentic experience, you really need to strike out on a leisurely drive along the intricate network of smaller backroads that criss-cross the countryside and eventually hook back up with the major routes. If you plan to explore these roads, obtain a copy of the highly detailed and valuable **Groff's Map of Lancaster County**. It has most small roads in the area, and it's available at the People's Place and many other sites in Lancaster County.

◆ OUTLETS FOR FINE CRAFTS

LANCASTER

The Weathervane Shop at the Landis Valley Museum *(also see page 117)*, where artists and artisans sell the items they make on the site. *2451 Kissel Hill Rd.; 717-569-0401.*

Rosa and Elmer Stoltzfus sell gorgeous locally made quilts out of their home. *Open daily; 9–5 except Sun. and holidays,;102 N. Ronks Rd.; (no phone).*

INTERCOURSE

Old Road Furniture Co. has antique reproduction furniture based on 19th-century Amish designs that are wonderful for their simplicity and beauty. There are harvest and farm tables, desks, chairs and cabinets. *3457 Old Philadelphia Pike; 800-760-7171.*

BIRD-IN-HAND

The Folk Craft Center and Museum has displays of traditional crafts: pottery, tinware, kitchen utensils, fabrics, and quilts. Similar items by local artisans are sold in the center's three gift shops. *One-half mile west of Bird-in-Hand in Witmer; 441 Mt. Sidney Rd.; 717-397-3609.*

◆ SITES OUTSIDE OF LANCASTER

The Amish Village
This living history museum features an authentically furnished Old Order Amish farmhouse. There is a barn with animals, blacksmith shop, schoolhouse, and many other exhibits. *Admission fee. Summer hours are 9-6; spring and fall 9-5; Rte. 896 in Strasburg; 717-687-8511.*

People's Place
One of the better places to get a good understanding of the Amish and other Plain People sects is this museum and bookshop in Intercourse. There's a documentary called "Who are the Amish?" and an interactive museum that answers a game of 20 questions about these contrarians to modernity. Next door is the Quilt Museum and shop where you can see Amish quilts being made, or purchase one of exceptional workmanship; *717-768-7171.*

Mennonite Information Center
Another required stop for those who wish to get a little more quality background information on the lives and history of the Mennonites. *2209 Millstream Rd., Lancaster; 717-299-0954.*

A Strasburg Rail Road train passes a corn maze near Paradise.

Railroad Museum of Pennsylvania

This state-maintained museum charts railroad history from its beginnings in the early 1800s to the present and does a great job of showing automobile-focused visitors how these machines transformed the state's economy and the face of the nation.

Visitors enter through a reconstructed train depot into a repair shop where they can walk underneath a 62-ton freight locomotive. Another highlight is the cavernous Rolling Stock Hall housing four railroad tracks where meticulously preserved rail cars and locomotives are on display. It is a much more polished, hospitable place than when it was the maintenance and repair garage for the Reading Railroad line. *Rte. 741, Strasburg; 717-687-8628.*

Strasburg Rail Road

Just down the road is a working version of the museum cars, the Strasburg Rail Road, which offers a nine-mile round trip run from Strasburg to Paradise and passes through some of the most beautiful Amish farm country in the state. On view through the train's windows are horse-drawn black buggies paying no mind to cars swooshing by on back country roads. As the tracks snake past farmland, passengers can see Amish men in their wide-brimmed straw hats directing horse-drawn plows along neat rows. Riders can bring their own picnic lunch for the stop in Paradise, or dine at The Red Caboose, a slightly updated version of an old-style dining car.

If you take the rail trip, be sure to reserve time to inspect the opulent private coach that catered to the president of the Reading Railroad. What train travel lacked in speed, it could make up for in leg room and amenities. The car cost more than $100,000 to build back in 1916 and features separate sleeping, dining, and meeting compartments. The lavish decor includes cut glass chandeliers and floor-to-ceiling mahogany paneling. *Rte. 741, Strasburg; 717-687-7522.*

◆ BACKROADS TO EPHRATA

Some of the most appealing, authentically Amish farm country lies between Intercourse and the town of Ephrata to the north. There are endless combinations of backroad routes that wind lazily through the heart of this bucolic countryside dotted with white farmhouses, and with a Groff's map you can follow whatever route strikes your fancy.

◆ EPHRATA CLOISTER *map page 87, C-3*

This community of religious celibates was founded in 1732 and practiced a no-frills existence with an emphasis on self-denial. Unlike other strict religious societies of the times, however, the group believed they honored God and themselves best when they were singing or engaging in artistic pursuits. The members, which numbered about 300 at the community's peak, were held to rigid dietary restrictions in the belief that singing through the discomfort of a near-empty stomach made voices purer. Ephratans were admired for their skill in a form of calligraphy known as *Frakturschriften*—broken lettering.

The cloister has a library filled with hand-lettered books, and many others that were produced here are held in rare book collections and research libraries.

The Ephrata Cloister is now open to the public.

A perfect time to tour the cloister is on a cold, gray winter's day, when you'll get a heightened sense of how drafty and austere the medieval-style buildings can be. Be sure to walk the entire length of the narrow corridors and imagine being reminded day after day that the path of virtue and humility is also straight and narrow—this according to the preaching of founder Conrad Beissel, who wrote much of the music sung by members. Also be sure to walk the grounds around the complex—still set off from modern society by a wooded park—and visualize how much more remote the community was over 250 years ago. *Admission $6; Follow Rte. 22 south to Ephrata and follow W. Main St. to the cloister complex at 632 W. Main. Mon–Sat, 9–5; Sun, noon–5; 717-733-6600.*

◆ LITITZ   *map page 87, B-3*

Just a few miles west of Ephrata along quiet Route 772 is the peaceful farming village of Lititz, founded by Protestant Moravians who came to Pennsylvania hoping to bag a few converts from among the "heathen" natives. It's a town that really is deserving of the grossly overused description "charming." The clean, tree-shaded main streets are lined with beautiful 18th-century buildings of fieldstone and aged red brick, many housing quality antique stores and craft shops. The town's center is wonderfully preserved Moravian Square, bordered by a 1787 Moravian church, Bretheren and Sister's houses, and Linden Hall, part of the oldest girls' residence school in the United States. You can pick up a walking tour map of the town at the General Sutter Inn, at the corner of Main Street and Route 501.

For the foodcentric traveler, Lititz has a couple of distractions sure to please. You can take a tour of the **Sturgis Pretzel House** *(219 E. Main St.; 717-626-4354),* the first commercial pretzel bakery in the country (it's $2 and you get to make—and eat—a pretzel); or follow the sweet smell of chocolate wafting on the air to the **Wilbur Chocolate Company's Candy Americana Museum and Store** where you can see can a variety of confections being made, and then wolf down a few samples. *48 N. Broad St.; 717-626-1131.*

◆ MOUNT JOY   *map page 87, B-3*

Leaving Lititz on Route 772 and heading west toward the Susquehanna River, you enter the town of Mount Joy, where you should stop and sample some pleasantly unpretentious Mennonite cuisine, though cuisine really is too chi-chi a word for the down-home meal served at **Groff's Farm Restaurant.***(650 Pinkerton Rd.; 717-653-2048.)* To wash down Betty Groff's creamed chicken specialty, stop in at the

150-year-old **Bube's Brewery** *(102 N. Market St.; 717-653-2056)* for a pint and a tour of a surviving 19th-century brewery. The tour leads down narrow, winding passages to a cave 40 feet below street level that once sheltered slaves moving along the Underground Railroad, and that now harbors the brewery's fermentation tanks.

◆ MARIETTA *map page 87, B-3*

About a 10-minute drive west out of Mt. Joy, Route 772 runs into Route 441 at the sleepy riverfront town of Marietta, where at least half of the town's buildings have earned designation on the National Registry of Historic Places. Stroll along Rockwell-esque streets lined with elegant Colonial, Federal, and Victorian homes, complete with manicured lawns, towering shade trees, and huge American flags flying from front porches. This newly polished former mill town is nurturing a growing artist's community, which is evident in the number of galleries, studios, and antique shops dotting the village center.

◆ CHICKIES ROCK COUNTY PARK *map page 87, B-3*

Give the Amish a break and pull off at this riverfront park to gawk at some different creatures for awhile: the swans and green herons gracefully plying the slow-rolling waters of the Susquehanna, and ospreys and bald eagles skimming the surface to snatch fish in their talons. Upon Chickies Rock itself, you may see rock climbers (the humans, not the birds) scaling the walls, for this site is considered the best place for the sport in the area. The 444-mile-long Susquehanna River is shallow and rocky here, its flow contained by hydroelectric dams. The park has two spectacular overlooks from which you can observe other forms of wildlife along the steep banks of the river. *Rte. 441; 717-295-2055 or 717-299-8215.*

◆ COLUMBIA AND ITS WATCH AND CLOCK MUSEUM *map page 87, B-3*

Eight easy miles farther south on 441 is the placid town of Columbia, stretching languidly along the riverfront and peppered with B&Bs, good restaurants, and antique shops. The town is best known for its more-interesting-than-it-sounds Watch and Clock Museum, where a vast collection of 8,000 items has been brought together under one roof by the National Association of Watch and Clock Collectors. Hanging over the reception desk at the museum entrance is the Latin motto *Tempus vitam regit*—"Time rules life." But time gets lost here amid the various timepieces, including an Egyptian pot that measures dripping water, Ameri-

(following pages) A sunrise fog hugs the dairylands of Lancaster County.

If you have time on your hands, visit the Watch and Clock Museum in Columbia.

can railroad watches, an entire room filled with cuckooing cuckoo clocks and, perhaps the museum's greatest treasure, a Stephen Engle Monumental Apostolic Clock, a 9-by-11-foot timepiece framed in an exquisitely carved case. The clock has 48 moving figures and eight separate movements. Engle worked on the clock for 20 years before completing it in 1877 and then sending it out across the country on a for-fee exhibit. *514 Poplar St., Columbia; 717-684-8261.*

■ HERSHEY *map page 87, A-2*

Imagine that the main street in your town is named Chocolate Avenue, that no matter the wind direction or the time of day, the distinct aroma of chocolate wafts through the air. Chocolate addicts will pay no heed to the historical significance of the place and follow their noses directly to Hershey's Chocolate World. To fully appreciate one businessman's ingenuity in turning an entire town into a giant marketing campaign for his candy factory, you need look no further than the street lights in the shape of foil-wrapped Hershey's Kisses.

After failed attempts to manufacture and sell candy in Philadelphia and New York City, native son Milton Snavely Hershey returned to Lancaster County, where his innovative use of fresh milk in making caramels proved highly successful. In 1900 he sold his Lancaster Caramel Company for $1 million, and 1903, he bought a cornfield, constructed a manufacturing plant, and set out to perfect the chocolate bar. His eponymous, quintessential company town sprang up around this operation.

Hershey ran his town with a firm but benevolent hand, and eventually Milton S. lent his name to a dozen other monuments to the public good in the region—including the Milton S. Hershey Medical Center and a home for disadvantaged boys.

Today, Hershey is basically a factory town grown into a fairly unappealing suburban area punctuated by a sweetened tourist destination. But that doesn't stop 1.5 million visitors from flocking here every year to pay their respects to the mecca of chocolate indulgence.

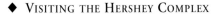

A Hershey's Kiss streetlight.

◆ VISITING THE HERSHEY COMPLEX

To get to the Hershey attractions, take Hershey Park Drive exit off Rte. 322. *The following sights are along Hershey Park Drive. Call 800-HERSHEY for more information, directions, and lodging reservations.*

The Chocolate World
Take an automated ride through the chocolate-making process and get a little reward at the end. This is also the town's official visitors center. *Free; 717-534-4900.*

Hershey Park
You won't see Mickey or Goofy here, but dancing Reese's Peanut Butter Cups and Hershey Bars bop around this 87-acre amusement park with 50 rides and attractions including five water slides and a 1919 carousel decked out with 66 hand-carved wooden horses. Admission $25; *information: 717-534-3916.*

Hershey Gardens
Purge the aroma of chocolate from your nose with a stroll through these 23 acres of stunning and fragrant botanical gardens. *717-534-3492.*

Hershey Museum of American Life
A memorial to Milton Hershey's life. Also, wonderful black-and-white photographs of the town's progression from one-horse waystop to world-famous city. Also on display are artifacts of early German immigrant life and American Indian history in the region. *170 W. Hershey Park Dr.; 717-534-3439.*

N O R T H E A S T
& T H E P O C O N O S

■ HIGHLIGHTS *page*

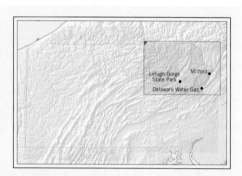

Food & Lodging
map 276; charts 277
listings by town, in alphabetical order 278

■ TRAVEL BASICS

In northeastern Pennsylvania forested mountains with spectacular views rise up from all directions. In the eastern section are the steep ridges of the Poconos; in the west, the rolling hills of the Appalachian Plateau. Exit the interstate anywhere in the Poconos for a backroad drive through mountain forest—especially in the fall to see the autumn leaves. The Poconos have several ski resorts where downhill and cross-country skiers, snowshoe hikers, and snowboarders glory in the consistently deep snows—an average of 60 inches of snow annually.

The Delaware Water Gap is where the Delaware River slices through a thousand-foot high ridge running across the borders of Pennsylvania and New Jersey. Views of the mountains and river are spectacular here, although dampened somewhat by the fact that I-80 also cuts through this same gap. The Delaware Water Gap National Recreation Area extends some 40 miles north along both sides of the river and affords ample opportunities for swimming, hiking, and canoeing.

Roads west of the Delaware River will take you through former coal towns, such as Scranton and Jim Thorpe, and the heavily forested nature areas of Lehigh Gorge State Park and the "Endless Mountains" of the western Appalachian Plateau.

Climate: The comparatively low elevation of the Poconos does not produce a true mountain climate, but temperatures are generally 10 degrees cooler than in the surrounding lowland regions. Summers are pleasant—high temperatures averaging in the 70s and 80s with occasional thunderstorms. Winters are cold—with temperatures averaging between 10 and 30 degrees. Spring (April and May) and fall (October) are gorgeous.

Food & Lodging: Although the Poconos are awash in tacky motels, there are gems in the region worth seeking out. Northeast communities are served by the standard range of chain hotels, but smaller towns often have a charming bed-and-breakfast or a cozy motel, a swank country inn or a couples-only resort. Along Route 209 in the Delaware Water Gap you'll find small resorts with landscaped gardens and cabins with wooden front porches. Many of the best restaurants are connected to pricey inns and B&Bs. **Food & Lodging map** page 276; **charts** page 277; **listings** in alphabetical order by town begin on page 278. Lodging reservations in the Poconos can be made toll free at 800-762-6667; internet: www.800POCONOS.COM

NORTHEAST BASICS

■ LANDSCAPE

The dominant landform in this area is the heavily forested Appalachian Plateau. A narrow section of the Allegheny Mountains reaches in from the southwest to touch the region around Scranton. The Poconos, rising up from the table-like Plateau, stretch from the Allegheny Mountains in the south to the Moosic Mountains in the west near Lehigh Gorge State Park, gradually subsiding northward into lower Wayne County and bounded by the Susquehanna River to the west and the Delaware River to the east. Here the Pocono Escarpment plunges from 2,300 feet above sea level down to the Delaware River, creating dramatic vistas along the way.

In the north, the Poconos are covered by second-growth forests of pine, beech, birch, oak, and maple; in the south and east with hickory-mixed oak; to the south along the Delaware River with chestnut; in Monroe and Pike Counties with hemlock and white pine. These are still young woodlands, as the virgin forests were logged off during the 19th and early 20th centuries.

The Delaware River, which forms the border between Pennsylvania and New Jersey, cuts through the mountains at a spot known today as the Delaware Water

Gap, but originally called "Pohoqualine," or "River passing between two mountains," by the indigenous Lenni Lenape. English trappers and settlers shortened the name to "The Poconos," a term which later came to refer to the entire area.

The northeast's forested Poconos and the shores of the Delaware and Susquehanna Rivers have remained beautiful, and for that reason a place of retreat. In spring, creeks and streams swell from melting snow and carry icy water on a sharp, winding descent to the rivers. Marking the steeper drops along that journey are 30 waterfalls, nearly half of all the significant falls in Pennsylvania. As the sun thaws the ground and the falling water warms to nurture wildlife, blossoms break out in brilliant colors. Mountain meadows and fields here are dominated by the pinkish white mountain laurel, Pennsylvania's state flower, which blooms from late May through July.

NORTHEAST LANDSCPE

PARALLEL RIDGES

*B*ut what moved me most deeply about Pennsylvania as a boy, and still does today, is her ancient symbol of freedom, the mountains; not a few isolated ranges, as in some states, but a whole province swarming with them, often one against the other with only narrow valleys between. The sight of their backs raised to the sky, sometimes humped or flared, green and lush in summer, brown, hairy and wild in winter, seldom failed to stir me. I liked to study them and learn the lay of their land, how some ran parallel for twenty or even fifty miles and then turned or joined or threw out spurs to form coves and pinnacles or plateaus; how their aspect changed when seen from different angles; how the benches lay like smaller ridges, often with intervening forest swamps or wild hemlock hollows that the old mountain trails and early roads invariably followed; and how water from one mountain tasted sweeter and purer than that from another.

—Conrad Richter, *Pennsylvania,* 1947

(following pages) The Nicholson Viaduct in Wyoming County was one of the largest bridges in America when it was completed in 1915.

■ HISTORY

Before the first European settlers arrived, northeastern Pennsylvania was criss-crossed by hunting trails followed by the Lenni Lenape, who took game along the rivers and in the Wyoming Valley. Indigenous tribes must have heard rumors of the growing European presence in North America, for by the time William Penn and his followers were entering the area around the lower Delaware River, settlements in Virginia were more than a century old. In 1725, a French Huguenot fleeing religious persecution became the first settler in the northeast. He was Nicholas DePui, who purchased 3,000 acres at the southern end of the Delaware Water Gap from the Wolf Clan of the Lenni Lenape and established good relations with the native tribes. DePui and his wife raised nine children here and supported their family by hunting, farming, and growing apples.

If the settlers who followed had been as honorable and peaceful as DePui, Pennsylvania might have been a very different place. Instead, English settlers drove out Indians, often by force or guile, in order to claim the homesteads they had been promised by the Penn family and its agents in London. Angered by increasing encroachment, the Lenni Lenape, Shawnee, and Nanticoke joined the French in fighting the English during the French and Indian War. Raiding parties descended upon small farms, terrorizing settlers. Entire families were butchered, farms burned, and children kidnapped.

◆ CONNECTICUT VS. PENNSYLVANIA

In the mid-1700s, Connecticut challenged Pennsylvania for control of the Wyoming Valley (see maps, pages 24 and 137). To establish their claim, Connecticut's governor sent hundreds of families to settle in the region, and the little town of Wilkes-Barre reflected their origins—it was designed like a classic New England town, complete with a central "green." The arrival of these Connecticut settlers, however, right in the middle of the Wyoming Valley, infuriated the Lenni Lenape, already dispossessed of much of their original territory. In 1763, a Lenni Lenape war party went on the rampage, destroying hundreds of settlements.

Pennsylvania's new colonial governor, John Penn, grandson of William, exhorted settlers streaming into the region to respect American Indian treaties but to no avail. The Indian raids continued, and Penn descended to offering bounties for the scalps of Indian warriors.

The conflict escalated into the Yankee-Pennamite Wars. And while the fighting was interrupted by the Revolutionary War, it began anew after the British surrendered. The dispute was ultimately resolved by the Decree of Trenton in 1782, ceding the valley to Pennsylvania.

◆ REVOLUTIONARY WAR

In 1778, in the midst of the Revolutionary War, a band of Native American tribes from the northeast joined British loyalists in defending the area's grain stores from confiscation by the Continental Army.

On July 3, 1778, the British and their Indian allies attacked the colonists in the Wyoming Valley. Outnumbered three-to-one, the ragtag farmer-soldiers were overwhelmed and more than 220 of them were killed. The Indians proceeded to ravage the unprotected homesteads—a series of events later referred to as the Wyoming Massacre.

In retaliation, after the conclusion of the Revolutionary War, the new American military forces destroyed scores of Indian villages which had supported the enemy. By 1795, Indian resistance had been overcome and peace finally came to the region. With borders secure and immigrants free to settle the territory, farms prospered and towns expanded.

◆ LOGGING, MINING, AND IRON

It was in the decade after the War of Independence that prospectors discovered huge anthracite coal deposits—"black diamonds" as this hard, hot-burning, and almost smokeless coal became known. In the decades before the Civil War, anthracite, along with timber, fueled Pennsylvania's economic expansion. Coal from Pennsylvania's new mines was hauled along roadways freshly cut through virgin forest, and as access improved, logging operations flourished. Bark was stripped from oak trees to supply tannin for tanneries in Stroudsburg and Tannersville, and hardwood trees—lashed together as rafts and floated down the Delaware—were milled into lumber for homes in the rapidly developing western settlements. By the 1840s, virtually all useable timber had been logged from the Poconos.

As the nation's railroads expanded, so did the demand for coal to fuel its engines and factories. The last barrier to widespread mining operations in the region—a cost-effective transportation system—ended when railroad tracks were laid to the Pocono Plateau. With its plentiful coal, iron foundries, and rail system, Pennsylvania emerged from the Civil War with its economy roaring full steam ahead.

◆ Union Movement

The center of the mining industry was in Carbon County and in the town known today as Jim Thorpe, and known then as Mauch Chunk. It was in this region that industrialists amassed fortunes while miners toiled away underground, going into debt buying their food in company stores. Many of the toughest mining jobs went to the Irish, who deeply resented their treatment in the mines as being a continuation of what they had endured under the British in Ireland. In the 1840s, laborers who dug coal were making 50 cents a day. There was no federal regulation of pay or working conditions, and the courts were vigorously anti-union.

In the coal-mining region, a secret terrorist group known as the Molly Maguires formed, its roots in a similar violent gang which targeted land barons of Ireland for assassination. The name is derived from the story of a Celtic woman who brought murderous vengeance on those who had wronged her.

It wasn't long before the Maguires' vigilante justice moved from sending greedy mine owners to their graves to targeting people in all levels in mine management, and any community people seen as industry sympathizers. Their hold on the region was so strong that killings often took place in public places in front of dozens of witnesses. But none would cooperate with police.

Eventually, the public became fed up with the violence and began to testify at trials. Ironically, it was an Irish contingent of the Pinkerton Detective Agency (a private police force employed with bloody results decades later in Pittsburgh steelworker union strikes) that infiltrated the Maguires and brought them down.

By 1902, an emerging labor movement crusading against unsafe conditions in the coal mines and an increasing reliance on oil as an industrial fuel source brought coal production nearly to a halt. By the 1930s, underground coal mining had been followed by strip mining, which left large scars on the land. By the 1980s the iron foundries were idle and once prosperous Scranton lay fallow in the heart of the "Rust Belt."

■ Northeast Today

The Lehigh and Wyoming Valleys and the forested Poconos bear little evidence of their blood-and-sweat-stained past. In most valley communities, the rusty skeletons of old steel mills, iron foundries, and mining operations stand as depressing monuments to the past. But in the larger former heavy industry powerhouses like

This Harper's Weekly *illustration shows Mount Pisgah and Mauch Chunk in the 1880s.*

Scranton and Jim Thorpe, those same facilities have been refurbished and turned into museums popular enough to draw several million visitors a year. Other old industrial sites have been reborn as "incubator" office parks for new, high-tech businesses.

In the mountainous areas, forests cover most of the peaks while spectacular waterfalls drop precipitously through two major plateaus, wearing down their edges and adding to the drama of the rock structures. These are all preserved in eight state parks totaling 35,000 acres, and the massive Delaware Gap National Recreation Area, a federal park along 40 miles of the Delaware River.

Although development continues to encroach on animal habitat, the region today is more protective than aggressive. Community groups and state environmental workers have been responsible for improving habitats for bald and golden eagles, ospreys, and white-tailed deer, the state animal, which was nearly hunted to extinction in the 1800s.

In the former industrial centers of the northeast and in the most remote mountain communities, the cycle has come full circle—from exploitation and bloody confrontation to preservation and a willingness to share.

(above) The abandoned Canton Steam Mill.

(opposite) Ricketts Glen in Sullivan County boasts some of the most beautiful waterfalls in northeast Pennsylvania.

■ ABOUT THE POCONOS

Coming out of the Lehigh Tunnel on the northeast extension of the Pennsylvania Turnpike (I-476), visitors will notice a dramatic change in the mountains. In this part of the Appalachian Plateau, the Poconos rise up steeply. A drive through the backroads of these woodlands will turn up dairy farms, charming villages, ski resorts, and—in the fall—a gorgeous display of autumn foliage. Alas, there is also a fair amount of ticky-tack along the way.

The Poconos stretch across four counties. Within them are golf courses, dense woodlands, and 13 recreation areas. In this part of the Appalachian Plateau, the mountains form peaks—in contrast to the long ridges of the Allegheny Plateau. However, they are not the Rockies; the loftiest elevations are at best a few thousand feet.

The Poconos reputation as a honeymoon destination began during World War II when servicemen rushed here with their brides before leaving for war. In 1963 Morris Wilkins introduced the first heart-shaped bathtub at his Cove Haven Resort. A photo feature about the tub in *LIFE* magazine earned the area, deserved or not, the reputation as the "Honeymoon Capital of the World."

A thrill ride at Knoebels Amusement Park in Elysburg. The Poconos have long been a family destination as well as a honeymoon retreat.

A sleigh rally in Forksville, Sullivan County.

Today, more than 200,000 couples honeymoon in the Poconos ever year, many of them at the nine couples-only resorts. These accommodations are likely to have in-room jacuzzis, fireplaces, and the now requisite heart-shaped tubs. (Many claim that the heart-shaped bathtub was in fact "invented" here.) Which isn't to say that the Poconos are only for those blinded by love. They're popular with hikers and with families who want to ski or to find a place to camp, hike, fish, and swim.

◆ SKIING

Thanks to an average of 60 inches of snow per year falling on its mountains, the Poconos are home to seven major winter recreation resorts, including Ski Camelback and Boulder Mountain, two of the state's best. Whether your tastes lean toward screaming on fast downhill runs, gliding over groomed cross-country trails, or plodding through powder on a snowshoe hike, most resorts have something for you. For a comprehensive listing of area resorts, look up *home.earthlink.net/eschr/skiguide,* o PA Ski Guide for a map and listing of Poconos ski areas, along with links to all individual resorts. *For information about fall foliage or skiing, call the Poconos hotline at 570-421-5565; or call Pocono Mountain Vacation Bureau, 800-762-6667.*

DELAWARE RIVER
NORTH

A — Delaware State Forest
Port Jervis — Matamoras
B — Tristate
To Middletown, NY
84
NEW YORK
NEW JERSEY
23
High Point 1,803 (highest point in New Jersey)

6
To Scranton
84

Milford
Montague
High Point State Park
Colesville

Raymondskill Falls
Log Tavern Pond
209

0   5 Miles
0   7.5 Kilometers

206
Stokes State Forest
519

739
Edgemere — Dingmans Falls
Layton

Dingmans Falls Visitor Center — Dingmans Ferry
Culvers Lake

Pocono Environmental Educational Center
Culvers Gap
NEW JERSEY
Lake Owassa
Halsey

PENNSYLVANIA
Delaware
Delaware State Forest

521
Swartswood
Egypt Mills
615
Delaware Water Gap National Park
Swartswood State Park
Swartswood Lake

402
Bushkill
Bushkill Visitor Center
627
Flatbrookville
617
Fredon

Bushkill Falls
209
Stillwater
94

Shoemaker
Echo Lake
602

Coolbaughs
602
Marksboro
659

Marshalls Creek
Blairstown

209
94
521
80
To Newark, NJ & New York, NY

Delaware Water Gap
Kittatinny Point Visitor Center
Hope

Stroudsburg
80
Great Meadows

To Williansport
611
Columbia
519

Portland
Delaware
Townsbury

Mt Bethel
46
46

191
Manunka Chunk
512
611
Buttzville

Belvidere
Oxford

Bangor
Richmond
626
31
57

Pen Argyl
512
191
Washington
NEW JERSEY

PENNSYLVANIA
519
Broadway

Martins Creek
New Village

Harmony
To Newark, NJ & New York, NY

33
611

Stockertown
57
To Allentown
78

Nazareth
Easton
Phillipsburg
Bloomsbury

■ DELAWARE WATER GAP

map opposite, A-4

An unsuspecting traveler heading west on I-80 through New Jersey might not be prepared for the dramatic entry point into the state of Pennsylvania known as the Delaware Water Gap. The Gap is literally a gap in the long ridge of Kittatinny Mountain carved by the Delaware River during a period of geologic uplift. The builders of I-80 might have been saying to themselves, *what is good enough for the Delaware River is good enough for us,* so they ran the interstate right through it. (Actually, a railway and several roads took advantage of the gap well before the interstate was built.) So, how did the gap come to be, one might ask? Back in a previous eon of geologic history, an uplift began beneath the river. The uplift was slow enough that the river's course eroded the rock underneath while the mountains rose on either side of it. As the mountains grew, so did the worn-away stone wall, creating a stunning cross-section. The twisted bands of metamorphic quartzite visible today cause geologists to pull off the highway for a closer look. Even those with little interest in geology might want to stop to take in the views.

■ DELAWARE WATER GAP NATIONAL RECREATION AREA

This 70,000-acre park protects both sides of the Delaware River, which for 40 miles forms the border between Pennsylvania and New Jersey. The protected area is, at its widest point, about six miles across. You'll want to travel the backroads along the river, stopping at small villages, swimming beaches, or canoe launches, or taking a hike from one of the marked trail heads.

The upper Delaware River is relatively slow-moving, shallow, and clear, lined with trees and home to fishing birds, beaver, and, in season, Canada geese. Following a serpentine course, the river makes a beautiful S curve on its mile-long journey through Kittatinny Ridge.

The Delaware is the only major waterway on the East Coast that has not been dammed, and it barely escaped that fate 35 years ago when the federal government announced plans to flood the valley and create a giant reservoir. Grassroots opposition grew and made its power felt in Congress, and in 1978, 73 miles of the Delaware were protected as a "wild and scenic" river.

At one time a covered bridge stretched across the Delaware River, below the Delaware Water Gap at Portland. (Underwood Photo Archives, San Francisco)

◆ WATER GAP BASICS

Getting there

If you come west from New York City on I–80, or north from Philadelphia on Highway 33, you'll arrive at the southern end of the park near the town of Stroudsburg. To reach the visitors center on the New Jersey side, Kittatinny Point Visitors Center, take the last exit before you cross the river. Route 209 is the main Pennsylvania thoroughfare north through the park. Halfway along it you'll find the Bushkill Visitor Center.

Swimming, Canoeing, and Tubing

In summer, you can swim, canoe, and ride inner tubes or rafts down the slow-moving Delaware. (Access points to the river are located every 8 to 10 miles.) Two beaches are recommended for swimming: Smithfield at the south end of the park near Shawnee-on-Delaware, and Milford at the north end. These are family-friendly, with lifeguards, and get fairly crowded. Water temperatures in summer (May to September) rise from the mid-50s to highs in the mid-70s in July. In spring and fall, wetsuits may be needed for comfort.

It is easy to arrange one- to five-day canoe and raft trips through the park. Look for Class I and Class II rapids. *For information on primitive camping and canoe and raft trips along the river, call 570-588-2451.*

(previous pages) Interstate 80 can be seen following the course of the river through the Delaware Water Gap near Stroudsburg.

Fishing

Shad, trout, walleye, muskellunge, and bass can be caught in the area; a fishing license is required.

Trails

Sixty miles of hiking trails meander through the forest. Interesting day hikes include the trial up Mount Tammany (1,527 feet) and Mount Minsi (1,463 feet), both of which have fine views at the top. A 25-mile segment of the Appalachian Trail, which traverses the East Coast from Maine to Georgia, winds through the park, most of it on the New Jersey side of the river.

Visitors Centers

Kittatinny Point Visitors Center. *Just off Interstate 80 in New Jersey (last exit before Delaware Water Gap toll bridge); open daily spring through late October, and most weekends in winter; 9–5 ; 908-496-4458.*

Bushkill Visitors Center. *On US Rte. 209 along the Bushkill Creek; open daily Jul–Oct; 9–5; 570-588-7044.*

Park Headquarters. *On River Rd. one mile off Rte. 209 in Bushkill; open Mon–Fri except holidays; 8–4. Website: www.nps.gov/dewa; 570-588-2451.*

Camping and Lodging

Overnight accommodations here include National Park–sponsored cabins and campgrounds; in nearby towns can be found youth hostels to hotels *(see above).*

A WALK RECOMMENDED, NOT

*T*he Appalachian Trail runs for 230 miles in a northeasterly arc across the state, like the broad end of a slice of pie. I never met a hiker with a good word to say about the trail in Pennsylvania. It is, as someone told a *National Geographic* reporter in 1987, the place "where boots go to die." During the last ice age it experienced what geologists call a periglacial climate—a zone at the edge of an ice sheet characterized by frequent freeze-thaw cycles that fractured the rock. The result is mile upon mile of jagged, oddly angled slabs of stone strewn about in wobbly piles known to science as *felsenmeer* (literally, "sea of rocks"). These require constant attentiveness if you are not to twist an ankle or sprawl on your face—not a pleasant experience with fifty pounds of momentum on your back. Lots of people leave Pennsylvania limping and bruised. The state also has what are reputed to be the meanest rattlesnakes anywhere along the trail, and the most unreliable water sources, particularly in high summer. The really beautiful Appalachian ranges in Pennsylvania—Nitanny and Jacks and Tussey—stand to the north and west. For various practical and historical reasons, the AT goes nowhere near them. It traverses no notable eminences at all in Pennsylvania, offers no particularly memorable vistas, visits no national parks or forests, and overlooks the state's considerable history. In consequence, the AT is essentially just the central part of a very long, taxing haul connecting the South and New England. It is little wonder that most people dislike it.

Oh, and it also has the very worst maps ever produced for hikers anywhere. The six sheets—maps is really much too strong a word for them—produced for Pennsylvania by a body called the Keystone Trails Association are small, monochrome, appallingly printed, inadequately keyed, and astoundingly vague—in short, useless: comically useless, heartbreakingly useless, dangerously useless. No one should be sent into a wilderness with maps this bad.

—Bill Bryson, *A Walk in the Woods,* 1998

◆ BUSHKILL FALLS *map page 144, A-3*

The most efficient way to get to Bushkill Falls, one of the natural wonders of the Delaware Gap area, is from I-80 at Stroudsburg, then north on Route 209.

The "Niagara of Pennsylvania," the Bushkill Falls are located on a 300-acre private estate and were first opened to the public by Charles Peters in 1904. The main falls, the most spectacular in a series of eight, can be reached by an easy 15-minute walk. The stream, which rises in the Poconos, drops over the edge of a 100-foot cliff. From the deep pool at the bottom, banked by ferns, mosses, and wildflowers, the creek drops another 70 feet through a long and spectacular gorge strewn with gigantic boulders. Access to other, smaller waterfalls, is along more challenging trails. Also within the property are a wildlife exhibit and an American Indian exhibit that includes a longhouse and artifacts: arrowheads and spear points, jewelry, tools, and pottery. *Two miles northwest of US 209; open Apr–Nov; $8 adults, $2 children; 570-588-6682.*

◆ POCONO ENVIRONMENTAL EDUCATION CENTER *map page 144, A-2*

This 38-acre compound dedicated to environmental education sits on the eastern slope of the Pocono Plateau, inside Delaware Water Gap park. Once a honeymoon

Deer abound in all parts of northeastern Pennsylvania.

getaway, the site was taken over by serious birdwatchers and environmentalists more than 26 years ago (who are more interested in the literal doings of the birds and bees), and is now the largest residential center for environmental education in the Western Hemisphere. More than 2,500 people come annually to stay and study a wide

The rattlesnakes of Pennsylvania are shorter and thicker than their counterparts in the Western states.

variety of nature-related topics, ranging from wildlife photography to the natural history of the Poconos. A three-day, two-night stay at the center will cost a family of four about $500 for the seminar course and spartan bed and board—a cabin fitted with bunkbeds and private bath (linens and towels cost extra), and daily meals served buffet style: simple but good fare like scrambled egg breakfasts, sandwich lunches, and five-course dinners. The staff is especially adept at teaching children —many classes are tailored to ages 3 to 14. The course material and teaching staff are equally superb. For those who would rather not overnight at the center, day passes for hikers are available.

The point of the PEEC (or "peak" as the staff calls it) isn't the indoor experience though. Within its 250,000 acres is a network of trails that traverse old hickory forests, open fields, and boggy wetlands. Otters, common in the Water Gap area, can be spotted here, as well as beavers, coyotes, foxes, porcupines, and snakes. Two poisonous snakes—copperheads and timber rattlesnakes—live here, and are most active in the spring.

Wildflowers are abundant. This is the place to see the pale pink mountain laurel, as well as mossy streamside rocks, and, if you're lucky, catch a glimpse of a bald eagle soaring in the late afternoon updrafts searching for fish in the Delaware River. *Open Mon–Sat, 9 A.M.–11 P.M. and Sun 9–5; Winter hours vary. 20 minutes north of Bushkill Falls on US 209; 570-828-2319.*

NORTHEAST
DEL. WATER GAP

The golf course of the Shawnee Resort, one of the premier hotels along the Delaware River, can be seen on the island below.

◆ **DINGMAN'S FALLS** *map page 144, A-2*

Quite close to the river, and well used as a canoe-launching site, is the charming small town of Dingman's Ferry. Here, a privately owned toll bridge spans the river.

Less than a mile west of US 209 is Dingman's Falls. This is a wonderfully non-commercial site, just a visitors center and a small picnic area. A half-mile trail (keep the stream in sight) threads through rhododendron and hemlocks to two waterfalls, the cascading Dingman's Falls and the more delicate Silver Thread Falls.

◆ **MILFORD** *map page 144, A/B-1*

Most first-time visitors to the Delaware Water Gap, especially hikers, find Milford a convenient and congenial base, with its many motels and restaurants. You'll find lovely Victorian houses here, as well as antique shops, artist studios, and cottage-style motels with open porches. Everyone seems to be either drinking lattes at a corner cafe, or wearing hiking boots and nibbling trail mix.

■ **ALONG SCENIC ROUTE 6** *map page 133, E&F-2*

Route 6 provides a scenic northern route across Pennsylvania. In the northeast it is most beautiful from Milford west to the outskirts of Scranton, and picks up again after Scranton as it traverses the state's northern counties.

◆ **MILFORD TO WHITE MILLS** *map page 133, E&F-2*

From Milford two-lane US 6 meanders west through forests of thick evergreens and hardwoods, and through several charming, country villages supported by area resorts. Although the road is well-traveled in warm-weather months, there is still a sense of being one with nature along this route. Stop at the town of **Hawley** to visit antique shops and have a bite to eat. Just south of the town is **Lake Wallenpaupack,** a man-made lake with a public beach, a nice place to stop for a picnic. Fishing here is for walleye, panfish, pickerel, largemouth bass, muskellunge, brown trout, and rainbow trout. You can swim, sail, water ski, power boat, canoe, hike and picnic.

Five miles north of Lake Wallenpaupack on US 6 is **White Mills** a charming village with upscale antique stores and cozy restaurants.

Along this part of Route 6 trees show off brilliant plumages in the fall. **For fall foliage driving tours**, and up-to-date information each autumn, call the hotline at the Pocono Mountains Visitors Bureau; *570-421-5565.*

Autumn leaves form a carpet of gold, obscuring the green of a grassy meadow.

A bucolic scene along the Susquehanna in Bradford County.

♦ DORFLINGER-SUYDAM WILDLIFE SANCTUARY AND GLASS MUSEUM
  map page 133, E-2

It *is* an unusual combination—a wildlife sanctuary and a glass museum—but, luckily, the wildlife isn't in the glass museum. The land was donated to the state by Dorothy Grant Suydam (granddaughter of 19th-century glassmaker Hank Loftus Dorflinger) who wanted to preserve her grandfather's land and his work.

Dorflinger Glass Museum, located near the entrance to the property, displays more than 600 pieces of cut glass and crystal including exquisitely etched vases, jewelry boxes, paperweights, and ornaments. Outside the museum, trails lead into thick forests, over fields, and around swamps; home to deer, fox, and Canada geese. The sanctuary is open year-round to hikers and cross-country skiers. *Long Ridge Rd., White Mills; Wed–Sat 10–4 and Sun 1–4; 570-253-1185.*

♦ "ENDLESS MOUNTAINS" OF THE NORTHERN COUNTIES
  map page 133

Scenic vistas overlooking mountains that seem to march over the horizon, rural farms in fertile valleys, and unspoiled waters comprise the Endless Mountains region of northeastern Pennsylvania. A part of the Allegheny Mountains, this area includes Bradford, Sullivan, Susquehanna, and Wyoming Counties. The name "Endless Mountains" was chosen in a public contest 40 years ago.

The region offers much to sports enthusiasts as well as to nature lovers: you can hike, ride a bike, or ski cross-country in one of the five state or county parks; you can also hunt on thousands of acres of state forest or game lands, and fish on lakes or rivers. There are several challenging golf courses here, too.

■ COAL COUNTRY

West of the Poconos is the coal country of Lackawanna and Luzerne Counties. If you come from the Poconos, you'll pass low rolling hills and manicured farmland.

◆ SCRANTON   *map page 133, D-2*

Those interested in Pennsylvania's railway and mining heritage should visit Scranton. It's a revitalized city of 81,000 through which the Lackawanna River flows. Some areas still bear the look of the coal-mining bust, and some residential streets reflect the tremendous wealth that once was created here.

A miner tends to a metal conveyor belt, which will carry anthracite coal for long distances underground. (Underwood Photo Archives, San Francisco)

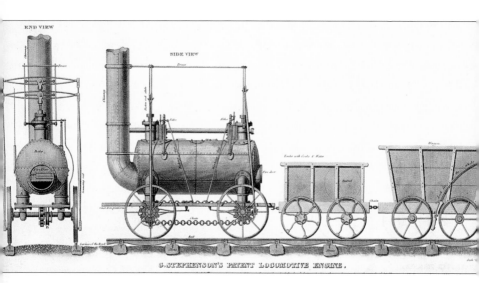

Pennsylvania has long been associated with rail history. The engraving above shows engineer and architect William Strickland's 1826 design for a locomotive steam engine. In the photograph below, Raymond Loewy stands atop the prototype for the S-1 he designed for the Pennsylvania Railroad. Loewy was instrumental in defining the streamlined aesthetic of 20th-century industrial design.

Lackawanna Railroad Depot

The city's two major gems are on Lackawanna Street and are related to railroads. The 1906 Lackawanna Railroad Depot has been restored and converted in to a fabulous hotel. Many of the original features of this French Renaissance building have been preserved, including the facade, sienna marble walls, brass fixtures, and the glass ceiling over the lobby restaurant. *700 Lackawanna Ave.; 570-342-8300.*

Steamtown National Historic Site

A few blocks away is Steamtown National Historic Site, a steam train museum and a large mall. This is one of the best train museums in the nation. The highlight of the 40-acre yard is a fleet of 29 steam locomotives and about 100 passenger and freight cars, donated by collector Nelson Blount. The museum features models of railroads and locomotives, undoubtedly one of the world's most difficult hobbies to maintain. Visitors can also explore a working rail yard. Steam train excursions lasting two hours are offered weekends from Memorial Day to early November. The train makes a 29-mile trip to Moscow, PA, twice daily. A trolley museum is being built at the river end of the site. *Admission fee; 150 S. Washington Ave.; 570-340-5200; 888-693-9391.*

A central green square at Washington and Spruce Streets has shade trees and welcoming benches that seem to invite passersby to sit and take in the statues that ring the 19th-century stone **Lackawanna County Courthouse**, or to pause for a drink from the courtyard fountain.

Scranton Iron Furnaces

Sheldon and George Scranton and their partner, William Henry, built the first iron furnace here in the mid-1800s to produce the heat required to make iron. Today, visitors can see four massive, stone-blast furnaces as part of a Steamtown National Historic Site tour by rail car. *Grounds open daily; free. 159 Cedar Ave. between Lackawanna and Moosic Sts.; 570-963-3208.*

Houdini Museum

Some of Houdini's most memorable contortionist tricks and speedy escapes took place in Scranton. Adoring fans—some magicians themselves—created this paean to the master: a collection of film clips, magazine articles, book excerpts, and photographs depicting his exploits.

Several Scranton businesses hired Houdini to perform as a way to advertise their products. Workers at hardware manufacturer J. B. Woolsey & Co., for instance, shut Houdini in a packing crate and secured it with seven pounds of nails. It took him six minutes to pop out. *Open daily Memorial Day to Labor Day; intermittently thereafter; admission fee; reservations required in winter; 1433 N. Main Ave.; 570-342-5555.*

McDade Park

In Scranton you'll find 200 acres of beautiful woodlands and wetlands. Here also are picnic groves, an Olympic-size swimming pool, ball fields, and a children's fishing pond. The story of coal mining is covered in sites following. *Free; Exit 57-B off I-81, off N. Keyser Ave.; 570-963-6764.*

Eckley Miners' Village is a restoration of a 19th-century company town. (See page 160.)

McDade Park Museums

The **Anthracite Heritage Museum** honors the difficult lives of the men and women who lived here in the 19th and early 20th centuries, when Scranton was a major mining and manufacturing center. Particularly poignant are the stories of hardships and obstacles overcome by immigrants who were on the bottom rung of the employment ladder during the state's industrial revolution. Some of the material is just as compelling and heart-rending as that at New York's Ellis Island museum. *Open daily; admission free; McDade Park off N. Keyser Ave.; 570-963-4804.*

At the **Lackawanna Coal Mine**, visitors descend 300 feet below ground (a modest depth by many mine standards) in railcars just as miners once did, to a former "working city" of underground stables, offices, storage rooms, and living quarters for hundreds of workers. Former miners lead the tour and give sobering lectures about the risks early miners faced, from poison gas eruptions to roof and wall cave-ins. *Open Apr–Nov; free; 51 McDade Park, off N. Keyser Ave.; 570-963-6463.*

◆ WILKES-BARRE   *map page 133, C-3*

Scranton and Wilkes-Barre are close to becoming one continuous city. The smaller of the two, Wilkes-Barre was named for John Wilkes and Isaac Barre, members of the British parliament who were sympathetic to the American colonies. This mostly working class city in Luzerne County lies along the banks of the Susquehanna River. The town centers on a traffic circle faced with hotels and stores.

FOREIGNERS

Theodore Dreiser was an Indiana native who often wrote about Pennsylvania. In 1915, already author of five novels, he and a friend took a motor trip, passing through the northeast part of the state. Here are some of his reflections on the many foreigners living in towns and working in coal mines there.

*W*hat becomes of all the Poles, Czechs, Croatioans, Serbians, etc., who are going to destroy us? I'll tell you. They gather on the street corners when their parents will permit them, arrayed in yellow or red ties, yellow shoes, dinky fedoras or beribboned straw hats and 'style-plus' clothes, and talk about 'when I was out to Dreamland the other night,' or make some such observation as 'Say, you should have seen the beaut that cut across here just now. Oh, mamma, some baby!' That's all the menace there is to the foreign invasion. Whatever their original intention may be, they can't resist the American yellow shoes, the American moving picture…the popular song, the automobile, the jitney. They are completely undone by our perfections. Instead of throwing bombs or lowering our social level, all bogies of the sociologists, they would rather stand on our street corners, go to the nearest moving pictures, smoke cigarettes, wear high white collars and braided yellow vests and yearn over the girls who know exactly how to handle them, or work to someday own an automobile and break the speed laws. They are really not so bad as we seem to want them to be. They are simple, gauche, de jeune, 'the limit'. In other words, they are fast becoming Americans.

—Theodore Dreiser, *A Hoosier Holiday,* 1916

◆ ECKLEY MINERS' VILLAGE   *map page 133, D-4*

This 19th-century anthracite mining village is about 25 miles south of Wilkes-Barre in the little town of Eckley, a fine example of the company towns of the industrial era, in which everything from the store to houses and schools were built and run by a company. About 20 people live here today. *Open Mon–Sat, 9–5; Sun noon-5; admission; 570-636-2070.*

■ LEHIGH GORGE   *map page 133, D-4*

Lehigh Gorge State Park, which follows the course of the Lehigh River for 26 miles through the rugged wilderness of the gorge, encompasses the most dramatic scenery in the Poconos. The Lehigh River is one of the most popular rivers in the East for Class III white-water rafting, kayaking, and canoeing. North of White Haven, the river is controlled at the Francis E. Walter Dam. During the dam's scheduled releases from mid-March through June the river's flow power ranges from 250 cubic feet per second to 5,000. A typical white-water rafting trip run by one of the companies operating in the park goes from White Haven to Jim

Abundant snowfall in the Poconos makes the region a prime destination for cross-country skiers.

Thorpe and takes 10 to 12 hours. (Inexperienced boaters should not attempt this trip without qualified guides. All boaters must enter and leave the Lehigh River at designated access areas.) You can fish here, too, as the lake behind the dam is stocked with trout.

The northern terminus of the **Lehigh Gorge Trail** is at White Haven. An abandoned railroad bed follows the river through the park, making it an ideal trail for hiking and mountain biking. Here, the landscape is a series of steep cliffs and jagged rock outcrops, which are set off spectacularly against deep blue skies on sunny hiking days. In the spring rhododendrons bloom along parts of these trails and in winter some of these trails are groomed for cross-country skiing and snowmobiling. *Exit 40 off I-80 to White Haven; 570-427-5000.*

❖

At nearby **Hickory Run State Park** you'll find directions for a unique auto tour called "Exploring Audubon's Lehigh." It focuses on famed naturalist John James Audubon's 1829 visit to the Rockport area. Brochures and tapes are available at several locations along the 53-mile route. The tour begins both at White Haven and the town of Jim Thorpe. *Call for information: 888-546-8467.*

■ JIM THORPE   *map page 133, D-4*

Built in 1815 on the sides of a narrow gorge of the Lehigh River, little has changed in the town of Jim Thorpe except its name. The original settlement was a company town, named appropriately but unromantically, Coalville. At the time of the development of the first railroad and the decline of the canal system, the town changed its name and became Mauch Chunk—"Bear Mountain" in the Lenni Lenape language (a step up). Then in 1954, the town took the name of one of the country's most famous Native American sons, Jim Thorpe (interesting, but can be confusing).

Mauch Chunk's economy had plunged into a tailspin after the United States began weaning itself from coal in the 1920s. A solution of sorts was found to this decline when three nearby towns merged into one municipality and assumed the name Jim Thorpe at the invitation of his widow.

The man Jim Thorpe (1888-1953) was born in Oklahoma of Fox and Sauk lineage and became one of the best all-around athletes in American history. He played football for coach Glenn Scobey "Pop" Warner at Pennsylvania's Carlisle Indian Industrial School, becoming an All American in 1911 and 1912. Thorpe won the pentathlon and decathlon at the 1912 Olympic Games in Stockholm but was stripped of his two gold medals when Olympic Committee members discovered he had played a season of professional baseball. To right this injustice, Mrs. Thorpe offered to have his body moved to the new town in exchange for its being renamed in Thorpe's honor. **Thorpe's mausoleum**—20 tons of granite—is set in a park along Route 903, one-half mile from the town's east side.

In 1982 the Olympic Committee reinstated Jim Thorpe's medals.

The town of Jim Thorpe bills itself as "Little Switzerland," which is a bit of a stretch, but the setting is pretty and the town center is well worth a walking tour. You can still get an hour's parking for a dime at any of the street meters.

From the 1888 Railroad Station, you can take a leisurely 40-minute **train ride** through miles of woodland over tracks that became part of the former Nesquehoning Valley Railroad in 1872. *Rail Tours, Inc.; Saturdays, Sundays, and holidays mid-May through October; 570-325-4606.*

St. Mark's Episcopal Church, on nearby Race Street, was designed by Richard

The citizens of Mauch Chunk, once a gritty coal town, renamed their city after athlete Jim Thorpe.

Upjohn and is a fine example of late Gothic-revival architecture. The windows are Tiffany stained glass and the altar is white Italian marble. The reredos is Caen stone and was donated as a memorial to the town's leading industrialist, Asa Packer, a philanthropist who helped found Lehigh University.

The Asa Packer Mansion is a quick drive up the hill on Route 209. Packer was worth $54 million in 1879, which made him one of the wealthiest men in the country. His mansion, built in 1850 and remodeled in 1877 for the then-staggering sum of $85,000, is open to the public. Among the items in the house: a gas chandelier from the 1876 Centennial Exposition and a crystal chandelier that was used as a model for Tara's chandelier in the movie version of *Gone With the Wind.*

Open weekends April–May, daily Jun–Oct; weekends through Nov; admission fee; Harvard Square Extension on Rte. 209; 570-325-3229.

■ WEST AND SOUTH OF SCRANTON

Outside of the Scranton–Wilkes-Barre metro area, to the west on Route 11 towards Blooms-burg, heavily forested rolling hills and farms

Jim Thorpe was one of the best all-around athletes in American history. (Cumberland County Historical Society, Carlisle)

fill the landscape. Here one encounters rural hamlets, some now shrunk down to just one street, with an abandoned house at the edge of town. Though many are tranquil and charming, many of these towns have long since lost their economic anchors and exist by the grace of pension checks from retiree residents.

Of the dozen or so towns in the industrial and mining heartland that borders this stretch of the Susquehanna River, only a few have had success in reinventing themselves for new industries and tourism. These are not the ever-so-tasteful getaways featured in *Martha Stewart Living*. These are the working-class communities where laundry hangs from clotheslines and shopkeepers wander into one another's stores to chat when business is slow.

◆ **BLOOMSBURG AREA**   *map page 133, B-4*

The area where the Susquehanna River splits into its west and east branches developed largely because of lumber and agriculture, thus sparing it the disfigurement that coal mining brought to other sections of the state.

Bloomsburg is a charming town of about 12,000 residents and a downtown with a startling total of 650 buildings designated on the National Register of Historic Places. It is anchored around Bloomsburg University, founded in 1839 and now serving about 7,200 students.

Outside of town, the land quickly becomes rural. From late spring through early fall, most of the wonderfully aged covered bridges of this area are surrounded by green woodlands. For a pleasant, winding, hilly drive, take Route 42 or 487 south from US 11 and turn onto backroads like Shakespeare, Parr's Mill, Bethel, and Glory Lake.

◆ **LAKE CHILLISQUAQUE**   *map page 133, B-3*

Located in the broad Appalachian valley between Montour Ridge and Muncy Hills and about 10 miles northwest of Bloomsburg is a region of gently rolling hills that converge on Lake Chillisquaque, an important waterfowl stopover.

The visitors center sits below the dike and out of view of the lake. The lake is an important rest-stop for more than a dozen species of migrating waterfowl. Common birds included Canada geese and hooded gansers, but even brown pelicans from Florida have been spotted in recent years.

The hiking trails vary in length from one-quarter mile to 4.2 miles and pass through beds of thistle, daisy, and clover. From late spring to early fall, the preserve's wildflowers are an artist's palette of colors that range from deep violets and reds to light yellows and ivories.

Fields of Indian pipes and buttercups are bordered by a wide variety of hardwoods and conifers—red, silver, and sugar maples, groves of white oak, shag bark hickory, and birch.

An environmental education center connected to the park offers regular programs but one of the most popular draws is the annual maple syrup festival. *From I-80 take Exit 33 to the village of Washingtonville and follow signs.*

CENTRALIA

Settled in the mid-1800s, for a century Centralia (about 15 miles south of Bloomsburg) was a thriving, hardworking town, with a population of almost 2,000, as many as 26 bars or taverns, and twenty trains a day arriving at its station. Today that is all gone. What remains is a true ecological wasteland: coal seams beneath the town have been burning since 1962.

The fire started when some trash dumped at the edge of town caught fire and spread into the coal seams and abandoned mines. Over the next two decades various plans were advanced to fight the fire. Huge volumes of water were poured onto the seams but simply evaporated due to the extreme underground temperatures. The only method proven effective against this sort of fire—digging out the blaze, extinguishing it, then refilling the dig area—also proved the most expensive, and funding for Centralia ran out.

The area had become a frightening place to live, with ground temperatures recorded at close to 1,000° F, and glowing hot spots visible across the landscape at night. Sudden cave-ins claimed backyards and basements and increasing levels of carbon monoxide seeping into homes made people sick.

Finally, in 1983, Congress allocated $42 million to purchase the town's homes, relocate its population, and bulldoze the buildings. The residents voted to accept the offer, and abandoned the town.

Today all routes into Centralia are officially closed, but remain passable. Its streets are deserted, driveways lead to empty lots, and a very few houses remain scattered around—some, amazingly, still occupied. An overall view of what's left of this once typical, anonymous, American town can be had from the mountain north of town. Some estimate the fire could continue to burn another thousand years.

Underground fires have long been a hazard in coal country. This photo from the 1930s shows a fire breaching an asphalt highway. (Underwood Photo Archives, San Francisco)

C E N T R A L
C I V I L   W A R   T R A I L

■ HIGHLIGHTS *page*

Food & Lodging
map 276; charts 277
listings by town, in alphabetical order 278

■ TRAVEL BASICS

Author Robert Louis Stevenson traveling through central Pennsylvania on a railroad journey in 1868 wrote in his diary:

> *I* saw one after another, pleasant villages, carts upon the highway and fishers by the stream, and heard cock-crows and cheery voices in the distance. …And then when I asked the name of the river from the brakesman, and heard that it was called the Susquehanna, the beauty of the name seemed to be part and parcel of the beauty of the land.

Stevenson said it well.

Central Pennsylvania is defined on its eastern boundary by the beautiful Susquehanna; its interior is criss-crossed by backroads that wind through hilly woodlands and small towns, and past family farms with barns made of fieldstone and logs. Gettysburg (just north of the Maryland border) was the site of the most devastating battle of the Civil War and remains a moving historical site. Further north lie woodlands, lakes, and streams which offer all the pleasures of the outdoors.

Nearly every state resident has a family connection to Pennsylvania State University built around the bucolic town of State College. Nearby are caves to explore, interesting historic towns, and hikes along the Allegheny Ridge.

CENTRAL BASICS

Climate: Temperatures here run about 10 degrees lower in every season than elsewhere in the state. Summers average 75–85 degrees with generally low humidity. Fall comes early, with nighttime lows dropping into the low 40s as early as the middle of September. Winters are long, cold, and snowy, the north-central area receiving as much as 100 inches of snow in a season and temperatures in the daytime averaging 15-30 degrees. Rainfall is evenly distributed around the year, averaging 3-4 inches a month. Keep an umbrella handy.

Food & Lodging: Restaurants and overnight lodgings run the gamut from a four-star resort in State College to Victorian-era bed-and-breakfasts in places like Williamsport and Boalsburg. Small town accommodations can be bleak. Outside of State College and Harrisburg, restaurant fare is generally unsophisticated but ample. **Food & Lodging map** page 276; **charts** page 277; **listings** in alphabetical order by town begin on page 278.

■ OVERVIEW

Except for the rolling farmland near Gettysburg, central Pennsylvania is a region of wooded ridges and narrow valleys. To the west is the Allegheny Ridge, rising above them all. Fed by dozens of creeks and streams, the wide Susquehanna River is the third-largest river in the state. It flows from Pennsylvania's northern border with New York, south through Harrisburg to the Chesapeake Bay. The indigenous Americans called it "Long Reach River."

Because the Susquehanna is not navigable along much of its course, and because the forests were once virtually impenetrable, Seneca and Iroquois Indians continued to live here largely undisturbed until the end of the 1700s when the land was annexed to the state for settlement. Soon, roads following Iroquois trails tied the region to the rest of the state, and dependable land routes—road and rail—allowed goods to reach navigable sections of the Susquehanna. Mining and refining operations exploited the region's coal, iron ore, and limestone deposits, but the chief export from central Pennsylvania was white pine from its vast forests. When these resources were exhausted, the area was abandoned, leaving its ridges stripped bare and its streams polluted from mine drainage.

Today, the land has begun to heal itself, and a great deal of the area's natural beauty has been restored.

CENTRAL
BASICS

CENTRAL

BEAUTIFUL SUSQUEHANNA

*T*he Susquehanna, though more than two hundred miles longer than the Hudson, is born among men. A few yards from the lake it is not quite four feet deep, and there children swim, shadowed sometimes by the high bank across from Riverbrink. Canoes drift here and fishermen, hardly expecting a catch, idle with short lines dangling in water so clear that the fish can see them. In spring and summer, lawn and stream and high bank across meld varying shades of green, making a lush and subtly arranged background for the fading hues of the house, like a landscape by the French painter, Corbet. And, somehow, ever consistent, through other backyards and through coal towns, through deep chasms and wide flat bottoms, the Susquehanna always keeps a relationship to the men on its banks. Sometimes dangerous, sometimes friendly, it ever maintains its unique unchanging quality, minding its own business, a "character" among streams.

—Carl Carmer, "The Susquehanna," 1955
from *The Way it Was*

■ HARRISBURG: STATE CAPITAL

Pennsylvania's capital city is situated on the eastern banks of the Susquehanna River, and most of the town commands a view of a one-mile stretch of the river. An important trading post was built on the spot in the 1700s, and later, a military fort during the French and Indian War. The city underwent several growth spurts and transformations, specifically as an important transportation center—first as a key link on the Main Line Canal from Pittsburgh to Philadelphia, and later as an interchange for several railroad lines. The city was chosen as the capital in 1812 because of its central location.

Today Harrisburg is a relatively small city of about 52,000 people, but institutional history abounds here—in the buildings and the momentous decisions made inside them. However, Harrisburg suffers the fate of many state capitals: the primary industry here is government, and the city's main purpose is to support it.

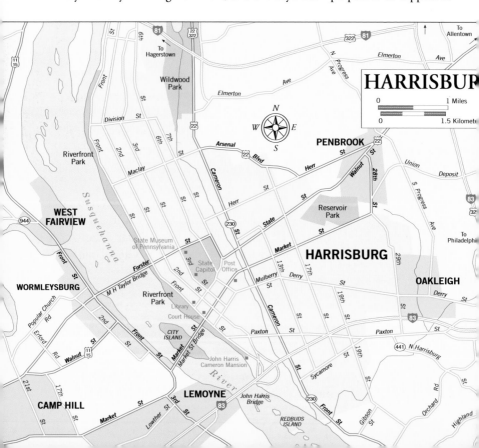

A choral group performs in the rotunda of the state capitol.

The majestic buildings of state are most often used by outsiders—legislators and lobbyists—and lack of ownership takes its toll.

The city is also known for its proximity to Three Mile Island, where in 1979 another toll was taken: the worst nuclear accident in U.S. history.

◆ STATE CAPITOL

When Theodore Roosevelt first walked into this building at its dedication on Oct.ober 4, 1906, and gazed upward at the great dome (modeled after St. Peter's Basilica in Rome) he removed his hat. "It is the handsomest building I ever saw," he told his hosts. Given the fact he was familiar with the U.S. Capitol building and the palaces and "great halls of Europe," this was high praise indeed. The five-story, 633-room building that Smithsonian Institution officials judged the finest of all the state capitols in the country, cost more than $4 million to build and more than double that to furnish and decorate. The Italian Renaissance style was the work of architect Joseph Huston, who commissioned mural artist Edwin Austin Abbey to do five paintings in the Hall of the House.

Abbey's crowning work is *The Apotheosis of Pennsylvania,* featuring 35 of the state's historic figures—among them, William Penn, Benjamin Franklin, and

Robert Morris—as a backdrop behind the Speaker's platform. On the back wall is "The Camp of the American Army at Valley Forge." On the ceiling 24 goddesses, representing the passage of the hours, float in a celestial heaven. *Third St. between North and Walnut Sts.; 717-787-6180.*

◆ STATE MUSEUM OF PENNSYLVANIA   *map page 170*

Directly across from the government operations center on Third Street is the **William Penn Memorial Museum and Archives,** where the state's original 1681 charter is displayed. Across the hall stands an imposing William Penn statue that honors his uniquely humanitarian stewardship. On the first floor, a colonial street is painstakingly re-created with storefronts, small businesses, and several rooms from a typical family home. The displays include exhibits on the state's wildlife, handcrafted furniture, and Pennsylvania folk art. *Third St., between North and Forster. Tues–Sat, 9–5; Sun, noon–5; 717-787-4978.*

◆ JOHN HARRIS CAMERON MANSION   *map page 170*

Early in the 18th century, John Harris, the first settler to the area, was sent by the Penn family to help mediate disputes between settlers and American Indians. He

The Millersburg ferry crosses the Susquehanna about 20 miles upriver from Harrisburg. The car ferry operates seasonally, closing during winter but is also available for charter. Call 717-692-2442 for more information.

An open house at the Harley-Davidson factory in York, York County.

established a trading post and a ferry business and began farming the rich soil in the ancient floodplain of the Susquehanna.

His son, John Harris, Jr. constructed the mansion in 1766, and later, in 1784, he and his son-in-law, William Maclay, founded the city of Harrisburg. The ornate residence is now the home of the Historical Society of Dauphin County, and 200 years of the city's history are well told here in a detailed tour that includes an impressive collection of colonial furniture and art.

A lithograph in the front room of the mansion portrays one of the enduring legends connected to Harris (one unsettling to the modern sensibility). Confronted by an angry band of intoxicated Indians demanding kegs of rum (he'd taken their land, but they were *drunk,* after all), Harris tried to negotiate his way out of the situation and failed. He was taken to a nearby mulberry tree where the Indians were preparing to burn him alive. One version of the story has him being saved by the intervention of his slave, Hercules. Others have him being rescued by a band of friendly Shawnees. In any case, it is historical fact that he survived and lived a long life. *Tours by reservation, $7; 219 S. Front St.; 717-233-3462.*

■ CIVIL WAR TRAIL

The Cumberland Valley in Franklin County endured more military activity during the Civil War than any other area in the North. Four important historical sites can be seen in this area, which is about one hour's drive from Lancaster. The most important was the site of the Battle of Gettysburg. More American lives were lost there in July 1863 than in any other single battle in American history. If you plan to drive through the area, get off the interstate onto the backroads. You'll see hamlets and farm centers at intersections and a few small towns. If you come here from Maryland you'll drive through Waynesboro, a beautiful town worth visiting.

◆ GETTYSBURG

Gettysburg is a town of 6,000 permanent residents, 2,000 college students attending Gettysburg College, and two million tourists wandering around over the course of a year.

Entering Gettysburg through the 6,000-acre Gettysburg National Park, which surrounds the town on all but its west side (a Route 30 strip mall), you will pass rolling hills and groves of oak and hickory. In town, the residential streets are lined with trees and Civil War–era woodframe homes. Closer to the town center are older, Federalist brick row houses with white painted wood trim.

At the center of town (see map) you'll find the site where President Abraham Lincoln delivered the Gettysburg Address. You'll also see, surrounding the park visitors center, many shops selling souvenirs relating to the battle. (The Park Service is presently proposing a controversial plan to move the visitors center into the middle of the park away from commercial development.)

A central square park contains memorials to the battle and is surrounded by historic buildings with bronze plaques explaining their significance. Many of the town's houses and buildings still bear the scars of bullets and cannon shells fired during the three-day campaign, which resulted in over 51,000 casualties.

Official army drawings of Union and Confederate cavalry officers in uniform.

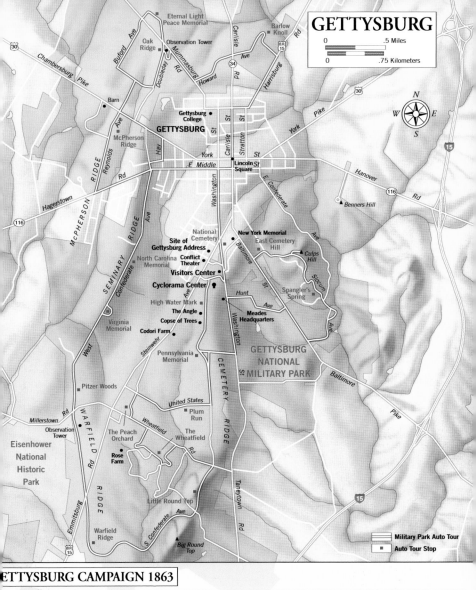

GETTYSBURG

0   .5 Miles

0   .75 Kilometers

Eternal Light Peace Memorial

Barlow Knoll

Oak Ridge

Observation Tower

Carlisle Rd

Harrisburg Rd

Chambersburg Pike

York Pike

Gettysburg College

GETTYSBURG

McPherson Ridge

Barn

Reynolds Ave

Doubleday Ave

Mummasburg Rd

Howard Ave

Carlisle St

Stratton St

York St

York St   E Middle St

Lincoln Square

Hanover Rd

Benners Hill

Hagerstown Rd

McPHERSON RIDGE

SEMINARY RIDGE

Confederate Ave

Washington Ave

National Cemetery

Site of Gettysburg Address

North Carolina Memorial

Conflict Theater

Visitors Center

Cyclorama Center

New York Memorial

East Cemetery Hill

Culps Hill

Baltimore St

Slocum Ave

Spangler's Spring

Virginia Memorial

High Water Mark

The Angle

Copse of Trees

Codori Farm

Hunt Ave

Meades Headquarters

Washington St

GETTYSBURG NATIONAL MILITARY PARK

West Ave

Steinwehr Ave

Pennsylvania Memorial

CEMETERY RIDGE

Baltimore Pike

Pitzer Woods

Millerstown Rd

Observation Tower

WARFIELD RIDGE

Wheatfield Rd

United States Ave

Plum Run

The Wheatfield

The Peach Orchard

Rose Farm

Eisenhower National Historic Park

Emmitsburg Rd

Little Round Top

Warfield Ridge

S Confederate Ave

Taneytown Rd

Big Round Top

Military Park Auto Tour

Auto Tour Stop

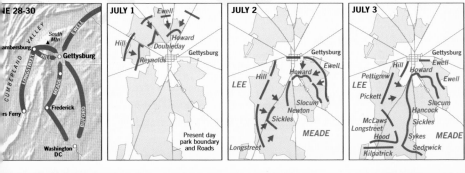

ETTYSBURG CAMPAIGN 1863

NE 28-30

CUMBERLAND VALLEY

South Mtn

EWELL

ambersburg

LONGSTREET

HILL

Gettysburg

MEADE

Frederick

BUFORD

rs Ferry

Washington DC

JULY 1

Ewell

Hill

Howard

Doubleday

Gettysburg

Reynolds

JULY 2

LEE

Hill

Gettysburg

Howard

Ewell

Slocum

Newton

Sickles

MEADE

Longstreet

Present day park boundary and Roads

JULY 3

Hill

Gettysburg

Ewell

Howard

Ewell

Pettigrew

LEE

Pickett

McLaws

Longstreet

Hood

Hancock

Slocum

Sickles

Sykes

MEADE

Kilpatrick

Sedgwick

BATTLE OF GETTYSBURG

In the third year of the Civil War, after an important, but costly Confederate victory at Chancellorsville (including the death of Gen. Thomas "Stonewall" Jackson), Virginia Confederate General Robert E. Lee urged the Confederate President, Jefferson Davis, to move the war north and strike at Pennsylvania. A victory there, he reasoned, could weaken the North's will to fight, raise Southern morale, and at the same time improve the chances for European recognition of the Confederacy. Furthermore, Pennsylvania's farms were supporting the Union Army, its factories were supplying weapons, shoes, and clothing, and its railroads were moving troops and supplies with great efficiency. Cutting the flow of supplies from Pennsylvania to Union armies could turn the course of the war.

In June of 1863, nearly 75,000 Southern troops crossed the Mason-Dixon Line, the border between Maryland and Pennsylvania.

DAYS PRECEDING THE BATTLE

The Union Army had received reports of the movement but was unsure of Confederate intentions. Lee kept enough troops in Virginia to deceive the Union generals into thinking that Washington, D.C. was his objective. When the newly appointed commander of the Union Army of the Potomac, Gen. George Meade, heard reports from fleeing civilians that Confederate troops had occupied the towns of Chambersburg,

Greenwood, and York in southern Pennsylvania, he immediately ordered 90,000 Union troops north.

Meade moved quickly. The Confederate Army was spread out over the rural area around Harrisburg, the state capital, and was planning an assault on it. A unit of Confederate General A. P. Hill's cavalry was just north of Gettysburg, reportedly looking for shoes among the manufacturers there, when they met with a division of Meade's advance cavalry commanded by Gen. George Buford. The Confederates drove the Union forces south of Gettysburg where they entrenched themselves along Cemetery Ridge, determined to fight until Meade's reinforcements arrived.

DAY ONE

On July 1, the great Battle of Gettysburg began with Confederate troops attacking Union troops on McPherson Ridge, west of town. Outnumbered, the Union forces managed to hold until afternoon when they were overpowered and driven back through town. In the confusion, thousands of Union soldiers were captured before they could rally on Cemetery Hill, south of town. Long into the night Union troops labored over their defenses while the bulk of Meade's army arrived and took positions.

DAY TWO

On July 2, the battle lines were drawn up in two sweeping arcs. The main portions of both armies were nearly a mile apart on two parallel ridges: Union forces on Cemetery Ridge facing Confederate forces on Seminary Ridge to the west. Lee ordered an attack against both Union flanks. James Longstreet's thrust on the Union left broke through D. E. Sickles's advance lines at the Peach Orchard, left the wheatfield strewn with dead and wounded, and turned the base of Little Round Top into a shambles. R. S. Ewell's attack proved futile against the entrenched Union right on East Cemetery Hill and Culp's Hill.

DAY THREE

On July 3, Lee's artillery opened a bombardment that for a time engaged the massed guns of both sides in a thundering duel for supremacy, but did little to soften up the Union center on Cemetery Ridge.

The climax of the Battle of Gettysburg came when Maj. Gen. George E. Pickett, his charge delayed most of the day by artillery tactics, spearheaded a massed infantry assault of some 12,000 Confederate troops across the open field toward the Union center on Cemetery Ridge.

Raked by artillery and rifle fire, Pickett's men reached but failed to break the

Union line, and the magnificent effort ended in disaster. In 50 minutes, at least 7,500 men and 5,000 horses were killed outright, and the attack—forever to be known as Pickett's Charge—was now history.

AFTERMATH

With the failure of Pickett's Charge the battle was over–the Union was saved. There were over 51,000 total casualties making Gettysburg the bloodiest battle in American history.

On July 4, Lee prepared for an attack that never came, and that night, under cover of a heavy rain, began his withdrawal to Virginia with an army that was physically and spiritually exhausted. Lee would never again attempt an offensive operation of such proportions. Meade, though he was criticized for not immediately pursuing Lee's army, had carried the day in the battle that has become known as the "High Water Mark of the Confederacy."

The war was to rage for two more terrible and tormenting years but would never again be fought north of the Mason-Dixon Line.

On November 19 of 1863, to dedicate a National Cemetery on the battlefield of Gettysburg, President Abraham Lincoln delivered his Gettysburg Address, a two-minute dedication that ranks as one of the great speeches of history.

The photographs in this essay were taken during the filming of the Civil War movie Glory.

GETTYSBURG ADDRESS

After the terrible battle of Gettysburg on July 1–3 of 1863, a national soldier's cemetery was established at Gettysburg, Pennsylvania. President Abraham Lincoln was asked to come and address those gathered at its dedication. Lincoln left Washington D.C. by train for Gettysburg on November 18th, his son Tad lying gravely ill at home. Fifteen thousand people were gathered on Cemetery Hill for the ceremonies, listening first to a former Massachusetts senator, Edward Everett, who spoke for two hours. Lincoln then rose to deliver the Gettysburg Address. He looked forward not upon a sculpted green memorial park, but upon the freshly dug graves of thousands of young men. The nation was filled with the sorrow of their deaths and the outcome and utility of the war was uncertain.

*F*OUR SCORE AND SEVEN YEARS AGO our fathers brought forth on this continent a new nation, conceived in liberty and dedicated to the proposition that all men are created equal.

Now we are engaged in a great civil war, testing whether that nation or any nation so conceived and so dedicated can long endure. We are met on a great battlefield of that war. We have come to dedicate a portion of that field as final resting place for those who here gave their lives that that nation might live. It is altogether fitting and proper that we should do this.

But, in a larger sense, we cannot dedicate—we cannot consecrate—we cannot hallow—this ground. The brave men, living and dead, who struggled here have consecrated it far above our poor power to add or detract. The world will little note nor long remember what we say here, but it can never forget what they did here. It is for us, the living, rather, to be dedicated here to the unfinished work which they who fought here have thus far so nobly advanced.

It is rather for us to be here dedicated to the great task remaining before us—that from these honored dead we take increased devotion to that cause for which they gave the last full measure of devotion; that we here highly resolve that these dead shall not have died in vain; that this nation, under God, shall have a new birth of freedom; and that government of the people, by the people, for the people shall not perish from the earth.

—Abraham Lincoln, 1863

The following day, Senator Everett wrote to Lincoln: "I should be glad if I could flatter myself that I came as near to the central idea of the occasion in two hours as you did in two minutes."

◆ GETTYSBURG SIGHTS   *map page 175*

Gettysburg National Military Park

Even a short walk along a portion of the battlefield here can be overwhelming, as you try to imagine the thoughts and feelings so many young men must have experienced in the early mornings before battle, and in the mass confusion of re-grouping in the wake of just one day's assault.

Guideposts and walking-tour brochures direct visitors to significant points in the region and follow the steps of Union and Confederate soldiers at key positions in the battle. More than 1,300 markers and monuments identify significant points and pay homage to soldiers and regiments.

Across from the visitors center you'll find the **Gettysburg Cyclorama**, a 50-foot-high, 400-foot-long, circular mural painted in 1884. An audio tape by actor Richard Dreyfuss describes events shown on the mural. *Park open daily 6 A.M.–10 P.M.; visitors center open daily, 8–5; cyclorama open 9–5. Admission free, but a $3.00 fee is charged to view the "electric map" and to view the cyclorama painting of Pickett's Charge. 97 Taneytown Rd.; 717-334-1124.*

Gettysburg National Cemetery

Two days after the Battle of Gettysburg, Pennsylvania's governor, Andrew Curtin, insisted on going through a day-long tour of the battlefield, where he viewed the bodies of hundreds of young men—Union and Confederate—buried in shallow graves or

A grave marker in Gettysburg National Cemetery.

A monument in Gettysburg National Military Park.

decaying in the hot summer sun. By nightfall, the shaken governor had ordered the immediate purchase of burial ground that would be turned over to the federal government as a way of honoring those who had given their lives.

It does not take much imagination to sense what President Abraham Lincoln must have felt when, four months after the battle, he came here to dedicate the cemetery. For the place where the address was delivered see map page 175. *The cemetery is open daily, 8–5.*

General Robert E. Lee Headquarters

At the 18th-century stone farmhouse commandeered by Lee as his battlefield headquarters you will find displays of Civil War military equipment, panels telling the story of Lee's life, and documents that offer insight into his battle strategy sessions. *Admission charged. 9–5 , mid-Mar to mid-Nov. Hours extended in summer; 401 Buford Ave. (Rte. 30 West); 717-334-3131.*

Eisenhower National Historic Site

A shuttle bus takes you from the Gettysburg Visitors Center to the Eisenhower property to view the home, barn and grounds. There is a bookstore on the premises, a biographical film of "Ike" as well as displays of memorabilia from his life. *Shuttle bus from 9–4 daily; closed Mon. & Tues, Nov–March. Admission fee; 717-334-1124.*

♦ CHAMBERSBURG *map page 169, C-5*

After the crucial Union victory at the Battle of Antietam in September of 1862, where General Lee's Confederate advance on Maryland was stopped, Chambersburg became an important hospital and supply center for the Union Army. When some 400 wounded soldiers were evacuated from battlefields to the town, residents opened up their homes to them.

Chambersburg was under Confederate occupation several times during the regional campaigns of 1861–63. A month before Gettysburg, Gen. Robert E. Lee and 65,000 Confederate troops camped in the area, and Lee and his generals held strategy sessions in the town center. It was here that Lee made the fateful decision to lead his troops east toward Gettysburg, about 25 miles away, after scouts reported that the Union Army of the Potomac was headed in their direction.

In 1864, an impoverished, ragtag Confederate force under the command of Gen. John McCausland held the town for $100,000 ransom. In an order read from the steps of the Franklin County Courthouse, McCausland threatened to burn the city if the ransom, payable in gold, wasn't paid. To dramatize the point, a Confederate cannon was fired into the west wall of the courthouse.

No gold was brought forward, the deadline passed, and the town's buildings were set ablaze as residents ran for refuge to the Cedar Grove Cemetery, on King Street at the edge of town. Only a few buildings were spared, including the **Masonic Temple** on Second Street near Queen, supposedly as a gesture of respect from Confederate brother Masons.

Despite nearly being burned down completely during McCausland's occupation, Chambersburg retains the same basic layout that was originally planned in 1788 by mill operator and town founder, Benjamin Chambers.

The main route to the town square follows Route 30 west, off Exit 6 of I-81. Just so you won't be expecting too much: it continues past a series of fast food restaurants and budget motels. Once beyond the Interstate service strip, Route 30 quickly transforms into a series of tree-line residential neighborhoods made up of tidy, 20th-century homes fronted by manicured lawns. The business district begins several blocks beyond a large hospital complex and continues to the town's center, marked by the intersection of Route 30 with Route 11.

Just beyond the intersection is the town square, which includes a four-tiered, cast-iron fountain created in 1878 as a monument to Union soldiers from the area who died serving in the Civil War. In front of the fountain, a cast-iron, full-size sculpture of a Union soldier faces south, the direction from which the invading

*These columns were all that remained of the Bank of Chambersburg after it was burned
by Confederate soldiers.*

Confederate Army came.

Also at the square is a marker, memorializing the burning of the town, and a
piece of the battleship USS *Maine,* which memorializes locals who fought in the
Spanish-American War. The town's best residential architecture—lovingly restored
1860s-era homes built of local gray limestone and wood—can be seen along
Philadelphia Avenue off Route 11 North.

◆ MERCERSBURG   *map page 169, B-6*

The seeds of the Battle of Gettysburg were sown in 1862 with a series of Confederate cavalry raids in the Cumberland Valley.

The townspeople of the tiny backcountry town of Mercersburg supported the
Union cause, and the Confederate raids made it a regular target. The **Steiger family
house**, at 120 North Main Street, was taken over by Confederate General J. E. B.
Stuart for use at mealtimes.

*More than 40 log homes and shops from all over Pennsylvania were transported to
Old Bedford Village, which simulates a pioneer-era settlement.*

When the fortunes of war turned against the Confederacy in 1863, hundreds of wounded Rebel soldiers were captured and placed in makeshift hospitals in the town. Many are interred in the local cemetery.

Much less conspicuous than the neatly kept and much honored soldiers' cemetery at Gettysburg is the **Black Cemetery** at the end of Bennet Avenue where hundreds of USCT (United States Colored Troops) are buried.

❖

Picturesque Mercersburg is surrounded by hundreds of acres of lush farmland and dairy pastures extending in every direction. Route 16 runs east to west directly through the small downtown, a four-block area centered with a small green square and bordered by large-limbed, shady oaks. The main business district contains several food stores, a restaurant, post office, and general store.

Most people come here to tour the 370-acre campus of **Mercersburg Academy** (alma matter of Jimmy Stewart), an exclusive prep school, and clearly visible from the main road with its distinctive gothic chapel resting on a hill.

■ SOUTHERN BACKROADS
AND SHAWNEE STATE PARK *map page 169, A-5*

In an area about 40 miles west as the crow flies from Mercersburg is a bucolic region of forested hills and valleys that is also known for having some of the finest **covered bridges** in the state. The Bedford County Visitors Bureau provides a useful map of covered bridges; drop by their office in Bedford. *141 South Julina St.; 814-623-1771.*

A recommended 24-mile tour visits some of the most interesting of these covered bridges. Although the route can be followed by car, it is much more worthwhile by bicycle. Mountain bikes are recommended because some bike tour routes run through dirt-and-gravel trails in Shawnee State Park. *Shawnee State Park, 814-733-4218.* Mountain bikes may be rented, and tours arranged, from Grousland Tours, *467 Robinsonville Rd., Clearville; 814-784-5000.*

Fishermen try their luck next to a covered bridge. South-Central Pennsylvania boasts a goodly collection of covered bridges.

CENTRAL
SHAWNEE PARK

The sun sets over the ridges and valleys of central Pennsylvania.

■ MAPLE RUN TRAIL HIKE   *map page 169, A-3/4*

In addition to bicycle touring, some great hikes are also to be recommended in this region. About 20 miles northeast of Shawnee State Park is a trail known as Maple Run. This seven-mile trail leads hikers through extensive forest and past fast-running mountain streams with moss-carpeted banks and beautiful native plants like sundew, tree huckleberry, and pitcher plants. It is located in state game lands in northern Bedford County near Saxton and Woodbury and explores the east side of Tussey Mountain between Loysburg Gap in the south and the intersection with Maple Run and Maple Run Road to the north.

The trail is marked with rectangular orange blazes on trees. You will need good hiking boots as most of the trail is rocky. The upper four miles of trail offers a day trip of spectacular scenery—a picture-perfect mountain stream filled with fat trout and shaded by giant hemlocks. The southern three miles follow more difficult terrain and require a good level of fitness to cover. This section heads to the west of Maple Run.

From Bedford, take Rte. 30 east about 3 miles to the warning-caution signal announcing a hospital zone. Turn left and follow to Loysburg. At Loysburg take Rte. 36 north for three miles. Turn right on Hickory Bottom Rd. (SR 1017). Look for the Shady Trail Riding School sign and follow for 2.3 miles. At Pulpit Rd., turn right. Look for the second Shady Trail Riding School sign and go 1.5 miles further on Pulpit Rd. to Maple Run Rd. Turn right onto Maple Run Rd.; go 1.3 miles to the trailhead.

■ ALTOONA AREA   *map page 169, A-3/4*

Set at the base of the Allegheny Ridge, Altoona is the largest town in Blair County and an old-time railroad center. In 1850, it was a tiny farm community next to an iron plant, but then the Pennsylvania Railroad made Altoona the site of its massive maintenance facility. At its peak, the workforce reached 17,000, and railroad life so dominated the city that even tasks as mundane as laundering clothes were governed by railroad schedules. Monday was the city-wide day for hanging clothes on backyard lines to dry because trains were inside maintenance buildings for repair instead of being run on the maze of switch tracks in the yard, where they blew thick clouds of coal dust over the city.

A train winds around the famous Horseshoe Curve in the Allegheny Ridge.

As coal-powered steam was replaced by diesel, the maintenance operation became increasingly obsolete, and Altoona's economy slumped. During the past decade, Conrail Corp., a descendent of the Pennsylvania Railroad empire, has retrofitted the old steam engine repair complex to accommodate diesel locomotives. Today, more tons of freight travel the Main Line rails through Altoona than at any previous time in the city's history.

Much of the historic detail of the boom years of Altoona railroading is captured in the **Railroaders Memorial Museum**, a memorial not to the tycoons who ran the corporations, but to the laborers who laid the track, repaired the cars, and worked on the lines. *1300 Ninth Ave., Altoona; 814-946-0834.*

❖

Nearby are the villages of **Tyrone,** with the Victorian homes of railway executives, and **Fort Roberdeau** in Sinking Valley, with a Revolutionary War–era fort. In the hamlet of **Spruce Creek,** visitors will find Indian caverns and massive rock formations. For antique collectors, **Hollidaysburg** and **Duncansville** are a short drive away.

◆ HORSESHOE CURVE   *map page 169, A-3/4*

The Allegheny Ridge rises steeply 1,200 feet above Altoona and Hollidaysburg, and long presented a major barrier to east-west traffic. One of the most dramatic solutions to this challenge is Horseshoe Curve, located just outside Altoona in the foothills of the Allegheny Mountain range. This expanse of track, now a national historic landmark, was designed by Pennsylvania Railroad chief engineer J. Edgar Thompson.

Thompson's plan called for a ravine to be filled between one of the main mountain ridges and a bed to be carved out of the mountainside. To accomplish this, 450 Irish immigrants worked for three years digging and sculpting the new grade. When it was completed, the two-day trip by horse from Hollidaysburg to Pittsburgh was slashed to 12 hours by train using the Horseshoe Curve. Even during World War II, the Horseshoe Curve was considered so strategically important that it was a target of an unsuccessful attempt by Nazis to sabotage it. (The would-be saboteurs were landed by U-boat on the East Coast, but were almost immediately apprehended, one of them in a bar; among their list of targets was Horseshoe Curve). *Approximately five miles northwest of Altoona, on Horseshoe Curve Rd. Information available at the Railroaders Museum office; 814-946-0834.*

CENTRAL ALTOONA

◆ ALLEGHENY PORTAGE RAILROAD HISTORIC SITE   *map page 169, A-4*

At the time of its inception in 1834, the Portage Railroad was not a railroad but a link in the Main Line canal system that ran from the Delaware River, near Philadelphia, to the Ohio River in Pittsburgh.

Here, passengers, cargo, and canal boats were transported over the summit of Allegheny Mountain between Hollidaysburg and Johnstown. A series of stair-step locks, connected by track, hauled barges from one platform to another up the mountain and then down the other side. The trip took five days, covering 36.5 miles over 10 inclines. By 1854, with the more practical Horseshoe Curve and Gallitzin Tunnels in operation, the Portage Railroad became obsolete. Visitors can view models of the horses and vehicles used to operate the system. *Twelve miles west of Altoona on US 22; 814-886-6150.*

A canal boat is pulled up an incline on the Allegheny Portage Railroad. (Pennsylvania Historical and Museum Commission)

George Storm's Lemon Inn on the Portage Railroad, *circa 1850.*
(State Museum of Pennsylvania)

ALLEGHENY PORTAGE RAILROAD

*T*he crowd and bustle attendant upon the arrival of every train—the change to the cars which stood ready for the mountain passage—the immense locomotives provided by the State to draw the trains to the foot of "Plane 10"—the anxious pause there while the clanking of chains indicated to the passengers that their car was being attached to the wire rope which was to draw it up the steep ascent—the halt at the top of the plane while this attachment was severed, and horses or a locomotive hitched on to draw it to the next summit, was continued until the train was made up again and went on its way to Pittsburgh—can never be forgotten by those who participated in the passage. This means of crossing the mountain was used until 1854, when the great tunnel was finished, and the trains then continued on from Altoona, without interruption.

—William B. Sipes, *The Pennsylvania Railroad,* 1875

■ BLACK MOSHANNON STATE PARK *map page 169, A/B-2*

Once the site of a waystop town on a stagecoach line, this small park lies on the Allegheny Plateau in Western Centre County about 30 miles northeast of Altoona and 15 miles northwest of State College. During the 1800s, it was the site of an extensive pine lumber operation.

Black Moshannon is one of the few parks in the state that has a well-planned network of trails. More than 20 miles have been groomed for bicycles and there are 16 miles for hiking. The longest and most interesting trail winds around the 250-acre Black Moshannon Lake, through stands of evergreens.

Winter is especially long in the park because of the plateau's elevation, so all the trails are maintained for cross-country skiing. Most of the park is open during hunting season and the lake, created from the damming of Black Moshannon Creek north of PA Route 504, is stocked.

Lodgings here include 80 campsites with fire rings and picnic tables; and 13 cabins for rent that can be charitably described as "rustic." *The park is located nine miles east of Philipsburg in Moshannon State Forest; junction of Rte. 504 and Julian Pike. Camping reservations are recommended; 814-342-5960 or 888-PAPARKS.*

■ STATE COLLEGE *map page 169, B-2*

In 1855, James Irwin, a Union general and co-founder of Centre Furnace Works, donated 200 acres of woodland as the site for an agricultural technology school for central Pennsylvania farmers. Today, his modest land grant is known as Penn State University. Alongside the university is the town of State College, which carries the double identity of university town and flagship municipality for the region.

Much of the downtown is the typical off-campus mix of cafes, watering holes, and shops that range from student budget to alumni expensive. On fall weekends when the nationally ranked Nittany Lions football team is proving its mettle at home, the downtown is a crush of returning alumni and fans from across the state. During the past decade, Beaver Stadium has been jacked up and stretched out to hold some 93,000 rabid fans.

◆ PENN STATE UNIVERSITY *map page 169, B-2*

This is a campus that has modernized and expanded while preserving its historic buildings and charm. Stroll from the point where town meets gown, the corner of East College Avenue and South Allen Street up through the main walkway across

campus to the university libraries—the highest point on campus. On the way, you'll pass **Old Main,** the building where top administrators have their offices. It's not the oldest building on campus, but it's worth going inside to see the excellent murals by Henry Varnum Poor that grace that grand entrance foyer. Poor painted the murals in two stages from 1939 through 1949, telling the story of the federal Land Grant Act that created Penn State and including major heroic figures as well as the university's contributions to engineering, mining, and agriculture.

Internationally known architects Charles W. Moore and Arbonies Vlock designed the notable **Palmer Museum of Art,** completed in 1993. Nine of 10 new galleries offer the museum's permanent art collections, celebrating artists and cultures from five continents spanning 3,500 years. *Free; Tues–Sat, 10:30 to 4:30; Sun, noon–4 ; Curtin Rd. on campus; 814-865-7672.*

■ BOALSBURG   *map page 169, C-2*

Charming, historic Boalsburg is just a 10-minute drive east from State College. Settled by Scotch-Irish immigrants in the early 1800s, Boalsburg bustles with activity. Strolling down Main Street is like stepping from a time machine into 1830s America. Businesses operate out of historic buildings and dozens of boutiques and antique shops beckon along the way.

Some people claim that the tradition of Memorial Day began in Boalsburg's military cemetery where, in 1864, residents began the practice of decorating soldiers' graves with flags and flowers.

In October of that year (two years earlier than Waterloo, NY, which the U.S. Congress marks as the birthplace of the holiday), Emma Hunter and Sophie Keller laid flowers and pine branches on the grave of Emma's father, a doctor who had died of yellow fever during the Civil War. At the cemetery they met their friend Elizabeth Meyers, who had lost her son on the last day of the Battle of Gettysburg and who was there for the same purpose. Together they decided to decorate the graves of all the war dead in the cemetery, a tradition that was quickly adopted by the rest of the town. These three women are now immortalized by a life-size bronze statue at the cemetery.

General John Logan officially established Memorial Day in 1868, and today, the holiday celebration at Boalsburg is observed by some 25,000 people.

(previous pages) Penn State football games draw massive crowds.

(opposite) A view of bucolic Boalsburg center.

◆ BOALSBURG SIGHTS

Pennsylvania Military Museum

This museum was formed by a partnership of U.S. Army officers from Pennsylvania who served in the south of France at the end of World War I. One of these soldiers was Col. Theodore Boal, great-great grandson of the town's founder. Each year he organized a group to place memorial plaques on a stone wall bordering Spring Creek "not to glorify war but to honor those who gave their lives in the defense of freedom." What became known as the Shrine of the 28th Division was purchased by the state in 1931 and became the site of the museum. A highlight is a tour through a replica of a World War I battlefield trench amid the re-created sounds and light flashes of rifles and artillery.

The museum also displays uniforms, weapons, and medals dating to the colonial militia and the Continental Army during the Revolutionary War. *US 322, Boalsburg Pike; 814-466-6263.*

Boal Mansion and Columbus Chapel

These buildings tell the story of a prominent and very unusual family. Work on the home was begun in 1789 by Capt. David Boal, an Irishman who founded the town and encouraged further Scotch-Irish settlement before leaving to fight in the Revolutionary War.

An expansion of the house was completed in 1798 by Boal's son, David—in whose honor the town was named. Nine generations of Boals made the mansion their home. Keepsakes and treasures establish links between the Boal family and those of Robert E. Lee in Virginia; Simon Bolivar, the revolutionary leader of Latin America; and Christopher Columbus.

One of the Boal wives was the niece of a direct descendant of Christopher Columbus, and since her uncle and aunt died childless, she inherited the contents of the Columbus family chapel—including significant relics. In 1909, the Boals shipped the entrance door and interior walls of the chapel along with all its contents from Spain to their Boalsburg estate. The admiral's desk Columbus took with him on his voyages is studded with gilt cockleshells, the symbol of devotees of the teachings of St. James of Compostella. Perhaps the most intriguing piece in the chapel collection is a silver reliquary containing two pieces of what is purported to be the True Cross. They were detached by the Bishop of Leon and presented to the Columbus family in 1817.

The period furniture alone is worth a tour through the home, but no visit is complete without a close inspection of portraits of family members. Many lived fascinating lives and most of the men were prominent in the country's important military campaigns. *Call for hours; open May–Oct 30. US Rte. 322 across from the Pennsylvania Military Museum; 814-466-6210.*

■ BELLEFONTE   *map page 169, B-2*

About 10 miles northeast of State College lies the town of Bellefonte, home to seven of the state's governors and the locally renowned Bellefonte Springs. The quality of the water here—and the significant flow of it—was noted by early surveyors working for the state of Pennsylvania. Poking around the steep hills and along the banks of a creek that flows through the area they found an enormous natural spring—the third-largest in the state—generating 11,500,000 gallons of water a day. In 1785, William Lamb saw the enormous value of such a resource and purchased 750 acres around the spring. Settlers flocked to the area and the community thrived on the banks of what became known as Spring Creek.

A chance visit by French statesman Charles-Maurice Talleyrand during his exile from France in 1795 changed the name of the town permanently from Big Spring to Bellefonte when he was said to have remarked upon tasting the water from the spring: *"Oh, Belle Fontaine!"*

Bellefonte's citizens, obviously impressed by Talleyrand's elocution, have named a creek-side park after him and designed it in formal French style; it includes a sculpture section and a gazebo. In every other aspect, Bellefonte is all-American.

◆ BELLEFONTE HISTORICAL RAILROAD   *map page 169, C-2*

A group of volunteer railroad buffs operate a two-car diesel train that runs along 60 miles of track snaking through several central Pennsylvania counties, into Bald Eagle Valley, and over Mount Nittany. The trip begins at Bellefonte's historic Pennsylvania Railroad Station, which has been restored and updated.

Other stops include a picnic trip to Sayers Dam, the tiny, picturesque village of Lemont at the base of Mount Nittany, the Curtin Village Iron Works, and the Keystone Gliderport, where sail planes have set world records riding Appalachian air currents. Half-hour air tours of the region are available. *High and Water Sts. in Bellefonte; 814-355-0311.*

■ MID-STATE TRAIL: BALD EAGLE STATE FOREST

map page 169, C-1

Bald Eagle State Forest is one of the state's largest forests and is dominated by tall, thick oaks whose broad leaves form canopies that allow only slivers of light to reach the ground. The forest covers a vast area to the east and south of State

College (not to be confused with Bald Eagle State Park north of Bellefonte) and is bisected by a section of the Mid-State Trail.

One section of the Mid-State Trail (requiring at least one night's camping) descends along the north flank of Thick Mountain and crosses Woodward Gap Road to a frigid natural spring, the perfect thirst quencher on a hot summer day after a strenuous hike. In part, the Mid-State Trail hike follows an abandoned Penn Central Rail road grade and trestle; the trail leads you under a mountain rather than over it, crossing under Paddy Mountain by way of a 280-foot tunnel.

Detailed trail maps are available at the R. B. Winter State Park Visitors Center, where most trail hikes begin and end. *Off Rte. 150 in Howard; 814-625-2775.*

◆ POE VALLEY STATE PARK   *map page 169, C-2*

This 9.6-mile leg of the Mid-State Trail begins in Poe Valley State Park at the blue-blazed hunters path at the park's concession stand. Following is an overview of the hike, but you should get a map if you plan to go. (No one wants to carry a guidebook to all of Pennsylvania on a hike.)

Follow the hunters path *(above)* to the intersection with the orange-blaze Mid-State Trail (MST) at the top of the ridge. Turn left on Thorpe Trail and follow it

The beautiful Kishacoquillas Valley in Mifflin County, not too far south of Poe Valley State Park, is typical of the scenery in this part of the state.

along Little Poe Mountain to Little Poe Road Creek. Beyond the creek, you will connect with Dry Hollow Trail; follow it until it veers off to the right and climbs to the top of Long Mountain. You will pass a section known as Panther Hollow that offers a spectacular view of a hollow flanked by tall oaks. Return via the Dry Hollow Trail to Big Poe Road, then bear right to return to Poe Paddy State Park. For two- or three-day extensions of this hike with sites for camping, consult park officials or *50 Hikes in Central Pennsylvania* by Tom Thwaites. *Poe Valley State Park; off Rte. 322 in Poe Valley; 814-349-8778.*

■ CAVES   *map page 169, C-2*

Chemical reactions between water and carbon dioxide that occurred underground in limestone here about 20 million years ago have left at least a thousand caves under central Pennsylvania land. All but a few of these caves have been explored and charted, but most are closed to the public. Two of the largest caves are open to visitors.

Penn's Cave: It seems appropriate that the mysterious Penn's Cave was originally bought in 1773 by a relative of Edgar Allen Poe's. The dark interior would seem a likely setting for one of his horror stories. Too-well advertised by billboards on every main highway around the area, Penn's Cave has been open for public tours since 1885 when owners Jesse and Samuel Long chipped in money for a flatboat to take people along the river than runs through the cave. The cave is filled with bizarre limestone sculptures that seem to take on whatever shape your imagination is willing to assign them. *Penn's Cave: SR 192, five miles east of Centre Hall; 814-364-1664.*

Woodward Cave: The largest cave in the state, Woodward was filled with water when nearby Pine Creek was running at capacity. But in 1923, engineers turned the creek flow away from the cave and removed tons of clay and river sediment. In the process they discovered Native American drawings and artifacts within.

Three years later, the cavern was opened for tours along trails that pass through five huge chambers. Several of these areas are crowded with stalactites (ceiling limestone formations) and stalagmites (those anchored to the floor). Inside the fourth chamber is Woodward Cave stalagmite: two million years old, 14 feet high, and weighing 50 tons. *Guided tours only; 22 miles east of State College on Rte. 45. Signs will direct you to the Woodward Inn. Turn right and follow more guide signs to the cave and campground entrance; 814-349-9800.*

■ SUGAR VALLEY LOOP DRIVE   *map p19 169, C-2*

Just north of Woodward is a valley named for its sugar maple trees and the town of Sugar Valley. This is a small enclave, where horse-drawn buggies are still a principal form of transport, thanks to the local Amish community. Drivers or bicyclists (in good shape) can take a 25-mile-long route past a grist mill built in the 1800s, a covered bridge, a one-room schoolhouse, and a number of old churches and graveyards, some with headstones dating back to 1806. *Take Exit 27 off I-80, south on SR 477 toward Loganton. After Loganton, turn right on Rte. 880, the Carroll-Tylersville Rd.*

■ LOCK HAVEN   *map page 169, C-1*

On the banks of the west branch of the the Susquehanna River some 20 miles west of Williamsport rests the town of Lock Haven. Logging operations during the late 1830s created millionaires out of many native sons in small communities like Lock Haven nearly overnight. Stroll down Water Street, the block known as mansion row, to see the elegant homes built to satisfy those few who found quick riches.

A Piper Cub pilots reunion taking place at Lock Haven as seen, appropriately, from the air.

Some homes have fallen into disrepair but a few have been kept up and are open to the public.

Lock Haven is known for its **Piper Heritage Aircraft Museum**. William T. Piper, back in 1937, was a natural entrepreneur. An oil prospector and businessman, Piper joined with aeronautics engineer Walter Jamouneau to build the first assembly-line produced, private airplane—the J3, or famous "Piper Cub." For 47 years, the company produced small aircraft for leisure flying and even assisted the Army Air Corps in World War II by modifying some models for combat flying. At the museum, you'll see prototype aircraft, photographs, and film footage. *Hangar One, One Piper Way, William T. Piper Memorial Airport, Lock Haven, 570-748-2586.*

■ WILLIAMSPORT   *map page 169, D-1*

Northeast of Lock Haven on US 220 is Williamsport. Its location along the scenic west branch of the Susquehanna River in the shadow of the Allegheny Mountains makes it worth a visit. Williamsport has never regained the glory it enjoyed in the mid-1800s, when it was at the center of the timber industry. Its Millionaire Row—where residents vied to have the most opulent home—has become a bit

A game in progress at the Howard J. Lamade Little League Baseball Stadium.

A mansion along Millionaire's Row in Williamsport.

shabby. With a population holding steady at about 32,000, the area does supply workers for several large industries, but it's most famous for the Little League Baseball World Series played here each year in late August. (Little League was born here in 1939.) The nearby **Little League Baseball Museum** plays videos of visitor's performances in the batting and pitching cages. Highlights of recent championship games are also available on video. *Located on US 15, 15 miles north of the intersection of US 15 and I-80 in South Williamsport; call 570-326-3607 for more information.*

Small businesses still thrive in this part of the state in spite of the demise of big coal. Esther Huff, egg artist (top right), sells her wares in Weedville. The Cannondale Bicycle factory (bottom right) in Bedford is another of the region's going concerns.

P I T T S B U R G H

■ HIGHLIGHTS *page*

• Pittsburgh

Food & Lodging
map 276; charts 277
listings by town, in alphabetical order 278

■ TRAVEL BASICS

Pittsburgh is a friendly city, with fine river views, handsome bridges, and memorable architecture. Surprised? So is everyone who hasn't been here for awhile, because old industrial Pittsburgh has reinvented itself. Mills along the rivers have closed and with them their smoke and pollution, revealing the city's beautiful natural setting along the Allegheny and Monongahela Rivers.

Pittsburgh lives in its ethnic neighborhoods—sites of both traditional and onion-domed churches, neat row houses and big, well-preserved Victorians, where people sit outside on warm summer evenings enjoying life along their tree-lined streets. Housing is affordable and crime rates are among the lowest in the country. Walk through the leafy river park at The Point; take the funicular (called "the incline") up Mount Washington for a panoramic view; and enjoy the funk and fun of The Strip.

Getting Around: If you arrive by plane and enter the city by car at night, you'll emerge from a tunnel to see a glittering cityscape, and cross a bridge whose lights reflect in the river below. Pittsburgh can be explored on foot and by car. Because it's a small and friendly city, it isn't hard to get around, though some streets zig-zag and climb hills, changing their names as they go. Major highways disappear into tunnels which run all over the city. Something is always under construction here—a road, a bridge, a building—diverting traffic into a maze of detours.

Climate: Pittsburgh has more cloudy days than Seattle, but when the sun shines, it is glorious. High temperatures in the summer average in the low 80s; high humidity in June, July, and August is common. Fall layers in gradually, beginning at the end of September when daytime highs reach only the low 60s. By November, the daytime highs are in the low 40s and rain is frequent. Winter snowfall averages about 40 inches. From December to mid-March, monthly temperatures average in the mid- to upper 30s.

Food & Lodging: A plethora of small, tucked-away ethnic eateries offer truly wonderful lunch and dinner fare at great prices. At the higher end—literally—some of the best sophisticated restaurants line Grandview Avenue on Mount Washington, which itself offers an appetizing view of the city. Other fine restaurants are on back streets around the Shadyside district of the city. Pittsburgh has several upscale inns just minutes from downtown and its Hilton on The Point commands a fine river view. **Food & Lodging map** page 276; **charts** page 277; **listings** in alphabetical order by town begin on page 278.

■ SETTING

At the narrow end of an island that seems to float in the Allegheny River just off Pittsburgh's North Side, a weathered steel bridge reaches across the water to connect well-manicured running-biking trails on both shores. No frou-frou design to this bridge; just heavy black metal with a brownish patina from a century of Pittsburgh weather. Joggers, walkers, bicyclists, in-line skaters, and mothers pushing babes in strollers cross from one idyllic setting to another. Few of them know this lovely island was once home to meat-packing plants. In fact, no Pittsburgher would have imagined even 10 years ago that the dramatic transformation that has taken place there today could possibly occur. But **Herr's Island, Washington's Landing** *(see page 228),* and the **Pedestrian Bridge** stand as symbols of a city that has scraped off the rust of its industrial past, cleansed its three rivers, and built up its skyline, becoming in the process one of the country's most livable cities.

❖

Pittsburgh was founded at the confluence of the Allegheny and Monongahela Rivers, which converge to form the mammoth Ohio River (which itself joins the Mississippi River and flows south to the Gulf of Mexico). Today, the place where the two rivers converge is the tip of a beautiful urban park. Downtown rises behind "The Point," and a ring of forested hills circles the city.

■ HISTORY

◆ BRITISH AND FRENCH FIGHT FOR CONTROL

By 1750, the French recognized that control of the point of land at the confluence of the Monongahela and Allegheny Rivers was key to the defense of an important inland trade route linking France's colonies in Canada with New Orleans on the Gulf of Mexico. The Ohio River, created by that confluence, led to the Mississippi River and directly to New Orleans.

The British also saw the strategic importance of this area, and sent soldiers into the area to appraise the situation. Their leader was 21-year-old George Washington, then a major in Virginia's colonial militia. He carried with him a letter from Virginia's Ohio Company (a group of businessmen granted a British charter for 500,000 acres of land in the Ohio Valley) to a French military commander, Contrecouer, protesting French plans to build forts in the area. "I spent some time in

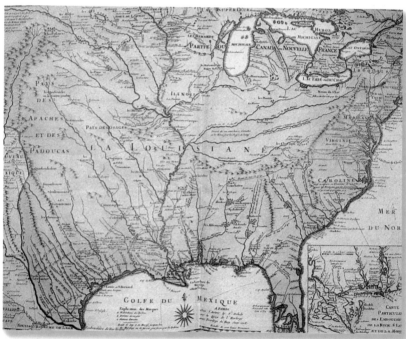

This French map dating from 1718 shows the importance of the rivers in the Ohio Valley in connecting French Canada to the French colonial city of New Orleans.

George Washington raises his hat as the British flag is raised over Fort Duquesne in 1758.
(Granger Collection, New York)

viewing the rivers and the land at the Fork, which I think extremely well situated for a Fort," he wrote in his journal in 1753.

The French officer who commanded Fort Le Boeuf on French Creek to the north, wined and dined George Washington but replied that the French were in western Pennsylvania to stay. The exchange was a polite preview of the bloody confrontation to come—the French and Indian War.

It was on this first trip through western Pennsylvania that Washington nearly drowned in the Allegheny River. His version of the story, told to dinner companions in his years as President, was that he saved himself from the river and also fought off an Indian attack. The version offered by a companion on the trip, Christopher Gist, a missionary, was that he was forced to dive in after the drowning man and haul him to the island now known as Washington's Landing.

Heeding Washington's advice, British forces were dispatched to the area to build a fort and establish a presence. The French, better supplied and manned, surrounded the fort, forced the British out, and set about building a larger defense post they named Fort Duquesne. Their fort at the confluence of the rivers gave them command of all points of entry.

In 1758, with their naval blockades proving highly effective against the French, the British attacked Fort Duquesne, but the French burned it to the ground rather than see it overrun. The British rebuilt the fort and named it for their prime minister, William Pitt, who had taken over management of the French and Indian War in 1757 and is largely credited for its ultimate success.

◆ PITTSBURGH AND THE REVOLUTION

In the fall of 1776, the first of many "Ohio Valley Volunteers" joined George Washington's army to fight in the Revolutionary War. As a reward to veterans, one of Pennsylvania's first official acts was to offer discounted land about a mile north of the confluence of the Allegheny and Monongahela Rivers. By 1786, the area had a fledgling settlement and its own newspaper, the ancestor of the largest newspaper in the city today, the *Pittsburgh Post-Gazette*.

If cheap land lured settlers to the area, rivers provided Pittsburgh with the means to grow and prosper. The nation's first steamboat, the *New Orleans,* was built in 1811 on a bank of the Monongahela near what is now Try Street. The popularity of steamboat travel combined with the efficiency of barge transportation made Pittsburgh a premier inland port. During the War of 1812, the city's location allowed for timely transport of military supplies and was key to American success. After the war, the economy of the city and the quality of the environment would change forever as it became one of the nation's major manufacturing centers.

PITTSBURGH HISTORY

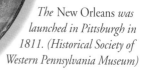

The New Orleans *was launched in Pittsburgh in 1811. (Historical Society of Western Pennsylvania Museum)*

Emma Gibson's View of the City of Pittsburgh in 1817. *(Historical Society of Western Pennsylvania Museum)*

◆ INDUSTRY AND IMMIGRANTS

By 1816, Pittsburgh was thriving and its citizens numbered 10,000. Word of job opportunities spread literally around the world, and soon immigrants were arriving in droves to work in the mills and build the city's bridges and roads.

Housing for workers sprung up in the shadow of their factories and mills, usually in ethnic enclaves. In 1852, the first rail line in the region—speeding Pittsburghers to Philadelphia in one day instead of four—was completed and immigrant neighborhoods also sprang up along the tracks.

In the late 1860s, Pittsburgh was home to some of the industrial revolution's most successful magnates: Andrew Carnegie built a steel empire; Henry Clay Frick produced the coke that fired the foundries; Col. Alfred Hunt built the Alcoa Aluminum plant; Henry J. Heinz established a processed-food empire; and George Westinghouse invented the air brake.

Steel refining and manufacturing prospered in Pittsburgh because the city offered abundant low-cost labor, water for processing and transportation, and coke (processed coal), a cost-effective fuel source for heating the blast furnaces. Unfortunately coke was a noxious pollutant. As blast furnaces along the rivers multiplied, a thick haze that would last over a century settled over the city. In the decades after World War I and through the 1940s when mills were chugging along at full capacity, it was common practice for business executives to go home on their lunch hours to change their white shirts—soiled during the morning from the coke ash in the air.

Pittsburgh industrialists also ran their labor forces as they saw fit, and working conditions, according to historical accounts, were horrific. Workers received barely enough to live on and there were no provisions for days off, vacation, health care, disability payments, or compensation for work-related accidents. In Pittsburgh, the gap between rich and poor was a yawning chasm with few opportunities for mill workers to move up.

Pioneering unions organized to help workers, but they all underestimated the ruthlessness and determination of businessmen who fought unions using every tactic available. In 1877, a strike by conductors and porters protesting a wage reduction turned violent, and 25 people were killed. The most famous union-management battle came more than a decade later when some 3,000 workers at

Andrew Carnegie's Homestead Steel Mill walked off their jobs to fight management changes in wages and work hours. Carnegie's chief executive at the mill, Henry Clay Frick, pitted a force of armed Pinkerton guards against the strikers. In the inevitable confrontation that followed, several guards and one striker were killed.

The Bessemer converter revolutionized steel production so greatly that a factory whose output had measured in the tens of tons began producing in the thousands of tons. (Library of Congress)

PITTSBURGH HISTORY

A pall of smoke from steel factories hangs over Pittsburgh in this 1903 stereograph. (Library of Congress)

The National Guard intervention that followed played right into Frick's strategy of depicting the strikers as lawless thugs. The largest union movement in the nation at the time —the Amalgamated Association—was shut down, and 20 years would pass before organized labor would re-emerge.

◆ RUST BELT REALITIES AND MODERN RENEWAL

For almost 150 years, Pittsburgh's scenic splendor was buried under the haze of mill smoke, and its rivers ran with industrial waste. But, with the election of a dynamic mayor, David Lawrence, in 1945, the city began an organized effort to clean itself up. The use of coal was either eliminated or severely restricted. Railroad engines were switched to diesel; coal-burning furnaces, the standard heating source for most Pittsburgh homes, were banned and residents had to pay for oil or gas-powered units. Yet, between 1975 and 1990, southwestern Pennsylvania lost nearly 800,000 residents, directly attributable to a decline in steel production. The mills and all their supporting industries withered as orders went to foreign countries whose labor costs were lower and production techniques more efficient.

Many riverside mill towns have never fully recovered. Pittsburgh's economy has survived by attracting high-tech industries, health care, medical research, financial management, banking, and some light manufacturing. Pittsburgh is still home to Fortune 500 corporations—there are seven headquarters buildings in southwestern

PITTSBURGH HISTORY

Concerned about the increased use of aluminum and plastic, in the 1950s J&L Steel ran advertising campaigns showing happy consumers glowing with pride over their steel products. (National Museum of American History)

Pennsylvania—one of them Alcoa's new glass-enclosed world headquarters which fronts the Allegheny River on the city's North Shore.

Under the leadership of another dynamic mayor, Tom Murphy, public-private partnerships launched more development in the city at the end of the '90s than occurred in the previous three decades. A commitment to wise use of the riverfronts may be Murphy's biggest legacy. His administration has focused on providing public green spaces and parks, and integrated walkways along the rivers, downtowns and in neighborhoods. Pittsburgh heads into the 21st century as an attractive, wonderfully livable city, with a population of 350,370 in the city itself and 2,361,000 people in the greater metropolitan area.

Pittsburgh's latest renaissance is centered on re-making its downtown to include work space, upscale retail space, residential space, and entertainment venues. More than $1 billion in new construction, including office buildings, new football and baseball stadiums, and a dramatic expansion of the Convention Center is now underway. Downtown's former red-light district is now a cultural district that includes a Michael Graves–designed theater to join with the gold-and-glitter Heinz Hall, home of the world-class Pittsburgh Symphony, presently conducted by Mariss Jansons. Nearby, the more modern Benedum Center for the Performing Arts hosts the Pittsburgh Ballet, Broadway musicals, and national dance troupes.

On Pittsburgh's North Side the Pittsburgh Pirates play in a new $261-million stadium on the North Shore and the Pittsburgh Steelers in another new $252-million stadium. No other period of cleanup can match in scale what has been going on during the past five years. Rand McNally's *Places Rated Almanac* has included Pittsburgh on its Top 20 Most Livable Cities list since 1985, and Pittsburgh's regional economy is so diverse that heavy manufacturing covers only about five percent of total regional employment.

■ WHO IS THE PITTSBURGHER?

Pittsburgh has produced some amazing people. Whether by birth or circumstance, those who have experienced Pittsburgh long enough to call it home know its power to nurture, especially in close-knit neighborhoods like Polish Hill, predominately Jewish Squirrel Hill, and the Serbian South Side. Pittsburgh still pulses with working-class blood and its ethnic enclaves are daily reminders of the immigrant backs and brawn that made this city work.

Famous Pittsburghers include impressionist painter Mary Cassatt and Pop artist Andy Warhol, authors Gertrude Stein and Annie Dillard, playwright August Wilson, and jazz great Billy Strayhorn, a graduate of Westinghouse High School.

*Three Rivers Stadium is home base for the Pittsburgh Pirates, a source of pride
for Pittsburghers.*

Pittsburghers are unpretentious and honest, sometimes clumsily so. A long-standing joke is that Pittsburgh is a big city with small-town customs. A driver pounding on the car horn in this town, for instance, is more likely to be signaling "hello" to someone on the street than to be trying to move stalled traffic. It's also common in many Pittsburgh neighborhoods to find a kitchen chair placed in front of a row house to guard a favored parking space.

■ DOWNTOWN

Packed in around the 11-by-11 block area bounded by the Monongahela and Allegheny Rivers, downtown is a medley of office towers, government buildings, hotels and river bridges, which form a dramatic skyline.

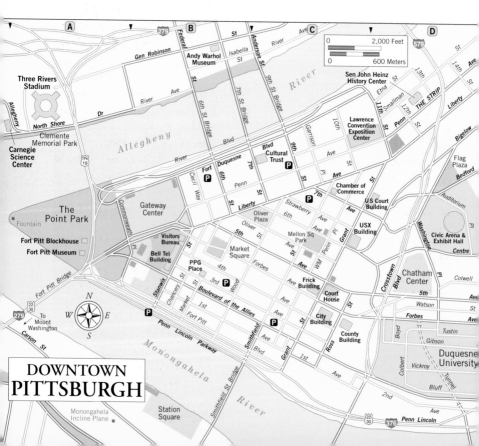

Beautifully situated at the confluence of two rivers, The Point is the site of many civic festivals.

The Point and Fort Pitt *map opposite*

Nearly every adventure in downtown Pittsburgh begins or ends at The Point, the peak of a geographical triangle that extends from a fountain at the confluence of the Allegheny and Monongahela Rivers to its base at a series of crosstown ramps and expressways known as I-579 West. By any comparison, this is a truly beautiful park, its grassy lawns green and inviting, its walks adjacent to one of two wide green rivers, and its center point, the place where the rivers meet to form the mighty Ohio, leading the eye toward forested green hills. If greenery and blue skies provide a beautiful setting, the people in the parks seem to be all polite, vigorous people, just out for a stroll. Both coal barges and pleasure boats ply the waters, the latter often docking at the concrete docking area. Strollers and, in summer, sunbathers, relax in the wide open area around a great fountain whose arched plume leaps 30 feet into the air.

The Point is the site of old earthworks and a wall of **Fort Pitt**, where the French and British soldiers contested this strategically important piece of land in the late 1750s. Artifacts and monuments at Fort Pitt Museum and Blockhouse give much of the credit for Britain's eventual victory to Gen. John Forbes. A Scotsman, Forbes was appointed to his post by British prime minister William Pitt in 1757.

Forbes knew that re-taking the fort (then called Fort Duquesne) from the French might require a long siege. In order to win he would need to outlast the French and would need a dependable route for provisions and weaponry. His response was to turn his soldiers into road builders—chopping down trees, hauling out boulders, and cutting away brush. Soon the road stretched from The Point east across the Allegheny Mountains. Wisely, the French abandoned Fort Duquesne to the British, but only after burning it to the ground.

"I have used the freedom of giving your name to Fort Duquesne," Forbes wrote Prime Minister Pitt in November 1758 after the French deserted it, "as I hope it was in some measure the being actuated by your spirit that now makes us masters of the place." *Museum located in The Point State Park; museum: 412-281-9284.*

Market Square   *map page 214, B-2*
About one-third mile due east of The Point on Fourth and Fifth Avenues is Market Square, the city center in the years just before the Revolutionary War. The Declaration of Independence was read aloud here in 1776, and the square acted as civic gathering place for public officials. Today, the square (and the restaurants on its perimeter) is a popular lunchtime hangout for office workers. At a Friday evening entertainment event called M Squared, people gather to drink, mingle, and listen to bands on an outdoor stage.

Highrise Grandees
The best place to see Pittsburgh's architectural splendors is from a view point on Mount Washington. There you'll see the city—compact, varied, and somehow eager—set between two rivers and both facing and backed by bridges. To the right of Market Square rises glassy **PPG Place**, world headquarters for Pittsburgh Paint and Glass Corp. Its buildings are made almost entirely of plate glass, one of the basic products made in PPG factories, and at sunset, with orange light bouncing off so many glass panes, the effect is pure magic. The building was designed in 1979 by pre-eminent New York architects Philip Johnson and John Burgee, and it remains a spectacular example of post-modern corporate architecture. *Blvd. of the Allies and Stanwix St.*

Pittsburgh's venerable and inspiring **Allegheny County Courthouse** is an 1888 relic from an era when buildings didn't need neon to be fixed in mind. Architect Henry Hobson Richardson's design of granite, castle-like towers and an inner courtyard with a 10-foot circular fountain works well from every angle. Critics, tongues in cheeks, dubbed the style Richardson Romanesque. Don't miss the frescoes on the building's first floor. *Self-guided tour available in Room 409A; 436 Grant St.; 412-350-5313.*

The **Frick Building** is a mix of black-and-white marble, gloriously colored stained glass, and filtered light, all in the Beaux-Arts style. Look for the bust of the formidable coke-and-steel baron Henry Clay Frick in the lobby. *On Grant St. across from courthouse (above).*

Frick might have preferred to have his bust in the lobby of the **USX Tower**, former headquarters of U.S. Steel. The rust-colored mammoth made of CORTEN steel rises 841 feet, making it the tallest building in the East outside of New York City and Chicago. An upscale restaurant, Top of the Triangle, offers a commanding view of the city from the 62nd floor. *600 Grant St.*

The Old Courthouse downtown is now dominated by towering highrises.

The urban transformation of the Golden Triangle from a forlorn downtown to a thriving city host to important corporations, is personified by a skyline of distinctive highrises.

Grant Street *map page 214, C-2*
Between Third and Liberty Avenues, Grant Street is lined with buildings that present a showcase of corporate and government architecture. Old trolley car tracks were ripped up from the street and red bricks laid down with a median strip of planters to provide a handsome promenade.

Mellon Square Park *map page 214, C-2*
A welcome respite from the heavy marble, stone, and steel is available one block off Grant Street at the square between Sixth and Oliver Avenues.

Here, Mellon Square Park bumps up against the **Westin William Penn Hotel,**

another Frick creation after he discovered there were no hotels of New York City standards in the city. Financier Andrew Mellon bankrolled Pittsburgh's industrialists and became a multi-millionaire himself. He and his son Paul built some of America's most important art galleries, which they endowed with their own important collections. Although none are in Pittsburgh, the Mellon name graces several Pittsburgh monuments.

Wood Street Galleries *map page 214, C-1*
One of the city's funkier art spaces, the Wood Street galleries hang over a "T" station stop, one of four in the city's fledgling downtown subway system. The gallery, a project of the Cultural Trust, a consortium of arts groups building a district in the downtown, features non-traditional exhibits. *601 Wood St.; 412-471-5605.*

■ THE STRIP   *map page 214, D-1*

Located just outside the Golden Triangle and northeast of downtown, The Strip is a 15-block-long, three-block-wide produce and wholesale district. Here the scent of freshly brewed coffee from gourmet coffee emporiums mixes with the scents of grilling ginger chicken (cooked by Vietnamese immigrants), and fresh flowers in the flower stalls. In early morning darkness, The Strip is lined with tractor trailers unloading their foods for warehouses and stores. During business hours, shoppers crowd the streets looking for savings by buying in bulk, like the full-pound cuts of gourmet cheeses at Pennsylvania Macaroni Co. on Penn Avenue.

In the evening hours, restaurants and a range of clubs to suit every taste fire up along Penn Avenue and Smallman Street. Several old warehouse buildings along The Strip route have been converted to loft condominiums.

■ OAKLAND   *map page 219, inset A-2*

The neighborhood of Oakland is old and prestigious, its streets lined with fine, century-old row houses, and its grand boulevards graced by the city's most venerable arts institutions. There are three, tree-shaded university campuses and, bordering lush Schenley Park, the four-block, L-shaped complex of aged sandstone buildings that house the Carnegie Museum of Art, the Museum of Natural History, the Carnegie Free Library, and the Carnegie Music Hall. Guarding the doors are life-size sculptures of Shakespeare, Bach, Galileo, and Michelangelo, each one signifying a specialization of the Carnegie Institute's four branches: literature, music, science, and art.

Carnegie Museum of Art
map page 219, A/B-2
The permanent collections at the Carnegie Museum of Art run the gamut from ancient Egyptian sculpture to classic Roman statuary to the modern art of Andy Warhol and Roy Liechtenstein. Works by Frans Hals, Peter Paul Rubens, and Maurice Prendergast are also part of the permanent collection.

Carnegie's credo as a collector was to stock up on the popular classical painters of his day but also reserve space for the "Old Masters of Tomorrow." Today, his legacy continues in one of the largest and most discussed annual art exhibitions in the country. *Tues–Sat 10–5, Sun 1–5; admission: one ticket good for adjacent museums; 4400 Forbes Ave.; 412-622-3131.*

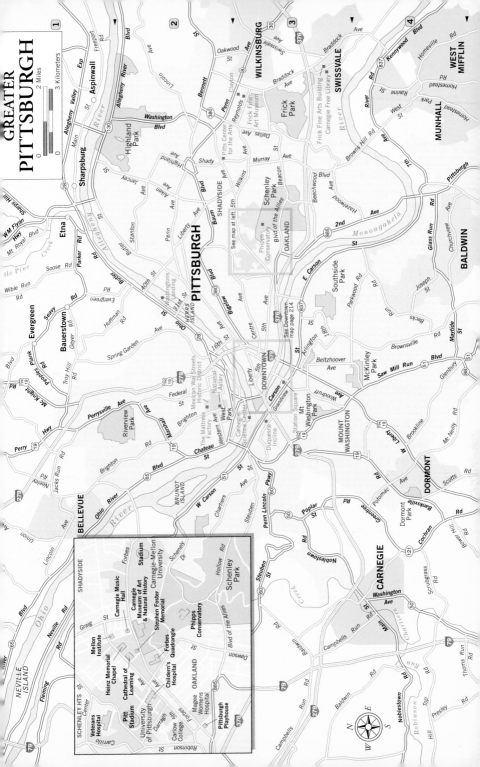

Museum of Natural History

map page 219. A/B-2

A walkway connects fine art to nature's version. Carnegie was a hands-on collector here, too, and dispatched one of the earliest teams of paleontologists to unearth fossils and dinosaur bones for reconstruction back in the museum. Knowing well where their funding was coming from, team members brought back a small fossilized dinosaur and named it *Diplodocus Carnegie* in the boss's honor. Almost as popular as its dinosaur collection are the museum's exhibits of Native Indian culture. *Tues–Sat 10–5, Sun 1–5; admission: one ticket good adjacent museums; 4400 Forbes Ave.; 412-622-3131.*

Hall of Sculpture and Architecture

Two grand halls, part of the Museum of Art, house the Hall of Sculpture and Architecture. John White Alexander's *The Crowning of Labor* graces the entryway. The Pentelic marble floor and columns in this building come from the same quarries that supplied the Parthenon in Athens. The superb background lighting makes the Hall one of the most popular backdrops for society functions and charitable fundraisers. There is a certain *je ne sais quoi* about sipping a drink in the shadow of a replica of the Temple of Athena that brings out the checkbooks. *Tues–Sat 10–5, Sun 1–5; admission: one ticket good for adjacent museums; 4400 Forbes Ave.; 412-622-5551.*

The Diplodocus Carnegie *in the Carnegie Museum of Natural History.*

Carnegie Free Library *map page 219, F-3*
Connected to the complex is the Carnegie Free Library, the mothership of Andrew Carnegie's network of library systems that extended first to southwestern Pennsylvania and then to other parts of the country. The library is an architectural gem which has undergone significant renovation and repair in recent years thanks to a regional funding system for cultural projects approved by Allegheny County voters. *4400 Forbes Ave.; 412-622-3116.*

Carnegie Music Hall *map page 219. A/B-2*
A key element of the complex is the Music Hall set in a hundred-year-old building with a green marble foyer, good acoustics, and offering the intimacy of an elegant 19th century theater. *4400 Forbes Ave.; 412-622-5551.*

CONTRADICTORY CARNEGIE

Andrew Carnegie's life is familiar in its general contours: At the age of 13 he arrived in the United States with his penniless family from Scotland, worked diligently, and invested shrewdly, becoming a millionaire in an age when millionaires really were rich. As a businessman he was ruthless toward both his competitors and his workers. Upon his retirement, he gave most of his wealth away, becoming in the process one of America's greatest philanthropists.

It is the particulars of this life that make Carnegie both contradictory and worth knowing. His father was a pro-labor activist. Young Andrew saw himself as a friend of the worker, but never allowed his sentiments to overcome his desire to maximize profits. He let his "bad-cop" partner Henry Frick take the blame for the bloody suppression of the Homestead Strike, but when it was over he wrote to a friend, "...it's fading as all events do & we are at work selling steel one pound for a half penny."

His charitable works were not just a guilty afterthought to a life of reckless acquisition. Carnegie wrote in a famous article known as the "Gospel of Wealth" that a talented businessman is entitled to great wealth, but he has a duty to live without ostentation, provide modestly for his dependents, and help his "poorer brethren, bringing to their service his superior wisdom, experience, and ability to administer, doing for them, better than they would or could do for themselves."

His tone is patronizing, his argument paternalistic in typical titan-of-industry style, but his works have the better of the argument. The wisest fields for philanthropy, he wrote in 1889, are universities, libraries, hospitals, parks, concert halls, swimming pools, and church buildings. Critics may carp (and they did) that homes should come before swimming pools, and that the "libraries" were just buildings

PITTSBURGH
OAKLAND

without books, but many of the 2,811 Carnegie libraries endure, as do the Carnegie Endowment for International Peace, Carnegie-Mellon University in Pittsburgh, the Carnegie Institute, of Washington, D.C., Carnegie Hall, and many other structures financed by his $350 million in gifts.

Social critics—such as the illustrator who drew this 1892 cartoon—pointed out that while Andrew Carnegie may have donated lavishly to cultural and educational institutions, he paid his employees poorly and opposed labor reform vehemently.
(Library of Congress)

◆ CARNEGIE MELLON UNIVERSITY
  AND THE UNIVERSITY OF PITTSBURGH *map page 219, A&B-2*

Connected to the museum complex and the park are the campuses of Carnegie Mellon University and the University of Pittsburgh. A building boom at well-endowed CMU celebrates the school's status as a premier scientific-technical institution well beyond founder Andrew Carnegie and Richard Mellon's wildest expectations. Many of the structures on Pitt's campus are historic landmarks.

The Cathedral of Learning stands on the campus of the University of Pittsburgh.

The 40-story **Cathedral of Learning**—with its 26 famous Nationality Rooms depicting ethnic origins of immigrant workers who helped build the city—was the fundraising brainchild of Chancellor John Bowman, who commissioned the work from architect Charles Clauder in 1925.

More than $10 million in donations poured in from average Pittsburghers, many of whom had never gone to college, to help pay for the building as the university moved from Perry Hilltop on the North Side to Oakland. *4200 Fifth Ave.; 412-624-6000.*

Across the main plaza and in the shadow of the secular "cathedral" is the **Heinz Memorial Chapel,** a French Gothic–style structure, whose ornate spires and detailed stone carvings contrast wonderfully with the smooth lines and mass of the Cathedral of Learning. The building, with its 73-foot-high stained glass transept windows, was commissioned by the Heinz family as a memorial to the family patriarch, Henry John, and to his mother, Anna Margareta. The chapel is often a busy place on weekends, given that Pitt students, employees, and extended families have wedding privileges there. *Heinz Memorial Chapel; 412-624-4157.*

❖

Across Forbes Avenue on Pitt's campus are three curious memorials that have much to do with Pittsburgh's colorful history but little in common with each other.

The Stephen Foster Memorial celebrates the life of the prolific Pittsburgh native, Stephen Foster (1826-1864). Foster wrote for black minstrel shows and is famous for composing tunes that have become American classics, including: "Oh Susanna," "Old Folks at Home," "Jeannie with the Light Brown Hair," and "Camptown Races." At the memorial there's a museum and a research library with 30,000 documents and artifacts connected to Foster. *4301 Forbes Ave.; 412-624-4100.*

Across the parking lot and housed in a mammoth and odd classroom building known as Forbes Quadrangle is the home plate of the historic **Forbes Field Baseball Park.** The plate where Babe Ruth put his eye on the ball for the last home run of his career is preserved under glass in the middle of one of the hallways. The left-field wall of the park is preserved on the sidewalk in front of the building.

The **Frick Fine Arts Building,** across the street from the Carnegie Free Library, was commissioned by Helen Clay Frick as a memorial to her father. The cloistered garden at the building's center is a wonderfully soothing quiet space. On the inner walls surrounding the glass-enclosed courtyard are replicas of frescoes painted by Nicholas Lochoff. Ms. Frick, having inherited much of her father's talent for negotiating deals, bought 22 of Lochoff's works for $40,000.

Ms. Frick offered to endow a larger museum along with the art department, but the university refused to accept her conditions for the bequest—which were that the museum contain no contemporary art and that no one of German extraction could work on the staff. *Schenley Dr.; 412-648-2400.*

Henry Clay Frick 1849–1919 (Underwood Photo Archives, San Francisco)

◆ FRICK FINE ART MUSEUM *map page 219, F-3*

When University of Pittsburgh officials declined to accept Ms. Frick's conditions for building a campus museum, she took her millions back home to Point Breeze and set about commissioning a museum to house her permanent collection of pre-20th-century European paintings.

The Frick Fine Art Museum is now part of a manicured six-acre complex that includes the restored family home, **Clayton.** A tour of the grounds, including the carriage house, offers insight into the pleasurable life led by Pittsburgh's multimillionaires at the time they stood staunchly against unions trying to better their workers' lives. The more modest homes surrounding Clayton were owned at the time of Frick's residency by middle-class workers, and not all who lived nearby then or now approve of the man who made millions but was known for greed. When the restored Clayton was opened for tours in 1990, graffiti vandals hit the complex over a period of weeks spraying out epitaphs and protests such as "oppressor of the worker."

You can discuss the good and bad of Frick's life over lunch at the linen-napkin cafe on the property. *7227 Reynolds St. near Homewood Ave. in the Point Breeze section of Pittsburgh; 412-371-0606.*

PITTSBURGH
OAKLAND

■ PUBLIC PARKS AND BYWAYS

Much of the city's East End is covered by a network of gorgeous public parks, but the premier green space is 300-acre **Schenley Park**, a gift of Mary Schenley, a wealthy expatriate who married a British navy captain and moved to England. The designer of the park was Frederick Law Olmsted, who created New York's crown jewel, Central Park.

At Schenley Park visit the Lord & Burnham–designed **Phipps Conservatory**. The structure is a prime example of Victorian "glass house" architecture and houses exotic indoor plants, trees, and exhibits. Nearly three acres of outdoor gardens surround the complex. *One Schenley Dr.; 412-622-6914.*

■ NORTH SIDE

The North Side combines Victorian-era and Craftsman-style row houses in a neighborhood of tree-lined streets The residential sector is separated from the commercial sector, where an H. J. Heinz plant employs 1,7600 workers adjacent to lush, 50-acre West Park.

Andy Warhol Museum   *map page 214, B-1*
Mayor David Lawrence no doubt would have scratched his head trying to figure out the work of artist Andy Warhol, Pittsburgh native, son of Carpatho-Russian immigrants. As soon as Wharhol graduated from Carnegie Institute in graphic design, he beat a hasty retreat out of town to pursue fame and fortune in New York City.

Located in an old warehouse, the museum's ultra-modern interior is devoted to the work, life, and times of one of America's most quixotic artist-celebrities. The museum is laid out according to the life periods of the artist. Among the most interesting exhibits is the earliest commercial graphics work he did while working for New York advertising agencies—portraits of an artist trying to break out of his forced discipline. Also not to be missed are the bulletin boards crammed with gossip stories and celebrity memorabilia, just the kind of stuff Andy loved. *117 Sandusky St.; 412-237-8300.*

National Aviary   *map page 219, C-2*
Once nearly eliminated in city budget cutbacks, another one-of-a-kind attraction flew the city coop and went for national affiliation. Now known as the National Aviary, the compound in Allegheny Commons Park is the main center for the breeding and study of exotic and endangered birds. More than 450 birds live here, some in cages, but many in tree-filled aviaries visitors can walk through. The main building is part of a glass-enclosed former plant conservatory. *Admission fee; 9–5 daily except Christmas; Arch St. between W. North and W. Ohio Sts.; 412-323-7235.*

Warhol's familiar celebrity portraits in the Andy Warhol Museum.

Carnegie Science Center *map page 219, D-2*
Mushed in the middle of stadium construction on the city's North Shore is the Carnegie Science Center, which duplicates the successful formula from other cities of making a science center interactive and entertaining. Funded by the Buhl Science Center and the Carnegie Institute, the complex opened in 1991 to rave reviews and features a planetarium, an interactive nutrition exhibit where food is prepared in a kitchen, and a miniature railroad. *One Allegheny Ave.; 412-237-3400.*

Mexican War Streets *map page 219, C-2*
This 1850s residential district was developed by architect and planner William Robinson. It is an eight-block rectangle of tree-shaded streets lined with narrow red-brick and stone homes. Robinson named the streets after generals and battles of note in the Mexican War. Many houses here were built for craftsmen, others for people of means. For years the neighborhood went downhill, but today it is reviving, and the modest homes with their pretty doors and front porches contribute to an intimate, harmonious environment.

Mattress Factory *map page 219, C-2*
This is an art museum that specializes in installations—large, sometimes interactional and/or multimedia works visitors can walk through—or by, around, or inside. The Mattress Factory is known nationally for mounting compelling installations and

environmental works.

The museum is named for its location in a former Stearns & Foster Mattress Factory Warehouse, where museum founder and executive director Barbara Luderowski and curator Michael Olijnyk also live. One of the most breathtaking installations is a permanent exhibit outside the building—a rock garden designed by Winifred Lutz. Here tranquility, rather than greenery, grows. Featured are passageways, uniquely shaped rock structures, and a small stream; *500 Sampsonia Way; 412-231-3169.*

Washington's Landing *map page 219, D-2*
Twenty-one year old George Washington made it ashore here in the mid-1700s after his boat capsized in the Allegheny River. He'd come on to western Pennsylvania to negotiate with the French on behalf of the British for control of this area. Today, Herr's Island is a residential area with lovely views and a running-jogging trail that follows the shoreline. *Reached by River Road on the city's North Side and by the 31st Street Bridge in the Strip District.*

■ MOUNT WASHINGTON   *map page 219, C-3*

Directly across the Monongahela River from downtown is 367-foot-high Mount Washington, the best place to go for a fine view of Pittsburgh and her rivers.

At the foot of Mount Washington is **Station Square**, a commercial development of shops, eateries, and a Sheraton Hotel. The former waiting room at the old Pittsburgh and Lake Erie Railroad terminal has been converted into a restaurant, the Grand Concourse, richly decorated in dark woods and stained glass.

Get to the top of **Mount Washington** by taking one of two "inclines," or cable cars that leave every few minutes. One dollar each way takes you on a two-minute ride. Looking down, you'll see Pittsburgh's fine downtown, set between the Allegheny and Monongehela Rivers that converge to form the Ohio. To your right, along the Monongehela, you'll see the city's South Side, a funky residential and shopping district, with well-preserved ethnic enclaves. Surrounding all of this are wooded hills, and the overall effect is one of space and beauty.

Monongahela Incline is located directly across the street from the Station Square development (*W. Carson St.; 412-231-5707*). **Duquesne Incline**, built in 1877, still has its original cars with cherry and maple interiors (*1197 W. Carson just opposite Fort Pitt Bridge; 412-381-1665*).

Atop Mount Washington you'll discover a mix of expensive homes, apartments, condos, and street-side restaurants, as well as fine overlooks of the city at the top of the inclines.

(opposite) A view of downtown Pittsburgh from Mount Washington.

PITTSBURGH
MT. WASHINGTON

S O U T H W E S T

Food & Lodging
map 276; charts 277
listings by town, in alphabetical order 278

■ TRAVEL BASICS

Much of southwestern Pennsylvania is farm country and rolling forested hills. Here, many people live simply on isolated produce and dairy farms, or in quaint villages with mom-and-pop businesses and homes with wide, wrap-around porches. On the grittier side, some parts of this region still lie in the shadows of abandoned steel mills. Along the Ohio River west through Beaver County and the Monongahela River south through Brownsville, the riverfront is lined with tired, ex-mill towns struggling to find new economies.

East of Pittsburgh, beginning at Greensburg, rise the beautiful Laurel Highlands where, during mid-September, hardwood forests turn brilliant red, orange, and all shades of brown, yellow, and green. By December, snow has cloaked these mountains in white, and until early March, skiers flock here to downhill and cross-country ski. During the spring and summer, the countryside north of Pittsburgh is especially beautiful, its green hills covered with buttercups, violets, and elegant white hemlock.

Climate: Temperatures during the warm-weather months range from the high 60s of mid-April to the humid 80s of summertime. Cloud cover is more common here than it is in Seattle, yet when the sun shines it is glorious. The wettest months are in spring and late fall. Cool, crisp fall temperatures heading into winter begin in late September with highs in the low 60s and nighttime temperatures as low as 35. By November, daytime highs are in the low 40s and rain is frequent. In deep winter, temperatures range from the high 30s to single-digit lows. Annual snowfall averages 40 to 45 inches.

Food & Lodging: Most food in southwestern Pennsylvania is the "comfort fare" of the small-town diner, where friendly waitresses still crack their gum and never let your coffee cup show bottom. No "healthy heart" symbols on the menu in these parts, what with entrees like homemade meat loaf with brown gravy or T-bone steak smothered in onions and served with thick-cut french fries. Every town has at least one Italian restaurant of the spaghetti-with-red sauce variety, usually run by the grandchildren of immigrants. There are a growing number of upscale restaurants, too, where the mesquite-grilled salmon has a tangerine sauce and the foie gras is perfectly seared.

Small town lodging near attractions like Fallingwater in the east and Washington's historic mansions in the south range from inexpensive family-owned motels to pricey resort condos and upscale B&Bs. Large chain hotels and motels are on all the major highways. For camping information on any of the state parks in the region, you can scroll through the Bureau of State Parks website at www.dcnr.state.pa.us, or call the toll-free central reservations number: 1-888-PA-PARKS. **Food & Lodging map** page 276; **charts** page 277; **listings** in alphabetical order by town begin on page 278.

■ LANDSCAPE

Amish farms prosper near New Castle and Ellwood City where wide valleys are ringed by hills and forests. In the south, ridges gather into mid-sized mountains and subside into canyons of lush vegetation fed by many creeks and streams. In the growing months, the scent of spruce and white pine is in the air. In the hilly counties at the border with West Virginia, shrubs mix with hardwood forests of oak, maple, and hickory.

The Laurel Highlands, the most southern end of the Allegheny Mountains in Pennsylvania, have moderate ridges that fold out in wide pleats like an accordion, a dramatic land mass that dominates the region.

Down from the hills and mountains rush rivers and streams—water cascading down sheer cliffs at McConnell's Mill State Park in the west; bumping and grinding in the rapids of the Youghiogheny in the east; tumbling wildly in hillside streams up north; and flowing gently through creeks and streams into the Monongahela River in the south. In the west, at many points along the rivers, the skeletons of old steel mills still haunt the land and the shrinking towns around them.

William Coventry Wall's On the Monongahela, *1860. (Westmoreland Museum of American Art)*

There is an air of independence about southwestern Pennsylvanians, perhaps fostered long ago by farmers and craftsmen—who, risking life and comfort by moving beyond the relatively secure confines of the Pittsburgh settlement, paid dearly for the patches of forest-covered land that their descendants now call home.

■ NORTH OF PITTSBURGH

A mix of high-end suburbs and wide-open farm land testifies to the competing forces at work in this region. In the far northwestern tier above Pittsburgh communities remain rural. Amish farms prosper in the country around New Wilmington and New Castle in Lawrence County. In Harmony, Zelienople, and Ellwood City, the architecture and local crafts reveal the towns' German immigrant roots.

◆ NEW WILMINGTON *map page 233, A-1*

Interstate 79 runs north of Pittsburgh toward Erie past suburbs, open country, scrub forest, and scattered farms. Crossing the Interstate about 15 miles north of Pittsburgh is Route 208, a winding, backcountry road that traverses the heart of

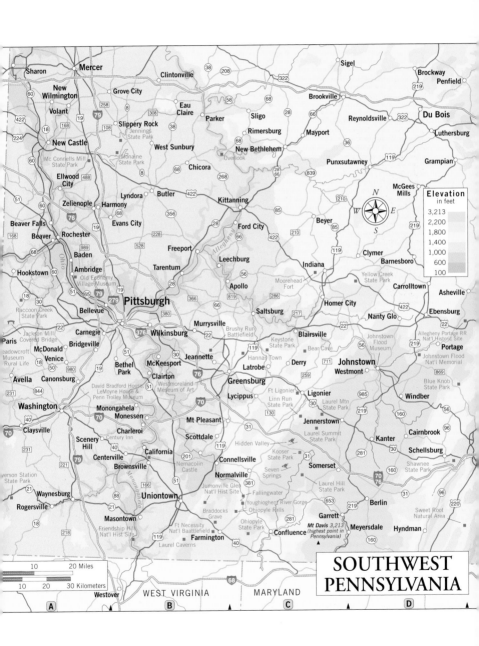

SOUTHWEST PENNSYLVANIA

An Amish hat shop.

western Pennsylvania's Amish farm country. Driving along this road, you may catch glimpses of Old Order Amish farmers in wide-brimmed hats tilling their fields with horse-pulled plows. No motorized machinery can be seen, and black buggies rather than cars are parked in their dirt driveways.

The peaceful borough of **New Wilmington** is a Main Street U.S.A. community. Home to **Westminster College** (an idyllic campus whose ivy-covered stone walls date to 1852) and the center of an Amish farming region, the town remains free of the exploitive commercialism that has sprung up around other Pennsylvania Amish enclaves. Residential streets are lined with graceful homes and maple trees; downtown is stately and thriving, with an assortment of antique and crafts shops.

The "Plain People" add a special dimension to village life, riding to town in their horse-drawn buggies and purposefully attending to business. Amish women come here to shop for sewing supplies, and New Wilmington's Grange Hall sponsors a quilt auction on the third Saturdays of April and October where more than 350 quilts are offered to bidders.

For a hearty meal, stop at the **Tavern Inn On the Square,** in its former life a family home and a refuge for escaped slaves following the Underground Railroad north to freedom. In 1931, two graduates of the town's Westminster College decided the area needed a good restaurant, bought the house and converted it. Today it's known for delicious, no-nonsense meals such as creamed chicken on a biscuit, grilled pork chops and apple sauce, or ham steaks, all served family style. *108 N. Market St.; 724-946-2020.*

Four miles east on Route 208 is **Volant**, a 19th-century farming town with a grist mill, quaint stores, and little restaurants.

◆ McConnell's Mill State Park   *map page 233, A-1*

A hidden gem, McConnell's Mill State Park is set in the deep gorge of Slippery Rock Creek. Within this spectacular 400-foot chasm are house-sized boulders, waterfalls cascading down sheer cliffs, and a restored gristmill. The mill was built in 1852 from hand-hewn oak timbers on a foundation of stone blocks. Fire destroyed the first mill, but it was rebuilt in 1868. The best place to view the mill and the creek is on the opposite bank by way of an old covered bridge.

Slippery Rock Creek alternates between rushing whitewater, and calm, deep pools. The seven miles of rugged trails touch only a small portion of the 2,512

McConnell's Mill was built in 1852 beside Slippery Rock Creek.

acres that make up the park. Hell's Hollow Trail winds through an area that in spring offers a spectacular wildflower display. Here, patches of violet and light blue merge into blazing yellows against the soft green leaves and tiny, white flowers of hemlock lining the valley.

With its multi-story rock formations, cascading waterfalls, and picnicking grounds, the park draws thousands of rock climbers, anglers, and rafters each year. Canoeing and kayaking are permitted. *Forty miles north of Pittsburgh on I-79, then west on Rte. 422; 724-368-8091.*

■ WEST OF PITTSBURGH: BEAVER COUNTY

In the 19th and early 20th century the titans of heavy industry built huge industrial mills and factories along the Ohio River in Beaver County. When steel production came to a halt beginning in the late 1970s, company towns like Aliquippa went through hard times, and much of the area's younger population moved away in search of work. Since then, some communities have been successful in creating a new economic base and forging new identities. In the borough of New Brighton, for instance, weekenders come to visit several architecturally interesting houses, a

Emil Bott's Beaver Falls, Pennsylvania, *1854. (Westmoreland Museum of American Art)*

St. Nicholas Chapel in Beaver County, which has a large Russian Orthodox population.

respected art gallery, and a revived "Victorian-era" business district. Other communities are still struggling.

If Beaver County's population and its aging industrial facilities are concentrated along its rivers, much of the rest of the region has remained rural. The region has a popular lake and a pristine state park, Raccoon Creek State Park *(see page 238)*.

◆ OLD ECONOMY VILLAGE MUSEUM   *map page 233, A-2*

A brick-walled time capsule in the middle of the working class town of Ambridge, Old Economy Village is a fine, if eccentric, example of early western Pennsylvania history. It was founded in 1804 by 1,500 members of the Harmony Society who moved onto 9,000 acres and established a system of communal living. Followers of George Rapp, a German preacher, they believed that the Second Coming of Christ was imminent and that a special visit would be made to their community, meaning that everything had to be kept in perfect order.

Several years later, the group decided to become celibate, believing that procreation was a waste of energy since the end of the world was due in 1829. In the meantime, the Harmonists were an industrious group, admired for their craftsmanship and the elegant simplicity of their artistic endeavors. The range of their achievements is evident in the workings of Old Economy Village Museum, the country's second-oldest, built in 1827. (Baltimore's Peale Museum is the oldest.) One side of the building displays arts and crafts and the other scientific inventions. Guided tours are conducted through the six buildings and gardens that supported the community. *Church and 14th Sts., Ambridge; 724-266-4500.*

◆ RACCOON CREEK STATE PARK IN HOOKSTOWN   *map page 233, A-2*

Twenty-five miles west of Pittsburgh on US 30, in farm country with some housing developments, Raccoon Creek Park includes a fine lake, bridle and hiking trails, the remains of a historic mineral spring, and an exceptional wildflower reserve. Swimming, boating, and fishing may all be enjoyed here.

The **wildflower reserve**, on the eastern edge of the park, contains five miles of trails and is the highlight of the park. The Max Henrici Trail traverses a wide mowed lane between field and woods to Raccoon Creek. The woods contain hickory, elm, black cherry, and a few huge sycamore trees. The peak blooming period for wildflowers is late April through mid-May, when sprays of yellow, white, pink, and purple poke out of the tall meadow. A blooming schedule of over 150 wildflowers (from mid-April through October) is available at the nature center. *Wildflower information: 724-899-3611.*

The **Frankfort Mineral Springs** were part of a well-known health spa in the 1800s. The remains of the spa are visible amid lilies and ancient oak trees, and the nearby footbridge offers a charming view of a waterfall pouring over a broken ledge into a rocky grotto. *3000 Rte. 18, Hookstown; 724-899-3919.*

◆ MEADOWCROFT MUSEUM OF RURAL LIFE   *map page 233, A-3*

In *Pittsburgh: An Urban Portrait,* University of Pittsburgh art and architecture history professor Franklin Toker points to landmarks of the early southwestern pioneering spirit in Avella, site of a recreated early settlement known as Meadowcroft Village. The setting, which is more like an outdoor museum, depicts everyday life in the 1800s.

The "village" was designed by Delvin Miller (a champion harness horse-racer at the Meadowlands race track in Washington County) and his brother, Albert. Together, they collected historic buildings from across the state and moved them to the family farm. Today, they include a log house built by the Millers' Scotch-Irish great-great grandfather in 1795, a one-room schoolhouse, a blacksmith's shop, and a covered bridge.

An on-going archeological dig on the Meadowcroft Village grounds has uncovered evidence of the earliest human occupation of the Western Hemisphere. Carbon dating tests, according to those at the village, put the remains found here back to 17,000 years. The dig area is not open to the public, but an exhibit details the work. *35 miles southwest of Pittsburgh on Rte. 50 in Avella; 724-587-3412.*

■ REBELLIOUS WASHINGTON COUNTY

In the area closest to Pittsburgh, suburbs with big upscale homes are burgeoning and high-tech industry is gaining a foothold. Farther south of Pittsburgh, the land folds out gradually into flat farmland, then back into hills where small country villages are tucked away. The people who live here own farms and supporting businesses, stores, and shops. Only a small percentage work in light manufacturing jobs or in service industries, and the pace of life is much more mellow than in urban Pittsburgh.

Historically, people in Washington County distrusted government, an attitude that can be traced back to the decade after the Revolutionary War when the area figured prominently in the Whiskey Rebellion, a violent campaign to thwart the federal government in its first attempt to tax its citizenry. In 1791, Congress resorted to raising excise taxes to help pay off the remaining debts of the Revolutionary War. It instituted a tax of seven cents per gallon on whiskey—which would surely decrease the amount of whiskey sold, and weaken the demand for the farmers' main cash crop, rye (the most popular grain at the time for making whiskey). What made people even madder was that jugs of whiskey were used as a form of currency, since money was hard to come by.

During that year, farmers who tried to obey the law were ridiculed and threatened; tax collectors were tarred and feathered; mail delivery was disrupted, and some tax money confiscated. The crisis came to a head when the "Whiskey Boys" tried to attack the Supervisor of Collections, Gen. John Neville. His home was burned to the ground and about 10 rebels were killed in the clash.

George Washington, acting on the advice of Federalist Alexander Hamilton, decided to make an example of the rebels and rode personally into Pittsburgh with 13,000 troops under the command of Gen. Harry "Lighthorse" Lee. While political differences could be tolerated, open lawlessness could not, and the rebellion was quelled.

An excise officer is tarred and feathered during the Whiskey Rebellion in this lithograph, circa 1794. (Washington & Jefferson College Historical Collection, Washington, PA)

◆ BRIDGES OF WASHINGTON COUNTY   *map page 233, A-3*

Spread out across Washington County on backcountry roads are 25 covered bridges, sometimes called "kissing" or "wishing" bridges. Those wanting to explore this peaceful farming area and hunt for these treasures should obtain a map from the Washington County Historical Society information center at the LeMoyne House in Washington. *LeMoyne House; 49 East Maiden St., Washington; 724-225-6740.*

One of the more popular routes begins on US 22 and is a bit more than 12 miles long, proceeding west from Pittsburgh International Airport, turning right on SR 18-N, and continuing along SR 18 through the intersection with CR 4004 (Pennsylvania Avenue). One-tenth of a mile on the left—heading west—is King's Creek Road, a seven-mile stretch to Jackson Mill, a covered bridge. King's Creek Road eventually loops back to the village of Paris where you'll find a small restaurant and a store.

◆ WASHINGTON   *map page 233, A-3*

Today, Washington maintains much of the spirited independence that bubbled to the surface in the Whiskey Rebellion. It is a bustling junior city about a 30-minute drive from Pittsburgh with a mixed economy built on light manufacturing, a nearby school, Washington and Jefferson College, and service industries.

SOUTHWEST WASHINGTON

LeMoyne House

Just outside of Washington proper is the residence of Dr. John Julius LeMoyne, one of the most courageous visionaries of 19th-century Pennsylvania.

He dared preach the idea of equality between the sexes and races and was treated as a pariah in his community as a result. LeMoyne practiced what he preached, helping 25 black slaves to freedom on the Underground Railroad. He also started colleges for women and for blacks.

LeMoyne House is a good place to go for maps and information on other sites of interest in the area. *49 East Maiden St.; 724-225-6740.*

David Bradford House

Among the Pennsylvanians who led the Whiskey Rebellion from behind the scenes was David Bradford, a bright, promising young businessman-lawyer. By 1786, at the age of 26, he had married, been appointed deputy attorney general of the state, and made a fortune from his grist and sawmills.

A hefty chunk of his money went into the building of the family estate, which became the unofficial headquarters for plotting various violent acts of the uprising. Though Bradford was never directly linked to any illegal acts, there was enough circumstantial evidence against him for President George Washington to sign a warrant

David Bradford House - rear view July 25, 1934   J. Gowynto Iams.

J. Howard Iams's General David Bradford House, *circa 1794. (Courtesy of Westmoreland Museum of American Art)*

for his arrest. When Washington rode into Pittsburgh to confront the rebels, one contingent of the army was sent to Washington County to search for Bradford.

Local history has it that the soldiers nearly caught their man. While they were heading down the road toward his estate, Bradford was hopping from the roof outside a bedroom window onto the roof of a cistern and then to his saddled horse. He eventually made his way down to the Louisiana Territory, where he resettled and prospered. President John Adams pardoned Bradford in 1799; he died in 1810 at 49.

Artifacts from the Whiskey Rebellion are on display in the David Bradford House, a Georgian mansion that still stands on Main Street. At $4,500, it was the most expensive and talked-about home in the region at the time, with mahogany from West India for the stairway and Italian marble for some of the fireplace mantles. It also was large enough to accommodate his five children. *Bradford House, 140 S. Main St., Washington; 724-222-3604.*

Pennsylvania Trolley Museum
map page 233, A-3

Several southwestern Pennsylvania communities still have trolleys as part of their public transportation systems but none carry as much nostalgia as those on display at the Pennsylvania Trolley Museum in Washington County, just a 20-minute drive south of Pittsburgh. Some 25 trolleys are on display, the oldest dating back to 1894. Children can ride a trolley that operates on a short track on the museum grounds. Trolley rides included in admission fee. *One Museum Rd.; Washington; 724-228-9256.*

Century Inn *map page 233, A-4*

Today an inn and restaurant, the Century Inn is tied to the Whiskey Rebellion, and was built the same year Bradford fled a few gallops ahead of federal soldiers. Tradition has long had it that instigators of the rebellion met here to drink and plot their next moves, and as if to confirm this story, a rare flag used by the insurgents was discovered hidden in the basement during a recent renovation. (It now hangs on a wall in the bar.) The inn, a National Historic Landmark, is the oldest continuously operating hostelry along the National Road, the first linking of the east coast to the western frontier.. *Rte. 40 southwest of Washington; in Scenery Hill; 724-945-5180.*

The Laurel Highlands, part of the Allegheny Mountains, rise east of Pittsburgh.

■ EAST OF PITTSBURGH: WESTMORELAND COUNTY

East of Pittsburgh rise the Laurel Highlands, where towns have remained remarkably the same in the face of some furious resort and condominium developments in the region. Many people who live here are employed in factories—including Sony's large television assembly center near New Stanton. Increasingly though, much of the economy is tied to outdoor recreation and tourism.

◆ BUSHY RUN BATTLEFIELD STATE PARK *map page 233, B-3*

In 1763, British general Henry Bouquet was sent to re-supply the soldiers of Fort Pitt who had been under siege by a 13-tribe war party led by Chief Pontiac. The Indians were angered over continued European encroachment on their lands, despite promises made in several treaties. On his trek to the fort, Bouquet camped at what is now Bushy Run State Park and was caught in a surprise attack by an Indian war party split off from the attack on the fort. Despite losing nearly one-quarter of his men, Bouquet rallied his troops, used supplies to build defense walls, and sent half his surviving forces to loop around to form a cross-fire when the Indians

(opposite) By the late 1880s, trolleys had enabled the growth of Pennsylvania's suburbs. (Historical Society of Western Pennsylvania, Pittsburgh)

re-grouped for a second attack. The maneuver was devastating to the attackers and they retreated. Bouquet continued on to the fort and covered the remaining 26 miles in four days. The rescue of the fort ensured victory over Pontiac, and later, the French.

Today, visitors find an idyllic park setting, perfect, weather permitting, for picnicking and hiking. *Rte. 993, 3 miles west of intersection with Rte. 66, in Jeanette, 11 miles north of Greensburg; 724-527-5584.*

◆ HANNA'S TOWN *map page 233, B/C-3*

Hanna's Town was once the seat of Westmoreland County government, but when it was burned by Indians at the behest of the British in 1782, it lost that honor to nearby Greensburg.

In its modern reincarnation, Hanna's Town guides and artisans dress in period costumes to dramatize the county's early history. Visitors can tour a reconstructed courthouse (with adjacent tavern after the verdict is in), and a log palisade fort among other attractions. *Call for tour information; Old Forbes Rd. in North Greensburg between Rts. 119 and 819; 724-836-1800.*

◆ GREENSBURG'S MUSEUM *map page 233, B/C-3*

Greensburg, the oldest county seat west of the Alleghenies, is a hilly, middle-size town with a beauty of a courthouse. The town's **Westmoreland Museum of American Art** draws art lovers from Pittsburgh and beyond, thanks to collections that focus on Pennsylvania painters. There is breadth, too. An entire gallery is devoted to landscapes from the likes of Winslow Homer, John Singer Sargent, and Thomas Eakins. Children will enjoy the Westmoreland's 2,000-piece toy collection; its dolls rum the gamut from antebellum belles to bell-bottom Barbies; *221 N. Main St.; 724-837-1500.*

■ LAUREL HIGHLANDS *map page 233, C-3&4*

East of Greensburg, gentle slopes rise toward the arching foothills of Laurel Ridge and the beginning of the Allegheny Mountains. The Pennsylvania Turnpike (I-76) and secondary roads cross over forests of oak and hemlock and trout-filled mountain streams. This is the Laurel Highlands, with its fresh mountain air and its spectacular valleys and ridges, including the dramatic and beautiful 1,700-foot-deep Youghiogheny River Gorge.

WELCOME TO PENNSYLVANIA!

Every summer we drove from Chicago to Baltimore to visit family. Our route followed the efficient, but prosaic turnpike system; the flat Indiana portion connecting seamlessly to the protracted dullness of Ohio. But gradually, as we moved east, the landscape would start to gently roll. This was our sign that Pennsylvania was soon to come. Pennsylvania was always the highlight of our trip. We would sit up high in our seats watching for the sign that said, "Welcome to

Koehler family getting ready to hit the turnpike.
(photo by Dad)

Pennsylvania," and once we entered the state we would eagerly await the first tunnel. The Pennsylvania Turnpike follows an old railroad bed and the distinctive character of the route is especially in evidence in the handcrafted stone archways of the tunnel entrances. (I always assumed that the Keystone State logo came from these archways.) As we entered each tunnel we would turn around in our seats and watch the window of light as it closed down to a pinhole and disappeared. Then we would whip back around and count the minutes of artificial night, awaiting the dot of light that would appear and grow in front of us.

Between tunnels we would marvel at the rich purple rock that was laid open for us in the road cuts. The chocolately look of it gave me a notion that it was connected, by some strange alchemy, with the children's paradise of Hershey at the other end of the state. Then, all too soon, we would drop off the Pennsylvania Turnpike for the dogleg down to Baltimore, and we would entirely miss the southeast corner of the state, the portion that many people imagine represents the entirety of Pennsylvania.

—Cheryl Koehler

Laurel Highlands has attracted city dwellers from Pittsburgh and surrounding communities since the early 1900s. Today, vacation homes, ski resorts, condo communities, and rustic backwoods hideaways can all be found here. The ski resorts at **Seven Springs** and **Hidden Valley** offer downhill and cross-country skiing. Other resorts cater to businesses as retreats and convention centers, with restaurants, golf courses, and health clubs. *For information on these resorts try the web at www.laurelhighlands.org or call Laurel Highlands visitors bureau at 800-925-7669.*

◆ LIGONIER   *map page 233, C-3*

The main route to the Laurel Mountain region extends northeast from Greensburg to Ligonier. This area was the last outpost for the British in Pennsylvania territory during the French and Indian War in the mid-18th century. Fort Ligonier, the only fort in Pennsylvania never surrendered to an enemy, was rebuilt in the 1950s according to plans supplied by the British War Office. The exhibits housed there, and the town itself, are popular tourist attractions. *Fort Ligonier, Rte. 30 West to Ligonier; 724-238-9701.*

Today, Ligonier is a quaint, gentrified town, the playground of the old-money crowd from Pittsburgh, some of whom keep horse farms nearby. Antique stores, country clubs, and bridle trails abound, as do families recovering from the rides at nearby **Idlewild Amusement Park**. Idlewild was created in 1878 by Judge Thomas Mellon, whose 350-acre estate was given over for "picnic purposes or pleasure grounds." One stipulation was that no trees or other plants would be disturbed in the park's construction. *Idlewild Amusement Park; Turnpike to Donegal Exit, then north to Rte. 711 to Rte. 30 west to the park; 724-238-3666. General information about Ligonier: 724-238-4200.*

◆ JOHNSTOWN   *map page 233, D-3*

Set at the beginning of the Ohio River, Johnstown is surrounded by high hills that once contained a precious resource: coal. It was a prosperous industrial town in the 19th century, with jobs aplenty in steel-making, river transport, and mining—which attracted immigrants from nearly every country of Europe.

The event that will forever set this city apart was its Memorial Day flood of 1889. Bad luck, scandalous indifference to public safety on the part of public officials and mill owners, and the wrath of nature all combined to make the calamity that hit this city one of the worst preventable disasters in American history.

Johnstown's historic district, a three-block-long area that survived the flood, is interesting to explore on foot. **The Johnstown Flood Museum** depicts the history of the tragedy in vivid exhibits and a 26-minute, Academy Award–winning documentary, "Black Friday," that identifies the culprits and causes of the disaster. *304 Washington St.; 814-539-1889.*

Johnstown Flood Disaster

High above the town of Johnstown at the head of the Little Conemaugh River stood the South Fork Fishing and Hunting Club, known locally as "The Bosses Club" because its membership included such leading lights as Andrew Carnegie, Andrew Mellon, and Henry Clay Frick, all residents of Pittsburgh. The club owned a reservoir-lake used for fishing and sailing and which was bordered by summer mansions.

The water in the reservoir was contained by a 72-foot-high dam, the largest in the United States when it was built in 1853 to create a reservoir for the Pennsylvania Main Line Canal. But the canal system had been abandoned by the time the dam was completed and it went through several other owners before being purchased by the sporting club in 1879.

Club officers ordered the dam repaired, but failed to authorize an engineer to oversee the work. To prevent the loss of the black bass that had been stocked in the lake, a screen was placed across the spillway. In addition, the hillsides around Johnstown had been stripped of timber to supply housing and land for a growing population, creating the potential for a dangerous erosion problem.

Years of complaints about the decrepit condition of the South Fork Dam, 14 miles upriver from the city, fell on deaf ears when, on Memorial Day 1889, human failings and nature's wrath combined to create a deadly disaster. A storm dropped seven inches of rain on the area, and the runoff rushed down the denuded hillsides and filled the reservoir. The fish screen quickly became clogged, preventing the water from escaping.

The dam burst with a thunderous roar. More than 20 million tons of water raced through the narrow valley creating a wall of water 35 to 75 feet high. The force was powerful enough to carry entire houses, train locomotives, and boulders along with it. The wreckage and water overwhelmed Johnstown, destroying the city and killing 2,209 people in what remains America's deadliest flood.

The flood disaster was the first relief effort organized by Clara Barton and her fledgling American Red Cross.

◆ OHIOPYLE STATE PARK AND
YOUGHIOGHENY RIVER GORGE   *map page 233, C-4*

In 1754, George Washington had high hopes that the Youghiogheny [YAWK-ah-gain-y] River would provide a quick route to speed his 300-man Virginia militia to oust the French from Fort Duquesne. But standing at the edge of Ohiopyle Falls, he was sobered at the sight of its 20-foot drop, and he decided to detour his troops through Great Meadows, near Farmington.

Nearly 19,000 acres surrounding one section of the **Youghiogheny River Gorge** has been preserved as Ohiopyle State Park. A testament to the restorative powers of nature, the Yough—"Yawk" as it is pronounced by natives—was for years considered a dead waterway after being polluted from a century of pit and strip mining. Thanks to a concerted clean-up effort, the Yough now supports a thriving ecosystem that includes trout. Several whitewater rafting companies operate in the area and the park is popular with mountain bikers, swimmers, and hikers. *Ohiopyle State Park: Turnpike to Exit 9 to Rte. 31 to Rtes. 381&711; 724-329-8591.*

Tolls for the old National Road (today Route 40) were collected at Searight's Toll House, erected in 1835 near Addison.

Among the many homes Frank Lloyd Wright designed, Fallingwater is generally considered to be his masterpiece.

◆ FALLINGWATER   *map page 233, C-4*

Just a 10-minute drive from the entrance to Ohiopyle State Park is Fallingwater, a private home built by architect Frank Lloyd Wright to blend in with its natural environment.

In 1936, Edgar J. Kaufmann, who had made a fortune as owner of Kaufmann's, Pittsburgh's premier department store, hired the architect to design a weekend retreat for his family on a piece of land they owned in Mill Run, near Ohiopyle. Wright's design incorporated much of what was already on the building site, including rock outcroppings, trees, and a rushing creek (the house sits directly over a waterfall). Battles of will between Kaufmann and Wright over the details of the design became legendary, but Kaufmann's pride in Fallingwater eventually overcame his frustration with Wright, and in the end he became his knight errant. When a contractor on the job remarked sourly that Wright's projects were often as much as 50 percent over budget and couldn't even keep out the rain, Kaufmann supposedly answered (illogically) "Works of art don't belong in the rain!" Perhaps in support of the thesis that beauty matters more than practicality, the American

FAITH IN OBJECTS: FALLINGWATER

*T*here are many who say that Frank Lloyd Wright's Fallingwater…was his crowning achievement. I am inclined to agree. If I am anywhere within a hundred miles of this historic house, I will always try to schedule a visit. A trip to Fallingwater is good for the soul. Well, it's good for my soul anyway. I can spend a few hours wandering from room to room on a brisk Fall afternoon and my faith in objects is restored.

Fallingwater is an absolutely wonderful object. I wish I could say the same for its architect and the people it was designed for. Frank Lloyd Wright was an egotistical, petty tyrant.

If you've been inside many Frank Lloyd Wright houses, you'll quickly notice that the ceilings are exceedingly low. Wright was a short man, but he firmly believed that his own height was the ideal human stature and designed his buildings accordingly. When Wright's taller brother accompanied him to Fallingwater, Wright asked him to remain seated while he was talking to the Kaufmanns because he was "spoiling the scale of the architecture."

Wright and the Kaufmann family are all dead now. Their many eccentricities and character flaws seem trivial when compared to the building itself. The building lives on. It has become objectified. After fifty years of study by architecture students around the world, Fallingwater has become transformed into an icon for truth and beauty.

—John Sealander, "Object Lessons," an essay from
The Road to Nowhere

Institute of Architects considers Fallingwater to be America's most beautiful home.

In 1963, Fallingwater was deeded to the Western Pennsylvania Conservancy, a not-for-profit land trust. In recent times, Fallingwater has made the news because it has needed structural work. Flawed or not, it remains one of America's most architecturally important homes. Tours are absolutely worth the effort, not only for what you see but for the stories you hear. *$8 Tue–Fri, $20 on weekends. Take the Pennsylvania Turnpike to Donegal Exit to Rte. 31 east to Rte. 381/711 to Mill Run and Fallingwater; 724-329-8501.*

♦ FORT NECESSITY NATIONAL BATTLEFIELD   *map page 233, B-4*

Young George Washington's first military campaign took place at Great Meadows, now called Fort Necessity National Battlefield. The battle, which helped begin the French and Indian War, occurred in 1754 after 22-year-old Washington, then a lieutenant colonel in the Virginia Militia, was sent by the colony's governor to force the French out of the Ohio Valley.

After Washington and about 300 Virginia volunteers stumbled across a contingent of 33 French soldiers, Washington ordered a surprise attack at dawn and 10 French soldiers were killed, including the French commander, Ensign Jumonville. Within 10 minutes the survivors had surrendered, but one soldier escaped and made his way to Fort Duquesne at (what is now) Pittsburgh. He told his superiors that Washington had ignored French cries that they were on a diplomatic rather than military mission. Washington later wrote that neither he nor any of his men had heard such protests.

Flush with his first victory, Washington camped at Great Meadows to re-group and ordered his men to build a slap-dash fort "of necessity" to offer some protection from a possible French counter-attack. In July 1754, as Washington's men were hacking their way through the woods building a road, a larger French force, led by the brother of the fallen Jumonville, did attack. Outnumbered, Washington surrendered after an eight-hour siege. In return for being allowed to march from the fort with swords and weapons, Washington agreed to sign a document of surrender written in French. Either deliberately or inadvertently, the English translation omitted a line in which Washington acknowledged that Jumonville's death was the result of an assassination instead of legitimate combat. The signed French document wreaked havoc in diplomatic circles in Europe, as the French used it against the British in their conduct of the war.

Demoralized, Washington was forced to resign his commission. He returned to Virginia, but redeemed himself militarily the following year and led a company of soldiers back into southwestern Pennsylvania. The famous British general, Edward Braddock, followed the road Washington's men had cut through the woods and headed toward Pittsburgh while Washington headed toward Brownsville.

When Braddock was fatally wounded in the Battle of the Monongahela in July 1755, Washington risked his own life to help remove the still-conscious general from the battlefield. After Braddock's death, Washington officiated at a memorial service at his grave which had to be unmarked along the road to keep Indians from finding it. Braddock's remains were later re-buried at Fort Necessity.

The fort has been renovated and also contains the **Mount Washington Tavern**, a rebuilt stagecoach stop from the early 1800s. *Fort Necessity National Battlefield: 11 miles southeast of Uniontown on Rte. 40; 724-329-5512.*

N O R T H W E S T

Food & Lodging
map 276; charts 277
listings by town, in alphabetical order 278

■ TRAVEL BASICS

Northwestern Pennsylvania is the least-visited corner of the state, but in many ways this is what gives it its unique character. Without the bright prospect of tourist dollars, the region has pretty much been left to the residents to style in whatever way they see fit. There is plenty to see and do, and the independent traveler is rewarded with dia-monds in the rough. Driving north from Pittsburgh to Erie, the city is quickly left be-hind. On either side of the major highways, wooded hills and farm fields recede as far as the eye can see, with the occasional red barn, cows in the pasture, or a country church with its adjacent, fenced cemetery.

The largest city in the northwest is Erie, with its Presque Isle Park jutting into Lake Erie. East of Erie lies an agricultural and wine region, and farther to the east is found the Allegheny Forest, a thinly settled, remote area, where you can canoe, hike, camp, and fish along creeks and lakes.

Climate: Temperatures range generally from 15-35 degrees during the daytime in winter to 75-85 degrees in summer. Springs are late, usually not until May and falls are late also, (mid- or late October) again because of the moderating effect of the lake although precipitation is evenly spread year around, and averages 35 inches. Heavy snow squalls blowing off Lake Erie between November and February may create haz-ardous driving conditions.

Food & Lodging: Today most of the best hotels and restaurants are on the highways outside the towns. Lodging inside these towns is mostly in B&Bs in Victorian homes. **Food & Lodging map** page 276; **charts** page 277; **listings** in alphabetical order by town begin on page 278.

■ EARLY HISTORY

Erie (city, county, and lake) was named for the Erie Indians, whose history has been largely lost after they were conquered and assimilated in the early 1600s by the Senecas, one of the powerful five nations of the Iroquois Confederacy (the Mohawk, Oneida, Onondaga, Cayuga, and Seneca). French explorers and trappers, working their way down from what is now Canada, were the first Europeans to set foot on Seneca land. The French, however, were allied with the Huron and Algonquian nations, the archenemies of the Iroquois, and fierce battles were waged against the French until 1696 when the French finally prevailed.

In the early 1700s, the French sought to control a direct route (via the Ohio River) south to the Mississippi River and to French colonies in Louisiana. When the English settlers began flooding into Iroquois land, the Iroquois turned on them. Capitalizing on their anger, the French recruited the Iroquois to help fight the British, initiating what came to be known as the French and Indian War. The French built defensive forts on Presque Isle and other key lakeside points, then abandoned and burned them after a wave of British attacks forced them to retreat.

Forts Presque Isle and Le Boeuf were rebuilt by the British, but lost again to the Indians led by Chief Pontiac. The forts were in Indian hands for several years until the treaty of Fort Stanwix, in 1768, returned the Northwest Pennsylvania territory to British control. The treaty also opened Indian land to settlement and by the end of the decade, immigrants were moving westward. Forced finally to accept their defeat, the second treaty of Fort Stanwix, in 1784, effectively ended the reign of the Iroquois Confederacy.

The first road in the Lake Erie area wasn't built until 1794, more than 40 years after the first settlement of Pittsburgh, but throughout the 19th century Lake Erie was of tremendous economic importance to the fledgling United States, as freight crossed from the interior into the port of Erie. During the War of 1812 Commodore Perry, aboard the brig US *Niagara,* defeated the British at the Battle of

Chief Pontiac of the Ottawa League smokes a peace pipe with Major Robert Rogers at the close of the French and Indian War. (Library of Congress)

Lake Erie, thus securing American control of that trade route.

It wasn't until after the Civil War that cities like Erie began to expand, and smaller outlying communities sprang up to link the port city to other areas of the state and to New York. In 1859, the town of Titusville became the site of the nation's first oil well and for a time the region rode the prosperity of an oil boom.

■ MODERN TIMES

Folks in northwest Pennsylvania are not the slightest bit ashamed to admit that their region may be the new Appalachia. While the economy across the United States, and throughout most of Pennsylvania, has boomed during the 1990s, the northwest region has continued to lose population and industry at a slow but steady rate. Factories have moved south, and farms have ceased production. As a result, nature has been able to reclaim land that was originally part of the vast eastern forest. Wildlife, such as the great herds of elk that used to roam the region, have been reintroduced, wildcats have been sighted, birds of prey have returned, and once distressed habitats now host a variety of songbirds. Meanwhile, the Amish and Mennonite populations have expanded in the area, no doubt due to the growing opportunity to be left in peace to practice the simple life that is central to their faith.

■ WOODED HILLS, SMALL TOWNS

There is no confusing the towns of northwest Pennsylvania as suburbs of Pittsburgh. They are Norman Rockwell–style towns, often with a town square and a bandstand, sometimes with a majestic county courthouse. They have big Victorian homes—for that was the era when towns like Mercer and Franklin flourished—and streets lined with smaller frame homes, all with front porches and porch swings. They are the kind of towns Americans dream of when they talk about wanting to move back to a simpler life.

Wellsboro in Tioga County exemplifies the charming towns of northwest Pennsylvania.

◆ MERCER   *map page 257, A-4*

With its population of 2,440, Mercer is typical of the charming, small towns in this area. Its courthouse is built on the highest elevation in the county and can be seen for miles around. Every year the town has a Victorian festival the last weekend in July.

Mercer is seven miles from the Grove City Shops, a huge outlet shopping mall.

◆ PYMATUNING RESERVOIR   *map page 257, A-3*

To control flooding and reclaim swamp land, the Pymatuning Dam was completed in 1934, creating in the process one of the largest man-made lakes in the eastern United States. Here you'll find a wide, placid lake with fishing, boating, camping, swimming, and beaches.

The name is derived from the Seneca name for the place, "Crooked Mouthed Man's Dwelling Place," referring to the Erie tribe who lived here, and their queen, known to them for her crooked dealings. (Another example, incidentally, of something that happened all over North America: European explorers would ask members of one tribe the name of a neighboring tribe, and, not understanding what the word meant in a native dialect, the European would record an unflattering name.) *One and a half miles north of Jamestown; 412-932-3141.*

■ LAKE ERIE   *map page 257, A&B-1*

The Great Lakes, including Lake Erie, were formed by the final expansions and contractions of the Wisconsin Glacier about 15,000 years ago. Much of the land was scraped to bedrock by the glaciers, and in some cases gouged down into deep craters. When the ice melted, water filled the craters and the Great Lakes were formed.

In the early 1800s, Erie became one of the busiest inland ports in the United States for both transport of people and goods and the construction of sailing vessels. The great sailing ships eventually gave way to steam-powered ships, and by 1850, Lake Erie and the other Great Lakes were bustling with hundreds of 300-foot steamers, popular with travelers because of their speed and comfort. (Interestingly, with the gradual cleansing of this once terribly polluted lake, the clearer water is revealing hundreds of sunken ships, the exploration of which has spawned a booming new business in scuba diving.)

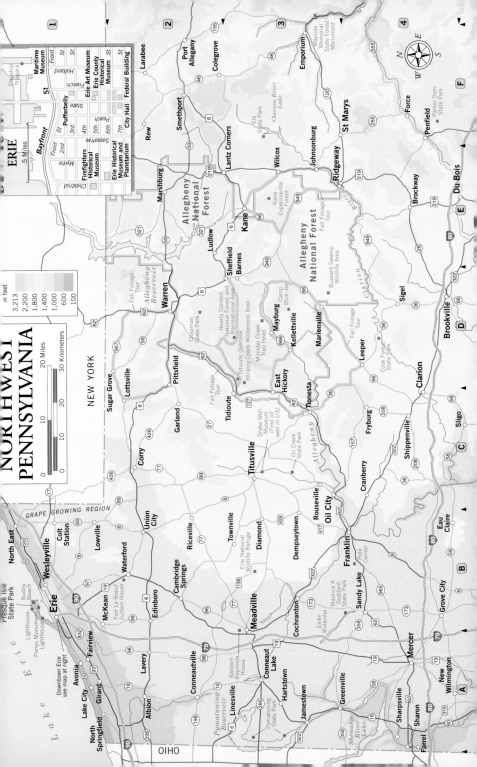

Transport businesses continued to search for a more efficient way to move goods from vessels docking in Erie to inland Pennsylvania. They found it in the Erie Extension Canal, a route that would ship goods on a man-made waterway from Erie to Pittsburgh. An eastern route stretched to the Allegheny River with stops at Conneaut Lake, Franklin, and Meadville. A western extension covered New Castle and points along the Beaver River. Burl Ives celebrated the canal in song with the famous, or infamous, chorus:

> Oh, the Erie was a'risin
> The gin was a'gettin low
> I didn't think we'd get a drink
> 'Till we got to Buffalo-ho-ho
> 'Till we got to Buffalo

By 1853, water transportation was supplanted by the railroad connecting Erie to Pittsburgh and Pittsburgh to the East Coast. Pennsylvania's town of Erie survived the economic U-turn by specializing in ship repair and fishing, but its boom era was drawing to a close.

Winter Travel Note: The waters of Lake Erie temper the heat of summer. In winter, it can get cold here, very cold, and restaurants and tourist attractions sometimes only operate "in season." From November through January intense snow squalls often blow off the lake making travel hazardous in localized areas within 20-30 miles from the lakeshore.

■ CITY OF ERIE   *map page 257, B-1*

Drive into Erie from any of the highways to the south, and you're suddenly on State Street, the wide boulevard that bisects the city.

Downtown Erie is level and major streets are unusually wide, having been designed for horse and ox-drawn wagons to make their wide turns. It's a good place to park the car and take a walk on State Street. It's easy to find your way around the city because everything on one side of State Street is west, and everything on the other side is east. Cross-streets are numbered, starting at the lake. The higher the number, the farther from the lake you are. Whether you walk or drive, check out West Sixth Street, once known as Millionaire's Row, where many elegant Victorian mansions still stand.

The US Niagara.

At the foot of State Street, on the city's bayfront, you will find the tallest of the Great Lakes tall ships, the US *Niagara*—unless she happens to be out on a sailing mission. Near her berth is the 187-foot Bicentennial Tower with two observation decks from which there are spectacular views of the lake.

Erie is a quiet, unhurried city of 105,000 people. General Electric is the biggest employer and Presque Isle (PRESK-ILL) is where everyone goes to sun and swim. On a warm summer evening, you're likely to pass people in bright blue T-shirts with a Seawolves logo on the pocket. They're heading for the new Jerry Uht Baseball Field, where the Erie Seawolves baseball team is playing. Erie's sports fans are equally enthusiastic about their hockey team, the Sea Otters.

◆ ERIE COUNTY HISTORICAL SOCIETY

For interesting trips through the backroads and around the city, stop by the Historical Society and pick up their driving-tour maps. The society maintains a superb collection of historical documents and a vast photographic archive, including glass plate photographic negatives taken from the Francis J. Bassett Collection, offering detailed views of life in Waterford and Erie from the late 1800s through the early 1900s. *State St. off the Bayfront Parkway; 814-454-1813.*

NORTHWEST
ERIE

From the historical society, you can walk next door to the **Cashier's House,** an 1839 Greek revival townhouse that served as the residence of Peter Benson, the chief executive of the Erie branch of the U.S. Bank of Pennsylvania. The house has been preserved as a typical example of the dwellings of the wealthy built during Erie's heyday in the mid- and late 1800s. Designed by noted Philadelphia architect William Kelly, the house has a no-nonsense, conservative exterior hiding an ornate interior—expensive wood carvings, marble fireplace mantels, and hardwood plank flooring. *Across the street from the Historical Society.*

◆ US *NIAGARA*

On September 10, 1813, the US *Niagara,* with Com. Oliver Hazard Perry in command, won the Battle of Lake Erie in the War of 1812. Perry's flagship, the *Lawrence,* had endured two hours of cannon fire from the British squadron, crippling it and either killing or wounding over 80 percent of his crew. Re-establishing himself aboard the *Niagara,* and bearing his signature flag with the words, "Don't Give Up the Ship," Perry daringly re-engaged the enemy and emerged victorious, the first time in naval history that an entire British squadron had been captured.

This print shows Com. Oliver Hazard Perry being rowed to the Niagara *after his ship, the* Lawrence, *was sunk. (Courtesy the Old Print Shop, New York)*

Following his victory, Commodore Perry sent the famous message: "We have met the enemy and he is ours." His victory essentially won the War of 1812, but during the era when schooners were routinely scavenged for useful materials, then scuttled in deep water, the victorious *Niagara* met that ignominious fate. It was returned to its rightful place in history in 1913, when a group of history buffs raised the money to pull the brig from the bay and rebuild it. The original craft finally fell apart in the 1980s but the Erie Historical Society came to the rescue, building a new version from the original plans. Early shipbuilding techniques were used, with nearly 100 pieces of the original vessel included.

The *Niagara* was re-commissioned in 1990 and now has the honor of being the flagship and symbol of the state of Pennsylvania. The reconstructed, two-masted, square-rigged vessel is officially berthed at the new Erie Maritime Museum on the bayfront. *Erie Maritime Museum; 150 East Front St.; 814-871-4596.*

◆ ERIE HISTORICAL MUSEUM AND PLANETARIUM

Exhibits on Erie's boating history are housed in the old Watson-Curtze mansion, an 1891 Richardsonian Romanesque creation with floors of exotic inlaid woods, decorative friezes, and coffered ceilings. While the artifacts featured in the exhibits are worthwhile, the mansion itself is a prime example of the good life that existed along Millionaire's Row on West Sixth Street. A planetarium is housed in the carriage house on the estate's grounds. *Historical Museum and mansion; 356 West Sixth St.; 814-871-5790.*

◆ FIREFIGHTERS HISTORICAL MUSEUM

Unconnected to Lake Erie history but nevertheless well worth a visit is this detailed homage to the firefighting profession featuring exhibits from around the world. Located in a retired Erie firehouse, the museum houses artifacts that include an 1889 Remington Howe horse-pulled water wagon and an interactive demonstration of the ancient system of fire call-boxes. The guides working here are all connected to firefighting and know the stories behind every piece on display. *Firefighters Museum, 428 Chestnut St.; 814-456-5969.*

Pufferbelly, a restaurant on French Street, also recalls the old days of the Erie Fire Department. It was Fire House No. 1, built in 1907 and used until 1979. On the walls are old fire-fighting equipment and pictures of the late 1800s when steam pumpers and engines (or "pufferbellies") put out fires in the city. Firehouse chili is on the menu.

■ PRESQUE ISLE STATE PARK   *map page 257, B-1*

Pennsylvania would be a land-locked state, were it not for a tiny bit of Lake Erie shoreline that appears to have been wrested away from New York State. Nature placed Presque Isle on this particular bit of shoreline, as if to give a special blessing to northwest Pennsylvania. Presque Isle is treasured by nearby residents who go there for water sports, kite-flying, and picnics, and often just for the serenity of looking out over the open water. Migratory birds also recognize that this is a likely place to stop.

The northern curve of the peninsula (which forms the isle) is mostly fringed by sandy beaches and is the favored haunt of three different types of sandpipers. The wetland areas on the southern facing, innershore are the domain of the blue herons, who strut majestically through the reeds. The song of a whippoorwill provides the soundscape for a quiet afternoon walk.

The peninsula's Misery Bay is where Com. Oliver Hazard Perry's second flagship, the *Niagara,* was scuttled in 1820. The Perry monument is at Crystal Point on Presque Isle.

(above) A dramatic sunset over Lake Erie, as viewed from Presque Isle.

(opposite) The Presque Isle Lighthouse was built in 1872.

Presque Isle is a National Natural Landmark, considered one the world's premier venues to study the ecological succession of plants. More than 500 species of plants grow here in several specific habitats reflecting the progression of development (succession) from dune stage, pond stage, through to climax, or final, forest stage. *Birder's World* magazine also calls it one of the top birding spots in the country, with at least 321 species spotted. In addition, 47 species of mammals have been recorded.

Presque Isle can be visited any time of the year (although it's awfully cold in winter). You'll find an 1872 lighthouse that overlooks the lakeshore; a 14-mile loop road connects the sites, and following it is a useful way to view autumn foliage or winter ice dunes.

Just before the park entrance, in the midst of an area that is typical seashore honky tonk, is Waldameer Park & Water World, a family park with some of the longest and steepest water slides in the country. Rides include a giant Ferris wheel that swings upward 100 feet in the air on the rise overlooking the peninsula.

Presque Isle State Park: Exit 5 on I-90 to Rte. 832 North to Sterrettania Rd., which becomes Peninsula Dr. and leads to the park; 814-833-7424.

Sunfish on Lake Erie, off the coast of Presque Isle.

■ GRAPE-GROWING REGION   *map page 257, B/C-1*

About 15 miles east of Erie is grape-growing country. While most of the grapes you'll see in this region are of the sweet Concord variety, and end up in jars of Welch's jams, jellies, or juice, processed at the local Welch's plant, some are wine varietals grown by local vintners. Wineries in the area are listed below.

(To bicycle through the area, drop by Lake Country Bike in the town of North East for maps and rentals. *21 E. Main St.; www.lakecountrybike.com.*)

Heritage Wine Cellars
12162 E. Main St. (Rte. 20);
814-725-8015
Run by five generations of the Bostwick family; it has the largest tasting room in the area and a restaurant too.

Mazza Vineyards
11815 E. Lake Rd. (Rte. 5);
814-725-8695
A hilly estate overlooking Lake Erie along scenic East Lake Road. Most crowded during its Labor Day festival. Mazza is known for its ice wine, a sweet dessert wine.

Penn Shore Winery
10225 E. Lake Rd.(Rte. 5);
814-725-8688
Vineyard views and wine and cheese tasting parties. Their specialty is kir, a dessert wine made from black currants.

Presque Isle Wine Cellars
9440 Buffalo Rd., off Rte. 20;
814-725-1314
Vineyard views and wine tasting. They produce cabernet sauvignon and chadonnay.

■ SOUTH FROM ERIE   *map page 257-B-1*

South from Erie, Route 19 quickly leaves the strip malls behind and enters rolling farm country sparsely dotted with modest homes on endless lawns, and the occasional tackle shop, and farm equipment dealer.

◆ WATERFORD   *map page 257-B-2*

Picturesque Waterford can take you quite by surprise. The town is dominated by the Eagle Hotel which is no longer run as a hotel, but as a historical exhibit operated by the Fort LeBoeuf Museum. The upper floors are open to the public and are jammed with interesting bric-a-brac. The first floor is now inhabited by a lively restaurant, Kellie's Sugar 'n Spice. At lunchtime it swarms with local businesspeople and grandmothers (their grandchildren trailing them like goslings), but rarely a tourist. Although Waterford offers little in the way of shops, the taxidermist keeps his shop door open and the couple who runs it is extremely friendly. When I visited they apologized for the strange aroma in the place, explaining that there was a bear's head being boiled in the back room. It's in such conversations that one learns the location of the local covered bridge.

Next to the hotel is a famous statue of George Washington. It faces the Fort LeBoeuf Museum and is close to the site of the old fort where Washington presented Britain's demands that the French leave the territory. Washington was treated cordially, but the consequence was the French and Indian War. The fort is no longer there but you can see a model of it in the museum. There are many exhibits on local history and information on curiosities such as the intriguing octagonal house in nearby Cambridge Springs. *Eagle Hotel (Kellie's Sugar 'n Spice), 32 High St.; 814-796-0060.*

♦ CAMBRIDGE SPRINGS   *map page 257-B-2*

A little farther down Route 19 lies splendid Cambridge Springs. In its heyday, during the Victorian era, the town hosted 10,000 people at a time, all because of the purported healing properties of the mineral waters that flow from local springs. Most of the magnificent old hotels are long gone, but the gorgeous Riverside Inn still carries on much of the tradition.

A walking tour of the town might include the intriguing octagonal house (now a private residence) which was built as a springhouse for taking the waters. To some, the more important waters in Cambridge Springs are those of French Creek. The creek was a major waterway for Indians and for French fur traders. It remained the primary access to the area until the coming of the railway. The bed of French Creek is especially deep near Cambridge Springs.

You can rent canoes from Budd and Carol Luce, who explained that they can drop off and pick up at any of 13 or more access points along French Creek and its tributaries. We put in for a leisurely paddle, imagining ourselves as intrepid French fur traders. If you manage to trap any furs, you can take them back to the taxidermy shop in Waterford. *Riverside Inn, One Fountain Ave.; 800-964-5173 or 814-398-4645. French Creek Canoe & Kayak, Rtes. 6N and 19; 4 miles south of Waterford; 814-796-3366.*

■ OIL COUNTRY   *map page 257, C-3*

Pennsylvania's Oil Heritage Region is not bleak—as a visitor from California or Texas might expect. Rather, it's a hilly, wooded, area just south of Allegheny National Forest, with lovely small towns, well worth visiting. Life may not be as exciting now in places like Pithole (15,000 people in 1865, abandoned by 1867) but they provide a look into those days gone by.

The country's first oil well was drilled near Titusville in 1859. Soon the region was pockmarked with "black gold" wells. Scores of small businessmen from sleepy towns such as Franklin, Oil City, and Pithole became millionaires virtually overnight. The boom continued until the early 1900s when more efficient extraction methods made backyard oil wells obsolete.

◆ DRAKE WELL MUSEUM   *map page 257, C-3*

Drake Well Museum south of Titusville provides a detailed history of the era when black gold was Pennsylvania's most valuable commodity. Exhibits tell the story of New York lawyer and entrepreneur George Bissell, who was fascinated by petroleum, then viewed as a messy substitute for kerosene. Working with a Yale University chemistry professor, Bissell developed a variety of uses for the product. In

Drake Well Museum just south of Titusville.

During Pennsylvania's oil boom days, derricks seemed to pop up everywhere.
(Drake Well Museum, Titusville)

order to get his petroleum products to market, though, he had to get it out of the ground in a way that would assure sufficient quantities to cover his extraction costs. The person who worked out the details was a retired railroad conductor, Edwin Drake, who built the first successful oil well in the United States on Bissell's country estate near Titusville.

A month after Drake perfected the first oil well machinery, a *New York Times* reporter wrote about the "excitement attendant on the discovery of this vast source of oil...fully equal to what I saw in California when a large lump of gold was accidentally turned out."

Soon well operations were chugging throughout the region and the refined petroleum was selling well, especially as "Rock Oil," a medicine that promised "wonderful curative powers." *Drake Well Museum, E. Bloss St. just south of Titusville on PA 8; 814-827-2797.*

◆ OIL CREEK STATE PARK AND TRAILS *map page 257, C-3*

Paralleling both sides of Oil Creek between Drake Well Museum to the north and the main park entrance at Petroleum Center, this 37-mile loop hike has both a walking and biking trail, with a 500-foot elevation change along the Westside trail. Four adults per day are permitted on the trail, and shelters with water and toilet facilities are strategically placed, but reservations must be made to use them.

In the 1860s oil wells, hamlets, and refineries lined this 13-mile stretch of the creek. Directions and maps at the main entrance park office. *Follow signs off Rte. 8 one mile north of Roseville. Oil Creek State Park, Oil City; 814-676-5915.*

◆ FRANKLIN *map page 257, B-3/4*

Few of the oil prospectors who flocked to this area in search of black gold realized their dreams, but many who rode the oil wave successfully came from the modest little town of Franklin which was turned into a trading and management center for the oil industry in the years after Drake's discovery.

Downtown Franklin. (photo by Kit Duane)

Thanks to the oil boom in this area, late-19th-century mansions line the streets of even very small towns.

Franklin remains a picturesque town with its fine, white-topped courthouse and wide streets. Buildings in the downtown business area are of red brick with white stone lintels and sidewalks are graced with elegant cast-iron street lamps. Within the town's park is a huge three-tiered cast-iron fountain, and several memorials, one placed there by a veteran of the Mexican War and dedicated to his mother. The setting is peaceful, lushly green, and quiet, the sky on a clear day, bright blue and filled with white cumulus clouds.

Late-19th-century mansions along Liberty, Miller Park, and Adelaide neighborhoods were built between 1860 and 1890 and range from Queen Anne to true Victorian to Arts and Crafts. Tours of some homes are available. *Venango County Historical Society, 301 S. Park St.; 814-437-2275.*

♦ **US 62 ABOVE OIL CITY**   *map page 257, C&D-3*

Above Oil City, you'll drive beneath green trees and among rolling hills. As you near McPhearson Road and the Allegheny General Store, you'll see signs along the road advertising their goods: old fashioned ring bologna, slab bacon, and Amish baked goods. Step inside the store for a homemade sandwich, or excellent cookies and breads, locally made jams and maple syrup.

As you continue north, hardwood forest is replaced by connifers. By Tionesta Lake the river is wide and beautiful, and the road, in September, is lined with goldenrod.

■ ALLEGHENY RIVER   *map page 257, C-3 & D-2*

From Oil City north to Kinzua Dam, the Allegheny River has been designated as a Recreational Waterway under the federal Wild and Scenic Rivers Act.

The drive along US 62, which follows the Allegheny River from Franklin to Tionesta and north past Warren, follows the river, which is slow moving, green, and peaceful. Canoe outfitters advertise their services, and there are several places to put in for a few hours and then be picked up downstream and brought back to your car. Many people go north to Warren and canoe down the Allegheny, camping on islands along the way.

A farm in Nauvoo in Tioga County.

Eagle Rock near Tionesta (May to mid-October); *814-755-4444.*
Outback Adventures near Tionesta (April to October); *814-589-7359.*
Allegheny Outfitters in Warren; *814-723-1203; allout@penn.com*
Be advised that anyone using outfitters, or canoeing on their own, does so at their own risk. Rates run from $25 a day per canoe for people planning their own pick-up/transportation, to more expensive guided weekend trips providing shuttle service beginning at $75 per person and including guides, meals, and tents. Experience isn't necessary according to river guides, although I have personally tipped over enough canoes to believe you'll benefit from instruction. People who float the river marvel at the beautiful green water and overhanging trees; some report seeing bald eagles, snapping turtles, great blue herons, and Canada geese.

■ ALLEGHENY NATIONAL FOREST   *map page 257, D&E-3*

The Allegheny National Forest is notable both for its rugged beauty and for its status as one of the few remnants of the ancient forest that used to cover most of the eastern United States. *Allegheny National Forest Headquarters; 222 Liberty St. in Warren; 814-723-5150.*

◆ HEARTS CONTENT RECREATION AREA   *map page 257, D-3*

This is a good place to look for virgin stands of ancient trees. Here one can find magnificent examples of Eastern hemlock, black cherry, sugar maple, and white pine, some as old as 300 to 400 years. The trail from Heart's Content to Minister Creek passes through some of these stands, which often have a dense understory of large ferns. The trail has an atmosphere of dark mystery, but astonishing views over the trees can be had by climbing the huge boulders along the way. The view is of ridge after forested ridge extending into the distance. This trail makes a good backpacking trip with good campsites to be found all along the way. Day hikes from either trailhead can be just as rewarding. A second, west-running 12-mile loop trail traverses the valleys and hills of nearby **Hickory Creek Wilderness Area** with meadows, hardwood forest, and narrow Jack's Run Creek, lined with hemlocks. *15 miles southwest of Warren; for information call Allegheny National Forest in Warren; 814-723-5150.*

◆ COUNTRY ROUTE ON 666   *map page 257, D-3*

Route 666 cuts east through wooded valleys, pine forest, and a few small towns, then settles into a steady diet of forest and wildland. The many side roads wind through woods, small farms with distinctive red barns and silos, and past many small white houses backed by forest and surrounded by lawn. It's an easy and enjoyable place to become somewhat lost; the last time I was wandering about turning this way and that, I came across seven wild turkeys.

◆ COOK FOREST STATE PARK
   AND THE CLARION RIVER   *map page 257, D-4*

Just south of the Allegheny National Forest is Cook Forest State Park. This delightful park was established by a private landowner, wanting to save his land from logging. The park is a popular spot, with an interpretive center, craft shops, and frequent music festivals. Be sure to climb the old fire tower for the view, and then take time to relax by the Clarion River and contemplate its deep and brooding green waters. *814-744-8407.*

◆ ELK COUNTY   *map page 257, F-3&4*

Just east of the Allegheny National Forest in Elk County is Elk State Forest where herds of elk have been re-established by the state. The plan has caused some controversy because elk from western states were introduced to encourage the development of the local herds. Being larger than the indigenous variety, they have produced a strain of voracious eaters with enormous racks of antlers. In order to placate local farmers, crops have been planted especially for the elk. Locals tell stories of seeing elk with especially large racks, and nature photographers are often observed seeking hard evidence to support what sounds occasionally like yet another fish story. **St Mary's,** the largest town in Elk County, would be a good place to seek advice on where the elk dude with the largest rack might be hanging out.

◆ AUTUMN LEAVES DRIVING TOURS

Between mid-September and mid-October backroads are vivid with color throughout the Alleghenies. For tours in this area see map page 257; routes are marked. *Because leaves change color depending on each year's weather, call ahead to the forest headquarters in Warren; 814-723-5150.*

NORTHWEST
ALLEGHENY FOREST

The Grand Canyon of Pennsylvania.

◆ GRAND CANYON OF PENNSYLVANIA   *map page 10–11*

The cliffs of this 50-mile gorge in some places rise a thousand feet above fast-flowing Pine Creek. Canoeists, kayakers, and whitewater rafters all come here to enjoy their sport. *For outfitters try Pine Creek Outfitters in Wellsboro; 570-724-3003.*

A "rail trail" follows the east bank of Pine Creek into the Grand Canyon of Pennsylvania, and the trailhead is found seven miles southwest of Wellsboro. Along the way you can fish for trout and small-mouth bass. In spring wildflowers are abundant, and in fall the hills are bright with the color of autumn leaves. *For maps and information call the Tioga State Forest District Office at One Nessnuk Lane in Wellsboro; 570-724-2868.*

*A polka dance in St. Mary's in Elk County (above)
and one of the elk the county is known for. (below)*

FOOD & LODGING

CHAIN LODGINGS IN PENNSYLVANIA

Best Western 800-528-1234	Holiday Inn 800-465-4329
Comfort Inn 800-228-5150	Hyatt 800-233-1234
Day's Inn 800-325-2525	Marriott 800-228-9290
Doubletree 800-222-8733	Radisson 800-333-3333
Hampton Inn 800-426-7866	Sheraton 800-325-3535
Hilton 800-445-8667	Westin 800-228-3000

Room rates:
Per night, per room, double occupancy:
$ = under $60; $$ = $60–95; $$$ = $95–125; $$$$ = over $125

Restaurant prices:
Per person, not including drinks, tax, and tips:
$ = under $10; $$ = $10–20; $$$ = over $20

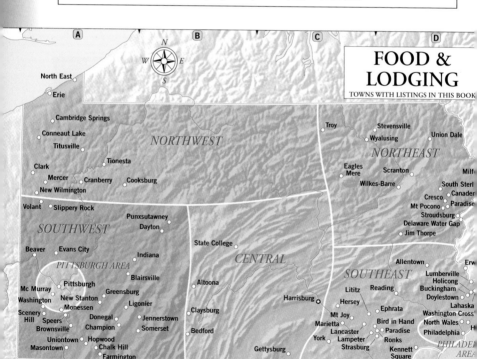

FOOD & LODGING

TOWNS WITH LISTINGS IN THIS BOOK

INDEX OF LISTINGS IN THIS BOOK

FOOD & LODGING

Altoona *map B-3*

X **Allegro Ristorante.** 3926 Broad Ave. at 40th St.; 814-946-5216 $$
For 20 years, this has been the place Altoona residents go for special occasions—Northern Italian food served in a refined atmosphere accented with fine linens, flowers, and candles. Veal, steaks, chops, and seafood also served. Lunch only on Friday, dinner Monday through Saturday.

X **Lena's Cafe.** 2000 Eighth Ave.; 814-943-9655 $
Who needs atmosphere when the food is so good? Wonderful, classic Italian food served in the oldest Italian restaurant in the county, in business 60 years.

Beaver/Beaver Falls *map A-2*

X **Giuseppe's.** Rte. 18, Beaver Falls; 724-843-5656 $$
This neighborhood Italian restaurant specializes in pastas, steaks, seafood, and hot Italian dressing on your salad. The ricotta-stuffed manicotti with meat sauce is terrific.

X **The Wooden Angel.** 308 Leopard Lane at Sharon Rd. on Bridgewater–Beaver border; 724-774-7880 $$-$$$
Superb all-American wine list and fine American fare to enjoy with it. Big, attractive restaurant with exposed brick walls and spotlights accenting paintings. Upstairs cafe serves light fare.

TODD HOUSE

⊞ **Todd House.** 330 Third St., Beaver; 724-775-1424 $-$$
Located on the main street of Beaver, this quaint B&B has six bedrooms with private or shared baths, two tasteful parlors, and a dining room decorated with Victorian antiques. Full breakfast.

Bedford *map B-3*

X **Gamble Mill Tavern.** 160 Dunlop St., Bellefonte, off Rte. 150; 814-355-7764 $
Romantic restaurant in an old mill. The water wheel may not run anymore, but the tavern has outstanding decor. Tradi-tional menu of beef, chicken, and pastas. Good desserts.

X **Jean Bonnet Restaurant.** Jct. of Rtes. 30 and 31; 814-623-2250 $
Meals are served in the ground floor restaurant of the tavern. Menus span the generations, from old-time oatmeal cake to contemporary dishes such as marinat-ed chicken salad. Lunch and dinner open to the public; breakfast for over-night guests only.

Food & Lodging map, page 276; index of listings by region/chapter, page 277.

✗ **Oralee's Golden Eagle.** 131 E. Pitt St.; 814-624-0800 $-$$
Breakfast is only for overnight guests; lunch and dinner is open to public. Menu changes, but you can usually count on quiche, sandwiches, salmon, steak, and pastas.

⊡ **Jean Bonnet Tavern.** Jct. of Rtes. 30 and 31; 814-623-2250 $
In use since 1760, the tavern boasts thick fieldstone walls, huge fireplaces, and chestnut beams. Four guest rooms; breakfast included.

⊡ **Oralee's Golden Eagle.** 131 E. Pitt St.; 814-624-0800 $-$$
Renovated colonial tavern with 11 comfortable guest rooms. Full breakfast included, and if you're lucky it will be a stack of sumptuous Belgian waffles.

Blairsville *map A-3*

⊡ **Chestnut Ridge Inn on the Green.** Rte. 22 and Rte. 119; 724-459-7191 $-$$$
Lunch in the La Fleur room, dinner in the elegant Crystal Terrace, Sunday brunch in big London Room. Take time to look around the beautiful building, with all its antiques and artwork. The view outside, over the golf course and wooded hills, is worth a lingering look, too. Confit of leg of duck with roasted duck breast is a big seller at dinner.

Brownsville *map A-3*

✗ **Caleigh's Thompson House.** 815 Water St.; 724-785-4744 $$
Continental-Italian restaurant located on the first floor of a mansion built in 1906 by the heir to a whiskey distillery fortune. Ambitious menu with different twists to popular entrees. Browse the boutique shops on the second floor before dinner.

Buckingham *map D-3*

✗ **Baci Ristorante & Heart of Oak Pub.** Rtes. 202 & 413; 215-794-7784 $-$$
A fireplace and stone walls set the mood of this restaurant specializing in Northern Italian classics such as veal piccata, calamari, bruschetta, and Italian soups. There's outside dining in pleasant weather and live entertainment in the pub.

Cambridge Springs *map A-1*

✗ **Concord Dining Room.** In the Riverside Inn, 1 Fountain Ave.; 800-964-5173 or 814-398-4645 $-$$
Nothing Victorian about the menu served in the big, sunny dining room or in the Riverside Lounge. Main course salads and sandwiches at lunch; prime rib, steaks, seafood, chicken, veal, and a light menu at dinner.

✗ **On the Green.** 24527 Rte. 19, at the Riverside Golf Course; 814-398-4692 $-$$
Overlooks the final holes of the golf course, which is not connected with the Riverside Inn. Lunch daily; dinner on Friday and Saturday, April to October.

⊡ **Riverside Inn.** 1 Fountain Ave.; 800-964-5173 or 814-398-4645 $$
The Victorian decor has been faithfully

preserved, from the caged cashier's window of frosted glass and gleaming marble counter just inside the entrance, to the 74 spacious guest rooms pleasantly devoid of televisions or telephones. Open from April through mid-December. Popular dinner theater in the hotel. Packages available for inclusion of breakfast or all meals, dinner theater, or golf.

RIVERSIDE INN

Canadenisis *map D-2*

✕ **Frog Town Inn.** Box 689;
570-595-6282 $$
Specialties include house-smoked salmon, grilled portabello mushrooms, roast duckling with blackberry brandy sauce, and rack of lamb roasted with dijon mustard and herbed bread crumbs.

▦ **Brookview Manor Bed &Breakfast Inn.**
S.R. 447 1 mile south of S.R. 390;
570-595-2451 or 800-585-7974 $$
Nine Victorian and country-style guestrooms with fireplaces or jacuzzis. This frame house, built in 1911, is perched on a hill with access to several acres of hiking trails, one of which leads to a hidden waterfall.

Chalk Hill *map A-3*

✕ **Stone House Restaurant.** Rte. 40 East,
2.2 miles from Fort Necessity;
724-329-8876 $$
Up-to-date, varied menu prepared by chef/owner Carl Fazio. Excellent spinach and brie salad. General George C. Marshall grew up near here and once told how he and his friends liked to go the old Stone House for chicken and dumplings, the best he ever tasted. It's still on the menu; you decide.

▦ **Stone House.** Rte. 40 East, 2.2 miles
from Fort Necessity; 724-329-8876 $$$
One of the original wayside inns on the National Road, opening in 1822. Today it has 10 handsome Victorian guest rooms, with either private or shared baths. Continental breakfast included. Close to Ohiopyle and Fallingwater.

Champion *map A-3*

✕ **Helen's Seven Springs.** R.R. 1, bet.
Somerset and Donegal; 814-352-7777,
ext. 7691 $$$
Don't let the rustic atmosphere fool you. This is actually a formal and sophisticated restaurant with waiters in tuxedos preparing lamb chops and chateaubriand tableside. Menu changes seasonally. Dinner only.

▦ **Seven Springs Mountain Resort.**
R.R. 1, bet. Somerset and Donegal; 800-452-2223 or 814-352-7777 $$$$
Big resort (375 rooms) with summer and winter activities. Price includes breakfast buffet.

SEVEN SPRINGS MOUNTAIN RESORT

Clark *map A-2*

✕ **Ashley's at Tara.** 2844 Lake Rd.; 800-782-2803 $$$
First-rate restaurant inside Tara country inn. Elegant seven-course dinners. Dinner guests may also tour the mansion to see all the *Gone With the Wind* memorabilia and other antiques. Reserve a day in advance. More casual are lunch and dinner in Tara's **Stonewall Tavern.**

🛏 **Tara.** 2844 Lake Rd.; 800-782-2803 $$$$
Fine, one-of-a-kind country inn, all about *Gone With the Wind.* Lots of antiques, and rooms have names like Fiddle Dee Dee and Miss Melanie's. Most have decidedly un—Scarlett O'Hara jacuzzis. Has to be seen to be believed.

Claysburg *map B-3*

🛏 **Blue Knob Four Seasons Resort.** Off I-99, bet. Bedford and Altoona; 800-458-3403 or 814-239-5111 $$
More than 100 condos with efficiency kitchens, open year-round. Rates higher

in the winter. Indoor and outdoor swimming, tennis, golf, and winter sports.

Conneaut Lake *map A-1*

✕ **Silver Shores on the Lake.** Rte. 322 on Conneaut Lake; 814-382-4471 $
This waterfront restaurant offers a spectacular setting to watch sunsets over the lake. Sandwiches, salads, varied American fare.

✕ **Victorian Room.** In the Hotel Conneaut, Rte. 16 inside Conneaut Lake Park; 814-382-5115 $
Big dining room with window-walls facing the lake. Breakfast and dinner only.

🛏 **Hotel Conneaut.** Rte. 16 inside Conneaut Lake Park; 814-382-5115 $
Renovated Victorian-style hotel, with an inviting wrap-around porch looking out onto the lake.

Cooksburg *map A-2*

✕ **Gateway Lodge.** Rte. 36; 814-744-8017 or 800-843-6862 $$
This quaint restaurant is known for their chicken salad (recipe was printed in *Gourmet* and it really is good); a dessert called Chocolate Lover's Delight (scoops of ice cream inside layers of rich chocolate cake, chocolate sauce over the top); and a 325-bottle wine list.

🛏 **Gateway Lodge.** Rte. 36; 814-744-8017 or 800-843-6862 $$$- $$$$
This lodge built in 1934 of pine and hemlock logs with gnarled chestnut

Food & Lodging map, page 276; index of listings by region/chapter, page 277.

walls has an indoor pool, sauna, and a newer addition. Cottages available, too. Every season offers an activity: bird-watching, hiking, summer theater, fishing, skiing, and leaf-peeping. Price includes breakfast; weekend and weekly packages available. No smoking.

GATEWAY LODGE

Cranberry *map A-2*

✗ **Tremont House.** In Sheraton Inn North, 910 Sheraton Dr.; 724-776-6900; $$-$$$
One-time chef for Leona Helmsley serves up imaginative menu. Example: roasted rack of lamb with chestnut crust and white wine shallot mint sauce.

Crescent Lodge. Paradise Valley, Jct. of Rtes. 191 & 940; 570-595-7486 or 800-392-9400 $-$$
Stay in the lodge or in one of the separate cottages beautifully furnished with canopy beds, sitting rooms, jacuzzis, and fireplaces. The beautifully landscaped grounds have hiking and fitness trails, an outdoor pool and a tennis court. Excellent dining room in the lodge.

Sheraton Inn North. 910 Sheraton Dr.; 724-776-6900 $$$
This five-story hotel has 200 rooms featuring modern amenities and a very good restaurant.

Cresco *map D-2*

The Homestead Inn. Sandspring Dr. off Rte. 390; 570-595-3171 $$-$$$
Tucked away in the woods, this peaceful restaurant has been one of the Poconos' best for several decades. Specialties include baby crab cakes with a roasted sweet red pepper sauce, stuffed pork loin, and rack of lamb. Dinners are inclusive. Open daily for dinner; closed Mondays from September to May.

Delaware Water Gap *map FD-2*

Dingmans Ferry Campground. Rte. 209, Dingmans Ferry; 570-828-2266 $
The official (and only) park camp has tent sites for $27 per night, first come first served. Canoe camping is also available in designated areas for those paddling along the river.

The Shepard House B&B. 108 Shepard Ave.; 570-424-9779 $
The seafoam-green Shepard House looks out over the valley. It has a side porch and four lovely country guest rooms. Breakfast is included.

Water Gap Country Club. Mountain Rd.; 570-476-0300 $
A full 18-hole golf course and simple countryside resort nestled in the Gap's

Food & Lodging map, page 276; index of listings by region/chapter, page 277.

mountains. There are 23 guest rooms and several two-bedroom cabins on the property. No restaurant on premises.

WATER GAP COUNTRY CLUB

Donegal *map A-3*

✗ **Lesley's Mountain View Bed & Breakfast.** 10 Mountain View Rd.; 800-392-7773 $$$
Elegant restaurant in the barn, outfitted with Chippendale furniture, now is open to the public, Wednesday through Saturday evenings. Swells who have big summer homes in the mountains come for the baked brie in puff pastry and Mountain View Wellington, paired with a selection of wines.

LESLEY'S MOUNTAIN VIEW

⊞ **Lesley's Mountain View Bed & Breakfast.** 10 Mountain View Rd.; 800-392-7773 $$$-$$$$
Four rooms in an 1850s farmhouse and another four in a chestnut barn, furnished with 18th-century American antiques and blessed with panoramic views of the Laurel Mountains. For 12 years, skiers, hikers, and tourists heading for nearby Fallingwater have spent a night here. Full breakfast.

Doylestown *map D-3*

✗ **Black Walnut Restaurant.** 80 W. State St.; 215-348-0708 $$$
Pale yellow liven up the walls inside this intimate and charming restaurant in an 1846 townhouse. Specialties include cedar-planked salmon, duck, and many mushroom dishes. There's outdoor dining during warm-weather months. Dinner only; closed Mondays.

⊞ **Sign of the Sorrel Horse.**
4424 Old Easton Rd.; 215-230-9999 $$
A rustic 1714 grist mill skillfully turned into an inn with five romantic guest rooms by its French proprietress. The inn's gourmet meals, served in the elegant Escoffier Room, have garnered many awards.

Eagle's Mere *map C-2*

⊞ **Eagle's Mere Inn.** Mary Ave.; 570-525-3273 or 800-426-3273 $$$
An 1887 country inn set on land given to William Penn and later owned by

FOOD & LODGING

Benjamin Rush, a signer of the Declaration of Independence. The area was developed as a resort in the 1800s and includes a country club, lake, and quaint shops. Guests have golf privileges at Eagle's Mere Country Club. Area activities include fishing, bicycling, horseback riding, and nature walks. There's an excellent dining room, too.

Ephrata map D-3

✕ **Doneckers Restaurant.** 333 N. State St.; 717-738-9501 $-$$$
The innovative French cuisine served in the fine-dining room has been lauded by *Gourmet* magazine, but the two-story restaurant also features great food in **Doneckers Bistro** (wild mushroom soup, roasted pork chops) and light fare such as quiche, salads, and sandwiches.

CLEARVIEW FARMS B&B

⊞ **Clearview Farm B&B.** 355 Clearview Rd.; 717-733-6333 $$
This lovingly restored 1814 limestone farmhouse is set among 200 bucolic acres of farmland, and is impeccably decorated with a fabulous array of an-

tiques. The breakfasts are hearty and healthy and served by candlelight. Open country surrounding the inn is perfect for a therapeutic walk. Five guestrooms.

⊞ **Doneckers.** 318-324 N. State St.; 717-738-9502 $-$$$
The Doneckers is really a complex consisting of four separate lodgings, a good French restaurant, shopping center, and a farmers market. All four inns—the Guesthouse, the Homestead, the 1770 House, and the Gerhart House—are dressed up in antiques and feature wonderful breakfasts and gracious hosts.

HISTORIC SMITHTON INN

⊞ **The Historic Smithton Inn.** 900 W. Main St.; 717-733-6094 $$-$$$
Wonderfully restored brick and stone building that has been operated as an inn for over 236 years. Fireplaces in each room, comfortable beds, and a hearty breakfast (if you're lucky, it'll be plate-sized, mouth-watering blueberry pancakes) is included. The small library has many books on the Amish and the proprietors are Pennsylvania Dutch and glad to impart their knowledge on the customs and culture.

Food & Lodging map, page 276; index of listings by region/chapter, page 277.

Erie *map A-1*

✕ **1000 French.** 10th and French Sts.; 814-454-6896 $-$$
Breakfast, lunch, and dinner. Close to Erie's ballfield. Lamb chops, pesto-grilled chicken. No credit cards.

✕ **Pie in the Sky Cafe.** 463 W. Eighth St.; 814-459-8638 $$
Don't let the scruffy outside fool you, because it's fine eating inside. Each weekend the menu is different, usually featuring a dozen selections, such as pork loin stuffed with wild rice and apricots with a blue cheese sauce.

✕ **Pufferbelly.** 414 French St.; 814-454-1557 $$
Renovated fire house with lots of touches from the old days, including the original brass pole firemen slid down. Name is a tribute to the steam pumpers and engines of the old days. Creative entrees such as horseradish-crusted salmon.

✕ **Waterfront.** 4 State St.; 814-459-0606 $$
At the foot of the Bicentenial Tower and right on Lake Erie, across the street from the Smuggler's Wharf, it's known as a power-lunch spot at noon and a romantic setting for dinner. Erie's best restaurant view and best lobster bisque.

🛏 **Avalon Hotel.** 16 W. 10th St.; 1800-822-5011 or 814-459-2220 $$
Comfortable, clean, no-frills, locally owned downtown hotel, formerly a Hilton. Free parking in garage. Eight floors, 196 rooms.

🛏 **Beachcomber Inn.** 2930 W. Sixth St.; 814-838-1961 $
A short walk from Waldameer Park; 58 rooms with baths, some with kitchenettes.

SPENCER HOUSE B&B

🛏 **Spencer House B & B.** 519 W. Sixth St.; 800-890-7263 or 814-454-5984 $$
Five rooms with private baths in a handsome restored Victorian mansion on what was once known as Erie's Millionaire's Row.

Erwinna *map D-3*

EVERMAY-ON-THE-DELAWARE

🛏 **Evermay-on-the-Delaware.** River Rd.; 610-294-9100 $$-$$$

FOOD & LODGING

Twenty-five acres with gardens on the Delaware River is the setting for this manor house and carriage house on the National Historic Register. There are 18 beautifully decorated guest rooms with private baths, and many public rooms to enjoy. A six-course dinner is served on Friday, Saturday, Sunday, and holidays.

Golden Pheasant Inn. 763 River Rd. (Rte. 32); 610-294-9595 or 800-830-4474 $-$$
Between the Delaware River and the canal is this 1857 fieldstone inn. Six antique-filled guest rooms and a detached cottage have queen-size canopy beds. French cuisine by chef-owner Michel Faure is showcased in the inn's full service fireside tavern.

Issac Stover House. 845 River Rd.; 610-294-8044 $$$-$$$$
Federal Victorian mansion overlooking the Delaware River and furnished with a mix of period antiques, collected worldly treasures, and a jumble of Victorian decor. Six rooms; choice of "organic spa" or traditional fattening-but-yummy breakfast included.

Evans City *map A-2*

Clifford's. 514 Upper Harmony Rd.; 724-789-9115 $$$
Tucked away deep in the country on a family farm, it's home-style cooking with many ethnic and contemporary twists. (The owners go to France every winter to brush up on the latest trends.) Fresh rainbow trout in garlic butter, tender

veal roast with a shallot apricot sauce, fresh sea scallops, and homemade rolls coming out of the oven all evening.

Farmington *map A-3*

✕ **Lautrec.** In the Nemacolin Woodlands Resort & Spa, Rte. 40, near Uniontown; 800-422-2736 $$$
Elegant and expensive. Beautiful, wood-lined dining room in Chateau Lafayette. Menu changes seasonally. You can get beluga caviar on ice complemented with chilled Russian vodka as an appetizer for $75, or entrees like pistachio-crusted lamb loin. Dinner only.

Newest of the Nemacolin's restaurants, **Seasons** ($$) is in a newly expanded world-class spa. It features "conscious paleolithic cuisine, a selection of regional, local, and organic ingredients nutritionally balanced to promote optimal vitality." Dinner might be southwestern-style chili-roasted free-range chicken, washed down with a glass of rice milk.

The **Golden Trout** ($) is a cafe where breakfast, lunch, and dinner and a popular Sunday brunch are served. More informal than Lautrec, but just as good.

Nemacolin Woodlands Resort & Spa. Rte. 40, near Uniontown; 800-422-2736 $$$$
One of the nation's premier resorts, featuring two golf courses, an equestrian center, full-service health spa, three swimming pools, tennis courts, and tree-lined lanes on 1,000 acres of the Laurel Highlands. English Tudor lodge with 96 rooms, condos, and 124 more rooms in

the opulent Chateau Lafayette, a copy of the Ritz in Paris. Three full-service restaurants, open to the public, are among nine eateries on the resort.

Gettysburg Area *map C-3*

✕ **Alexander Dobbin Dining Rooms.** 89 Steinwehr Ave.; 717-334-2100 $$ Dine in six historic rooms built in 1776, including The Dining Room, Library, Parlour, Study, and Spinning Room. Enjoy traditional delicacies updated, prepared from fresh ingredients. Delicious homemade breads and desserts such as warm colonial gingerbread. Main dishes include Adams County roast duck, William Penn's pork tenderloin with cherries, drunken scallops, and prime rib of beef.

✕ **The Altland House.** Center Square, Rte. 30, Abbottstown; 717-259-9535 $-$$ Located 15 miles east of Gettysburg, this was one of President Eisenhower's favorite eating establishments. Operated as a public tavern in 1790, the home has undergone many renovations but still retains its genteel country charm. Best known for its turtle soup, chicken waffles, and crab casserole, the restaurant offers contemporary cuisine at lunch, dinner, and Sunday brunch. *Central Pennsylvania Magazine* voted it the finest restaurant in Adams County. Lighter, informal fare is served in the downstairs **Underside Restaurant and Bar,** which also offers entertainment Friday and Saturday nights.

✕ **Centuries on the Square.** One Lincoln Sq.; 717-337-2000 $-$$ Located in the Gettysburg Hotel, this casual fine-dining restaurant has picture windows that look out onto Lincoln Square and Windsor chairs pulled up to the cloth-covered dining tables. A Continental menu including chicken Chesapeake, Woodman steak, and seafood is served in the fireplace-cozy dining room, with more casual service in the outdoor cafe (weather permitting).

✕ **Farnsworth House Inn.** 401 Baltimore St.; 717-334-8838 $-$$ This inn was once occupied by Confederate sharpshooters during the Civil War. Specialties in the candle-lit dining room are recipes from the innkeepers' great grandmothers including spoon bread, game pie, goober pea (peanut) soup, sweet potato pudding, rum cream pie, and black walnut apple cake. The dinner menu is also available in an open-air garden along a stone-lined stream that once provided water for both the Union and Confederate troops. The **Killer Angel Tavern** behind the restaurant was used as the officers club for the film *Gettysburg.*

✕ **Gingerbread Man.** 217 Steinwehr Ave.; 717-334-1100 $ This casual eatery specializes in soups and hot sandwiches, with steaks and seafood served at dinner. Always on the menu are cream of crab and French onion soups, and hot crab dip served in a bread bowl. Large variety of imported and Pennsylvania-brewed beers.

Food & Lodging map, page 276; index of listings by region/chapter, page 277.

X **The Herr Tavern and Publick House.**
900 Chambersburg Rd.; 717-334-4332
$-$$
Five dining areas in the main house built the same year Napoleon fought the Battle of Waterloo. Featuring casual American cuisine in a faithfully restored 1815 tavern. All foods are made on site. Specialties of the house include soups made fresh daily, blackened prime rib, marinated duck breast with cherries, Herr Tavern cheesecake and pecan pie.

X **Hickory Bridge Farm.** 96 Hickory Bridge Farm Rd, Orrtanna; 717-642-5261 or 800-642-1766.
Unique country dining in a beautiful 150-year-old barn decorated with antiques. Specializes in serving bus groups farm-style meals; lunch and dinner daily. Excellent food and atmosphere.

X **Hofbrauhaus.** Lincoln Way West (Rte. 30), Abbottstown; 717-259-9641 $
Complete German dinners are the specialty at this chalet-style restaurant 15 miles east of Gettysburg. The house-cooked specialties are a variety of wurst, sauerbraten, schnitzel, and smoked pork loin with apples. German side dishes include red cabbage, beet salad, and potato dumplings. Seafood and sandwiches are also on the menu.

X **Hotel Oxford Restaurant.** 7 Lincoln Way West (Rte. 30), New Oxford; 717-624-2500 $-$$
This establishment hasn't served as a hotel for many years, but it's a reasonable, nice place to eat while you're shopping in the "Antique Capital of Central Pennsylvania." The restaurant includes a neat, narrow wooden bar and specializes in fresh fish. The large, white brick building is a mainstay of the town's main street.]

X **The Springhouse Tavern.** 89 Steinwehr Ave.; 717-334-2100 $
This cozy and romantic colonial tavern features fresh deli sandwiches and salads, generous dinner platters, tasty desserts, and a variety of spirits. The homemade soups include baked onion soup, made with beef and served in a tureen.

⊡ **The Barker House Bed & Breakfast.**
10 Lincoln Way West (Rte. 30), New Oxford; 717-624-9066 or 888-546-1520 $$
This brick-over-log house is the second oldest structure in New Oxford, and was occupied by Confederate general John Gordon of Georgia and his officers on the way to the Battle of Gettysburg. The five rooms are furnished in antiques, and all have private baths. The home—within walking distance of 40 antique dealers—has lovely wood floors, a large parlor, and a library. Lodging includes a bountiful breakfast of fresh, good food.

⊡ **The Brafferton Inn.** 44-46 York St.; 717-337-3423 $$-$$$
A stay at the Brafferton Inn may be the most pleasant way to get a full sense of Gettysburg's historical richness. The 14-room stone house, built in 1786 as the first residence in town, faces a mid-19th century street and has an adjacent seven

room pre–Civil War clapboard addition. On the first day of the battle a bullet shattered an upstairs window; it lodged in the mantel and is still there today. During the war, services were held here while the church was being used as a hospital. Just down the street is the house where Lincoln wrote his Gettysburg Address.

The Doubleday Inn. 104 Doubleday Ave.; 717-334-9119 $-$$
This beautifully restored country inn is located directly on the battlefield and filled with cozy antiques and Civil War memorabilia. Candle-lit country breakfast and afternoon tea. Civil War lectures on some evenings. Splendid views of the battlefield from atop Oak Ridge.

FARNSWORTH HOUSE INN

Farnsworth House Inn. 401 Balt St.; 717-334-8838 $$-$$$
The walls of this inn built in 1810 still show the scars of 100 bullet holes shot during the Battle of Gettysburg. The nine guest rooms in this building on the National Register of Historic Places are decorated in Victorian style, and some

have working fireplaces. Guests can relax in the patio gardens. A Civil War–oriented bookstore is on the premises.

Gettysburg Hotel (Best Western). One Lincoln Square; 800-528-1234 or 717-337-2000 $-$$
This white-brick hotel located on Lincoln Square is a National Historic Landmark. The building was recently reconstructed to include spacious guest rooms decorated in reproduction period furnishings. Luxury suites feature fireplaces and jacuzzi baths. Guests can relax in the swimming pool or enjoy tennis and jogging at nearby Gettysburg College. Covered parking and shuttles to battlefield tours available. Restaurant.

Gettystown Inn. 89 Steinwehr Ave. (Rte. 15 South); 717-334-2100 $$-$$$
This bed and breakfast with five charming guests rooms is a historic Civil War-era home comfortably furnished with beautiful 19th-century antiques and reproductions. Lodging includes a hearty breakfast served in the sunny parlor of The Dobbin House next door. The hostelry is ideally situated to overlook the spot where Lincoln gave his Gettysburg Address and within walking distance of the Gettysburg visitors center.

The Herr Tavern & Publick House. 900 Chambersburg Rd.; 717-334-4332 or 800-362-9849 $-$$$$
The Battle of Gettysburg began in the fields surrounding this 1815 Federal-style building listed on the National Register of Historic Places. The bed-

and-breakfast consists of 12 guest rooms all offering private baths, fireplaces, cable TV, and phones, some with Jacuzzi tubs, queen-sized canopy beds, and sitting areas. Rates include a full breakfast and afternoon tea. The hotel's dining rooms serve lunch and dinner.

☒ **James Gettys Hotel.** 27 Chambersburg St.; 717-337-1334 $$$
Built in 1804 and restored in 1996, this 195-year-old historic hotel has served as a tavern and roadhouse to accommodate those traveling west, a hospital for wounded soldiers during the Battle of Gettysburg, an apartment building, and a youth hostel. This handsome European-style suites-only hotel offers 11 lovely quarters with sitting room, kitchenette, bedroom, and private bath. Each suite is named for a business that existed within the building or in the adjacent downtown city blocks. Located in the building is the **Thistlefield Tea Room.**

☒ **Keystone Inn.** 231 Hanover Street; 717-337-3888 $-$$
As you step through the large, leaded-glass entrance of this 1913 late-Victorian brick house, you'll see the handsome chestnut staircase marching majestically to the third floor. Built by a local furniture maker, the inn features natural oak and chestnut throughout. Each bright, cheerful guest room has a reading nook with chairs and ottomans, books, and a writing desk overlooking Gettysburg. Breakfast might include fruit pancakes, Pennsylvania Dutch scrapple, eggs, fresh fruit, and home-baked breads.

Greensburg *map A-3*

✗ **Vallozzi's.** Rte. 30 east of town; 724-836-7663 $$
Upscale Italian-American bistro with an exceptional wine list. Family owned and operated.

☒ **Mountain View Inn.** Rte. 30, 5 minutes east of town; 800-537-8709 or 724-834-5300 $$-$$$
Long-established hotel with recent addition; all rooms individually decorated in period styles. Rooms in addition are more spacious. Dining room and tavern in the inn.

Harrisburg *map C-3*

✗ **Appalachian Brewing Co.** 50 N. Cameron St.; 717-221-1080 $
Housed in an impressive three-story brick and heavy-timber structure built in 1918. Antique brick walls, massive wooden beams, hardwood floors, and ceilings give warmth to the brewpub. The menu includes soups, stews, salads, sandwiches, pizza, and pasta. The brewery produces 15,000 barrels of beer per year. Tours Saturdays at 1:00 (free).

✗ **Empire Restaurant & Bar.** 149 N. Hanover St., Carlisle; 717-258-4888 $$-$$$
There's a big-city sophistication to this restaurant just north of Carlisle's downtown square, 10 miles west of Harrisburg. The chef serves a globally infused menu of innovative dishes such as vanilla

Food & Lodging map, page 276; index of listings by region/chapter, page 277.

-cured duck with mashed sweet potatoes and grilled venison in a port sauce with sweet potato cakes and figs.

✗ **Firehouse Restaurant.** 606 N. Second St.; 717-234-6064 $-$$
This 1871 firehouse has been completely restored into multi-level restaurant specializing in New American Cuisine. The clever "four-alarm" menu includes appetizers, salads, sandwiches, and entrees including the "Hook & Ladder" (half rack of ribs with a lobster tail) and "The Backdraft" (a grilled tuna, chicken, or filet mignon sandwich).

✗ **The Golden Sheaf.** In the Hilton, One N. Second St.; 717-237-6400 $-$$$
Coat and tie are required in this fine-dining restaurant specializing in regional American cuisine. Winemaker dinners are held monthly, and the restaurant is a member of the Chaine des Rotisseurs. No smoking.

☷ **Ashcombe Mansion Bed and Breakfast.** 1100 Grantham Road, Mechanicsburg; 800-580-8899 or 717-766-6820 $$-$$$
This turreted Queen Anne mansion was built in 1891, and sits on 23 acres of rolling countryside. Waterfowl frequent the property in summer and fall. The 10 bedrooms—some with porches—have beautiful views and are individually decorated with antiques. Intricate parquet floors and ornamental woodwork are the hallmark of the public rooms. Continental Breakfast included. No children under 12, no pets, no smoking.

ASHCOMBE MANSION

☷ **Felicita Golf Spa Garden Resort.** 2201 Fishing Creek Valley Rd.; 717-599-5301 or 888-321-3713 $$$
A 54-room country inn located on hundreds of acres, this resort has a golf course, lighted tennis court, hiking trails, and a full-service spa. Rooms are furnished in country decor.

☷ **Harrisburg Hilton and Towers.** One N. Second St.; 717-233-6000 or 800-445-8667 $$
Centrally located near the Amtrak station and the capitol building, this 351-room hotel has a heated indoor pool and fine-dining restaurant *(see above)*. Guest rooms are stylishly decorated and guests receive a free newspaper daily.

☷ **Pheasant Field Bed & Breakfast.** 150 Hickorytown Rd., Carlisle; 717-258-0717 $-$$
A former stop on the Underground Railroad, this 200-year-old, federal-style brick farmhouse is in a serene location close to the Appalachian Trail. An extensive breakfast is included.

FOOD & LODGING

PHEASANT FIELD B&B

⊡ **Radisson Penn Harris Hotel.** 1150 Camp Hill Bypass, Camp Hill; 717-763-7117 or 800-333-3333 $
Across the river from Harrisburg is this faux-Colonial hotel on 16 acres of wooded grounds. The charming property has an outdoor pool, an exercise room, and picnic grounds.

RADISSON PENN HARRIS HOTEL

⊡ **Towne House Suites Hotel.** 660 Boas St.; 717-232-1900 or 888-532-1900 $$
If you're having an extended stay in Pennsylvania's capital city, this hotel offers apartment living in attractively furnished suites with kitchens, sundecks, evening hospitality room, and complimentary newspaper.

Hershey *map C-3*

✕ **Catherine's.** In Spinner's Inn, 845 E. Chocolate Ave.; 717-533-9050 $-$$
Interesting American cuisine featuring beef, veal, and seafood is the mainstay of this casual fine-dining restaurant. Dinner only; closed Sunday and Monday.

✕ **The Circular Dining Room.** In the Hotel Hershey, Hotel Rd.; 717-533-2171 $$-$$$
Coat and tie are required for dinner in this elegant restaurant set amid Mediterranean decor. Breakfast buffet, lunch, and Sunday brunch are also served. Live entertainment Thursday to Sunday. Prix fixe menu at dinner Mondays and Tuesdays. Innovative, sophisticated dishes.

⊡ **The Hershey Lodge and Convention Center.** W. Chocolate Ave. at University Dr.; 717-534-8600 or 800-HERSHEY $$-$$$
All the amenities you'd expect of a huge, 665-room motor hotel are available at The Hershey Lodge. On the property are an indoor pool, wading pool, saunas, whirlpool, lighted tennis courts, miniature golf, game room, and three restaurants—everything but a roller coaster. The rooms are modern and the lodge is attractively set on spacious grounds.

⊡ **The Hotel Hershey.** Hotel Rd.; 717-533-2171 or 800-HERSHEY $$$
If you enjoy staying at upscale, famous historic hotels, this is the area's grande dame. Set on a hilltop overlooking the entire area, the elegant dowager has im-

Food & Lodging map, page 276; index of listings by region/chapter, page 277.

maculate grounds, a fountain in the lobby, and a variety of sports including golf, tennis, an indoor pool, sports court, and sand volleyball. Also available, for an extra fee, are cross-country skiing, tobogganing, balloon rides, bocci, carriage rides, and bicycles. Excellent restaurant.

THE HOTEL HERSHEY

☒ **Ogden's Country Bed & Breakfast.** 407 N. Hanover St.; 717-566-9238 $
This redbrick, white-frame home is located in a quiet village setting five minutes from Hershey Park and the outlets. There's a front porch to loll on, and the guest rooms are decorated with Amish quilts and crafts.

☒ **Spinner's Inn.** 845 E. Chocolate Ave.; 717-533-9157 $-$$
Fluffy duvets and lots of pillows make the nicely decorated bedrooms inviting at this two-story motor inn. Located only a mile from Hershey Park, the 52-room facility has a heated swimming pool and game room. Continental breakfast is included, and there's a good restaurant (Catherine's) on the premises.

Holicong *map 3-A CHECK*

☒ **Ash Mill Farm.** Rte. 202; 215-794-5373 $-$$
This 1790 Federal manor house with a large veranda sits on 11 pastoral acres, and is only 10 minutes by car from both New Hope and Doylestown. The manor house is furnished with American antiques, Shaker reproductions, and the owners' eclectic treasures. Full breakfast.

ASH MILL FARM

☒ **Barley Sheaf Farm.** Route 202; 215-794-5104 $$-$$$
This 1740 mansard-roofed fieldstone house was the hideaway of playwright George S. Kaufman in the 1930s. Today this charming 30-acre farm retains the quiet gentility that prevailed when Lillian Hellman, Alexander Woollcott, and Moss Hart visited here. A swimming pool, duck pond, and the bank barn are near the home, which is a National Historic Site. Oriental rugs are scattered over the wide-plank floors. Guest rooms are decorated with floral prints and brass-and-iron beds. Full breakfast and afternoon tea.

Holland *map D-3*

⌂ **Mill Race Inn.** 183 Buck Rd. (Rte. 532); 215-322-2010 $$
Excellent steaks, fresh seafood, and innovative chicken dishes are served in a restored 18th-century grist mill overlooking the little Mill Creek waterfall. Outside dining is on the patio. A salad bar accompanies the main dishes.

Hopwood *map A-3*

⌂ **Chez Gerard.** Rte. 40; 724-437-9001 $$
French food served in a historic stone house, once a stop of the National Road. Owners, who also have the B&B Inn of the Princess in nearby Uniontown, make frequent trips to Paris, bring back latest French recipes. Servers are sometimes young French students here on internships, and are exceptionally easy to pick-up on. Exceptional selection of French cheeses and wines. A la carte and prix fixe meals. Closed Tuesdays.

Indiana *map A-2*

✕ **Benjamin's.** 458 Philadelphia St.; 724-465-4446 $
Casual dining in an old Victorian house. Summer dining on the patio or under the grape arbor. Popular entrees: chicken Savoy, chicken breasts sauteed in cabernet, and stuffed chicken Romano, with prosciutto and Monterey jack cheese in the stuffing. Closed Sunday.

Jennerstown *map B-3*

✕ **Green Gables.** 7712 Somerset Rd.; 814-629-9220 $
Old-fashioned roast turkey with stuffing and gravy, chicken salad, and more up-to-date entrees like ostrich tournedos. Homemade desserts. Lovely old building in wooded area, across the lawn from the Mountain Playhouse.

Jim Thorpe *map D-2*

✕ **Black Bread Cafe.** 47 Race St.; 570-325-8957 $-$$
A wood-burning oven bakes wonderful whole-grain breads to accompany international and innovative bistro dishes. Casual fine dinners and light fare.

✕ **The Emerald.** In the Inn at Jim Thorpe, 24 Broadway; 570-325-8995 $$
The restaurant specializes in Irish food —shepherd's pie, bubble and squeak, fish-and-chips—as well as standard American dishes, while the attached **Molly McGuire's Pub** serves hot sandwiches, appetizers, and perfectly poured pints of Guinness. In nice weather, dine on the front porch.

⌂ **The Harry Packer Mansion.** Packer Hill; 570-325-8566 $$$
The most impressing lodging in Jim Thorpe, this 1874 Second Empire Italianate mansion was home to a coal magnate. Built from local brick and New England sandstone, the mansion has Tiffany windows, Minton tiles, and period antiques. There are 13 rooms in the

mansion and its carriage house. Murder Mystery Weekends are held year-round in the slightly haunted looking house.

HARRY PACKER MANSION

☷ **Inn at Jim Thorpe.** 24 Broadway; 717-325-2599 $-$$$
Built in the 1840s, the inn has a New Orleans–style balcony with wicker rocking chairs very conducive to loafing. There are 25 comfortable guest rooms, and the suites have fireplaces and whirlpools. Breakfast buffet is included.

☷ **Rendon House Bed & Breakfast.** 80 Broadway; 717-325-5515 $
This 1827 Italianate Victorian home is located in the heart of the town, once known as Millionaire's Row. Antiques and fresh flowers adorn the inn, which has outdoor terraces where you could sit and sip. Full breakfast included.

Kennett Square *map D-3*

✗ **Sovanna Bistro & Pizza Kitchen.** Rtes. 926 and 82; 610-444-5600 $-$$
Homemade pastas, fresh fish, and fancy pizzas are the specialty of this sharp-looking casual eatery.

☷ **Meadow Spring Farm Bed & Breakfast.** 201 E. Street Rd. (Rte. 926); 610-444-3903 $
Set in the fields of Brandywine Valley, this family farmhouse has six guest rooms—all with working fireplaces, Amish quilts, and private baths. An outdoor pool, billiards, and ping pong are free to guests. Canoeing on the nearby Brandywine River, tennis courts, and public golf courses are other diversions.

MEADOW SPRING FARM B&B

☷ **Scarlett House.** 503 W. State St.; 610-444-9592 $-$$
This late 1800s stone manor is furnished with Victorian antiques; it is within walking distance to the downtown area, and a 10-minute drive from Longwood Gardens. Breakfast is included.

Lahaska *map D-3*

✗ **Buckingham Mountain Brewing Co. and Restaurant.** 5775 Rte. 202; 215-794-7302 $-$$
There's a beautiful view of the mountain and valley from the upstairs dining room of Bucks County's first microbrewery.

Food & Lodging map, page 276; index of listings by region/chapter, page 277.

FOOD & LODGING

Patrons can take a tour of the brewhouse and sample four five-ounce glasses of the various beers made on site. The menu includes mountain onion soup, barbecued shrimp, beef, and a variety of vegetarian specialties. A beer garden is open seasonally. A free hourly restaurant shuttle picks up passengers of the New Hope –Ivyland Scenic Railroad at the station.

✕ **The Cock 'n' Bull.** Rtes. 202 and 263 in Peddler's Village; 215-794-4010 $-$$$
Servers are garbed in colonial attire and the dining rooms are richly decorated with colonial-style accoutrements and the owner's personal collection of fine art and antiques. Light or hearty traditional American fare and some contemporary dishes are included on the menu.

✕ **Jenny's Bistro.** Rte. 202 and Street Rd., in Peddler's Village; 215-794-4020 $-$$
This French country cafe offers fresh seasonal fare with a new American flair. Both casual meals and special-occasion dining are available. Open daily for lunch and dinner; bar menu from 3 P.M. Piano Bar Fri. and Sat. evenings.

GOLDEN PLOUGH INN

▦ **Golden Plough Inn.** Rte. 202 and Street Rd.(in Peddlers Village); 215-794-4004 $$-$$$
Of the 66 rooms, 20 are suites in this luxury country inn. Many of the richly appointed rooms have canopy beds, whirlpools, and/or gas-lit fireplace; all have a coffeemaker and refrigerator.

Lampeter *map C-3*

▦ **Australian Walkabout Bed & Breakfast.** 837 Village Rd.; 717-464-0707 $$-$$$
Mosquito netting canopies the beds in this historic, authentic Australian-style B&B in a rural setting. An English garden, pond, fireplaces, and "Outback" fantasy suite adorn the inn. Complimentary breakfast is served by candlelight. Champagne, soft drinks, and snacks upon arrival and breakfast are included.

Lancaster *map C-3*

✕ **Center City Grill**, 10 Prince St. in the city center; 717-299-3456 $$
An upscale neighborhood bar with delicious International cuisine like Thai chicken in peanut-ginger sauce and gourmet pizzas. Live jazz on Sunday nights.

✕ **D & S Brasserie Bar & Restaurant.** 1679 Lincoln Hwy. East; 717-299-1694 $$
Specialties of this historical restaurant and bar, converted from a 1925 home, include tomato bisque, broiled crab cakes, whole Maine lobster with char-

broiled beef filet, and fettucine Alfredo with house-smoked salmon and snow peas. Choose from several cozy dining rooms; outdoor deck open in summer.

✕ **The Log Cabin.** 11 Lehoy Forest Dr., 6 miles northeast of Lancaster on Rte. 272; 717-626-1181 $$$
This former speakeasy from Prohibition days is now perfectly legal as a welcoming roadside inn with wonderful American standards like braised lamb chops and seafood pasta. Candlelight and a nice collection of early American paintings make for an elegant atmosphere.

COUNTRY LIVING INN

🛏 **Country Living Inn.** 2406 Old Philadelphia Pike; 717-295-7295 $
Although this is a new inn, the 34 rooms are furnished in authentic Shaker style with hand-stitched quilts. There are plenty of inviting rocking chairs on the front porch. Free coffee, tea, and hot chocolate daily; complimentary pastries served on the porch May to October.

🛏 **Greystone Manor Bed & Breakfast.** 2658 Old Philadelphia Pike; 717-393-4233 $-$$

A Victorian mansion and barn have been made into a B&B and carriage-house accommodations. Many of the 13 guest rooms and suites have stained glass windows, cut-crystal doors, and original woodwork. A lavish breakfast (included in room rate) is served in the formal dining room.

KING'S COTTAGE B&B

🛏 **King's Cottage B & B.** 1049 E. King St.; 717-397-1017 or 800-747-8717 $$-$$$
On the top-10 list of American Historic Inns, this Spanish-style B&B is on the National Historic Register and has nine elegantly decorated guest rooms with private baths and fireplaces. A separate carriage house is a honeymoon suite with a jacuzzi and fireplace.

🛏 **Stockyard Inn.** 1147 Lititz Pike; 717-394-7975 $-$$
Built as a farmhouse in 1750, this large, family-owned restaurant was once the home of President James Buchanan. Adjacent to real stockyard pens and the railroad, this inn specializes in prime rib, steaks, and seafood.

Food & Lodging map, page 276; index of listings by region/chapter, page 277.

VILLAGE INN OF BIRD-IN-HAND

🖿 **Village Inn of Bird-in-Hand.**
2695 Old Philadelphia Pike;
717-293-8369 or 800-914-2473 $-$$
This historic inn was built in the late 1800s, and was a convenient rest stop along the Old Philadelphia Pike. The handsome reception desk was once the inn's bar. Guest rooms and suites are beautifully decorated in mahogany reproduction furniture; the included continental-plus breakfast is served on the enclosed sun porch. Complimentary wine and cheese served in the afternoon.

Ligonier *map A-3*

🖿 **Sleepy Hollow Inn.** Rte. 30 bet. Latrobe and Ligonier; 724-537-5454 $$
Outside, it looks like an old log roadhouse (which it is). Inside, it's a modern, white tabecloth restaurant with a solarium along the back overlooking the woods and Loyalhanna Creek. American cuisine (salmon with dijon-dill glaze).

Lititz *map C-3*

🖿 **General Sutter Inn.** 14 E. Main St.; 717-626-2115 $$
This circa 1764, redbrick Georgian-style mansion overlooks the charming town square and is said to be the oldest continually operated inn in the state. The decor is smooth blend of Victorian furnishings and Pennsylvania folk art. Also in the inn is a tavern serving meals.

GENERAL SUTTER INN

🖿 **Swiss Woods B&B.** 500 Blantz Rd.; 717-627-3358 or 800-594-8018 $$-$$$
This modified Swiss chalet inn has seven guestrooms, all with bath and either a patio or balcony. Situated on 30 rolling acres of land, the house is surrounded by an amazing flower garden. There's bird watching, hiking and biking trails, and a canoe. Breakfasts are a creative culinary affair, and might feature french toast stuffed with strawberry cream cheese, eggs florentine, pastries, quiche, and fruit and berries from the garden.

Food & Lodging map, page 276; index of listings by region/chapter, page 277.

Lumberville *map D-3*

⊓ **Black Bass Hotel.** 3774 River Rd.;
215-297-5770 $$$
Set on the banks of the Delaware River,
the elegant Black Bass has been a lodging
and dining establishment for more than
250 years. Guest rooms are decorated
with antiques, and rooms facing the river
have balconies. The restaurant is excel-
lent, and on warm summer nights you
can dine on the riverside veranda, enjoy-
ing such dishes as coffee-lacquered duck
with fresh ginger pear chutney.

BLACK BASS HOTEL

⊓ **1740 House.** 3690 River Rd.;
215-297-5661 $-$$
The 1740 House takes full advantage of
its picturesque location just a few feet
from the Delaware Canal and the
Delaware River. All 24 guest rooms have
balconies looking over the waterways
and are decorated in beige and Wedg-
wood blue; many have wicker furniture
and exposed beams. The romantic inn
has been touted by numerous magazines
as one of the best in the country.

Marietta *map C-3*

⊓ **Railroad House.** W. Front and S. Perry
Sts.; 717-426-4141 $$-$$$
This little nine-room hotel on the National Historic Register was built in the
1820s to provide accommodation for
travelers on the nearby canal and Susquehanna River. The old railway station
across the street is part of the hotel's
property. Rooms vary in antique decor.

Masontown *map A-3*

✕ **Lardin House Inn.** Rte. 21, 10 miles
from Uniontown; 724-583-2380 $-$$
Old Victorian house that's not really an
inn, but a restaurant whose signature
dish is chicken Lardin—sauteed chicken
breast, portobello mushrooms, and sun-
dried tomatoes.

McMurray *map A-3*

✕ **The Classroom.** 133 Camp Lane; 724-
942-4878 $-$$
This restaurant in a 1904 one-room
schoolhouse consistently gets an A+.
Everything made from scratch—bread
baked twice a day, real whipped cream,
restaurant-made sauces and desserts.

Mercer *map A-2*

✕ **Springfield Grille.** Route 19, south of
Mercer; 724-748-3589 $$
Club-like restaurant featuring fire-grilled
Black Angus beef, pork, mahi mahi, and

more. Not to be missed: crab cakes, turtle soup, 14-layer cinnamon chocolate mousse torte, and apple dumplings.

Milford *map D-2*

⊞ **Cliff Park Inn & Golf Course.**
155 Cliff Park Rd.; 570-296-6491 or 800-225-6535 $$-$$$
A fifth generation of innkeepers oversees this inn that had its beginnings as an 1820 farmhouse. The inn is on 500 acres and features a nine-hole golf course. Guest rooms are decorated with family heirlooms.

Monessen *map A-3*

✕ **Lucchesi's.** 372 Donner Ave.; 724-684-9889 $$
People from Pittsburgh come to this old steel town along the Monongahela River to enjoy this fine, traditional Italian restaurant featuring dishes such as garlic shrimp, veal in wine, or sea bass with capers. Owner personally prepares every dish. Dinner only.

Mount Joy *map C-3*

✕ **Bube's Brewery.** 102 N. Market St.; 717-653-2056 $$
Looking much as it did in the 1880s, this brewery-tavern is listed on the National Register of Historic Places. The complex functions as a museum of 19th-century brewing. It has three restaurants, a beer garden, and a microbrewery. One of the eateries, the Catacombs, is several

stories underground in a former hideaway for slaves following the Underground Railroad. Today it harbors the beer-aging cellars. Open for dinner only.

✕ **Groff's Farm Restaurant.** 650 Pinkerton Rd.; 717-653-2048 $$
Arguably the best restaurant in Pennsylvania Dutch country. The all-inclusive meals are served family style at your table and include meats, seafood, and the famous Amish wedding dish, chicken Stolzfus. The authentic cooking is taken from old family recipes and given a gourmet touch by co-owner Betty Groff, who has written four award-winning cookbooks. *Everything* is homemade. Reservations required for dinner.

CEDAR HILL FARM

⊞ **Cedar Hill Farm Bed & Breakfast.**
305 Longenecker Rd; 717-653-4655 $
Built in 1817, the limestone barn and farmhouse overlook peaceful "Little Chickies Creek," named for an area Indian tribe. The house, with its winding staircase, is furnished with many family heirlooms and antiques. Breakfast is served by the open hearth where cooking was done in the 1800s.

⌂ **The Olde Square Inn.** 127 E. Main St.;
717-653-4525 or 800-742-3533 $
A portico supported by white columns
greets guests today just as it once sheltered horse-drawn carriages visiting this
redbrick mansion. A separate "Enchant-
ed Cottage" is privy to a garden-sur-
rounded whirlpool. A fireplace, stereo
system, VCR, microwave, and wet bar
complete the amenities.

Mount Pocono *map D-2*

✗ **Hampton Court Inn.** S. R. 940 East,
2 miles east of Jct. at S.R. 611;
570-839-2119 $$
There's a quaint Olde English ambiance
in this 100-year old farmhouse specializ-
ing in veal, duck, steaks and seafood.
Dinners include bread, salad, and ac-
companiments. Desserts are homemade.

✗ **The Original Baileys Grille &
Steakhouse.** 604 Pocono Blvd.;
570-839-9678 $-$$
The menu at this eatery, housed in an
old stone and plaster building, offers
something for every appetite. Soups, appetizers, salads, hot sandwiches, barbecue, steaks, chops, and fish are available
lunch and dinner daily. This is also a
popular happy hour gathering place.

New Hope *map D-3*

✗ **Centre Bridge Inn.** 2998 N. River Rd.;
215-862-9139 $$$
The first Centre Bridge House was built
on this property in 1705. A ferry across
the Delaware River existed here until a
bridge was built in 1814. The current
inn was rebuilt in 1962 after fires de-
stroyed the previous two. The inn has
panoramic river views, period furnish-
ings, private baths, and canopy beds. A
full-service restaurant is on the premises.

✗ **Karla's.** 5 W. Mechanic St.;
215-862-2612 $$-$$$
There's a mix of both the spicy adventur-
ous and tried and true on the menu. An
open terrace for al fresco dining or a
more formal dining room with a beauti-
fully tiled bar.

✗ **The Landing.** 8 W. Mechanic St.;
215-862-3558 $$
Tourists and locals are drawn to the
healthy New American fare in a tavern
atmosphere but this is also a restaurant
on the river with a fantastic view of the
Delaware and across to Lambertville.

✗ **Logan Inn Restaurant.** 10 W. Ferry St.;
215-862-2300 $-$$$
American continental cuisine is served in
this historic inn built in 1727. Enjoy a
wide variety of entrees including crab-
stuffed shrimp, twin lobster tails, crab
cakes, grilled meats, pasta, as well as veg-
etarian and daily specials. Outdoor din-
ing in season offers a lighter menu
including soups, salads, burgers, and
seafood.

✗ **Odette's Restaurant.** S. River Rd.;
215-862-2432 $-$$
Odette's has provided patrons a beautiful
view of the Delaware riverside in this
200-year-old building for decades. Din-

Food & Lodging map, page 276; index of listings by region/chapter, page 277.

ner menu main dishes include pancetta-wrapped filet mignon, buffalo ribeye, and pine-nut crusted swordfish. Salads, sandwiches, and hot dishes are available at lunch. Nightly award-winning piano bar. Seasonal weekend cabaret shows.

Fox & Hound. 246 W. Bridge St.; 215-862-5082 or 800-862-5082 $$-$$$
This stately brick and white-trim Victorian has been lovingly restored but not at the expense of comfort when housing a full complement of guests. A recent addition to the back of the home has added several rooms to the five in the main house. All have private baths. In warm months, the full breakfast is served on a brick side patio.

Logan Inn. 10 W. Ferry St.; 215-862-2300 $$-$$$
If you like being right in the center of things, this is your inn. The charming 18th-century restaurant and inn with its ample sloping lawn is right on the main street of the historic town. The 16 rooms all have private baths and cable TV. A full-service restaurant is on the premises; outdoor dining in season.

New Hope Inn. 36 W. Mechanic St.; 215-862-2078 or 888-272-2078 $-$$
Just up the hill from downtown is this rambling inn. Its 33 renovated rooms all have private baths; many have gas-lit fireplaces. The heated outdoor pool is a great place for energetic kids to frolic. There's a full-service restaurant for fine dining and a pub for more casual fare.

New Hope Motel in the Woods. 400 W. Bridge St. (Rte. 179); 215-862-2800 $
Homey, budget lodging in a quiet five-acre spot with a pond and heated pool. A mere quarter mile from the congestion of downtown. The 28 units have porches, TV, phones, refrigerators, and private baths. Two night minimum on weekends. Pets welcome with advance booking. A lounge is on the premises and room service by local deli is available.

New Stanton *map A-3*

La Tavola. 400 S. Center Ave.; 724-925-9440 $-$$
Take the New Stanton exit off the Pennsylvania Turnpike into the town of New Stanton and this surprisingly good Northern Italian restaurant. Seafood La Tavola, a feast of shrimp, scallops, crab, and lots more, is a signature dish. Owner comes to your table to prepare flaming desserts. Have plenty of water on hand.

New Wilmington *map A-2*

Tavern on the Square. 108 N. Market St.; 724-946-2020 $-$$
Old-fashioned restaurant in home of the original town doctor. Nostalgic favorite of alumni of Westminster College, the town's centerpiece, for more than 60 years. Servers recite menu.

Food & Lodging map, page 276; index of listings by region/chapter, page 277.

North East *map A-1*

✗ **The Gathering.** Heritage Wine Cellars, 12162 E. Main Rd.; 800-747-0083 or 814-725-8015 $-$$
Rustic restaurant, with deck, in former winery barn. Quiche and sandwiches for lunch; pork, chicken, and steak for dinner. Open Wednesday through Saturday.

North Wales *map D-3*

☵ **Joseph Ambler Inn.** 1005 Horsham Rd. (Rte. 463): 215-362-7500 $$
"Elegance in a country setting" describes this 1734 inn, now home to 37 guest rooms filled with antiques and reproductions; all have private baths and telephones. Full country breakfast.

JOSEPH AMBLER INN

Paradise *map D-3*

✗ **Historic Revere Tavern.** 3063 Lincoln Hwy. East; 717-687-8601 $$$
This historic fieldstone inn built in 1740 offers casual dining in a colonial atmosphere. The dining rooms have fireplaces. Seafood and steak dominate the menu.

☵ **Maple Lane Farm Guest House.** 505 Paradise Lane; 717-687-7479 $.
Owned by a Mennonite couple, this B&B is a working dairy farm. Immaculate country guest rooms are in the red-brick main house. Guests are encouraged to stroll through the meadows and woodland crossed by a winding stream, or watch the dairy in operation. You'll spend a restful night out in the country, awakening to the lowing of cows.

Paradise Valley *map D-2*

✗ **Crescent Lodge Restaurant.** Jct. Rtes. 191 and 940; 570-595-7486 or 800-392-9400 $$-$$$
The chef really knows his seafood in this lovely, candlelit, multi-room dining venue run by the same family for decades. Dinner includes a marinated vegetable appetizer, house-made breads, salad, and side vegetables. Piano music Thurday, Friday, and Saturday nights in the attractive wood-paneled bar room.

Philadelphia *map D-3*

✗ **Astral Plane.** 1708 Lombard St.; 215-546-6230 $$$
You know when you walk into this restaurant that dinner will be an event. Parachute material is quilted across the ceiling, a cloud-like contrast to ruby-colored walls. Atmosphere is low candlelight and kitsch with tables cozied up in nooks and crannies for privacy The cuisine is New American, with dishes

like seared tuna and leeks over wilted spinach with balsamic vinaigrette.

✗ **Brasserie Perrier.** 1619 Walnut St.; 215-568-3000 $$-$$$
Georges Perrier of Le Bec-Fin opened this less formal, more American version of a brasserie, complete with a lively bar. The delightful menu includes contemporary food such as a halibut with potato ravioli and olive jus, and brik (flaky pastry) of salmon with bok choy and lime sauce. The chef prepares four- and five-course tasting menus after consulting with the customer. This is one of the most happening places in town—not cheap but worth it.

✗ **Bridget Foy's South Street Grill.** Second and South Sts.; 215-922-1813 $-$$
Before the bar starts hopping, the kitchen at this popular South Street establishment cranks out a varied bag of New American cuisine, including Javanese pork tenderloin, sauteed New Zealand mussels, grilled buffalo, and fresh fish such as wahoo and ahi.

✗ **Ciboulette.** 200 S. Broad St.; 215-790-1210 $$$
In the historic Bellevue Building is this French restaurant with one of the city's most beautiful dining rooms. The menu includes more than 30 elegant Provencal dishes. Reservations recommended. Open daily for dinner.

✗ **City Tavern.** 138 S. 2nd St. at Walnut; 215-413-1443 $$-$$$
The National Park Service owns this faithful re-creation of the colonial

tavern that originally occupied this spot. The food has been less than great in the early '90s, but today's menu is much improved. All the dishes are researched and are from historic recipes. Special touches are the costumed wait staff, candlelit rooms, and seasonal outdoor dining on a second-floor porch overlooking a lovely garden or adjacent to the garden itself.

✗ **Dante & Luigi's.** 762 S. 10th St. at Catharine St.; 215-922-9501 $$
Dante & Luigi's has been around since 1899, and the dining rooms have an old-world parlor atmosphere, and the food is straight from mama's kitchen. Specialities on the extensive menu include the largest—at 20 ounces—veal chop in the city, seafood cioppino, osso bucco, veal Catharine, and homemade desserts such as ricotta cheesecake and tiramisu.

✗ **DiNardo's Famous Seafood.** 312 Race St.; 215-925-5115 $$
Philly's best steamed hard-shell crabs are the specialty of this restaurant five blocks from the Liberty Bell. Many chicken, beef, and pasta dishes are also available.

✗ **Engine 46 Steakhouse.** 10 Reed St.; 215-462-4646 $$
This American family restaurant is housed in a historic 100-year-old firehouse decorated with firefighter memorabilia. Large portions of ribs, chicken, seafood, and, of course, steaks. Free parking. Located near Penn's Landing.

Food & Lodging map, page 276; index of listings by region/chapter, page 277.

✗ **Fork.** 306 Market St.; 215-625-9425 $-$$

This unpretentiously stylish bistro in Old City serves up New American cuisine that gracefully manages to be innovative and fresh while avoiding creative culinary overkill. Roasted beets and Greystone Farm chevre with watercress and toasted walnut vinaigrette and Pan-crusted striped bass with a lemony sorrel sauce. The service is attentive and friendly; great wine list.

✗ **Fountain Restaurant.** One Logan Sq., Benjamin Franklin Pkwy.; 215-963-1500 $$$

Dining at this mahogany-accented restaurant in the Four Seasons Hotel is a glamorous, sophisticated experience. The flawless service is surpassed only by the fabulous cuisine. The menu changes with the seasons. Among the favorites are fingerling potatoes Lyonnaise with caviar cream; pot-au-feu of rabbit and artichokes; and sauteed venison medallions on pasta. Reservations essential.

✗ **The Garden.** 1617 Spruce St.; 215-546-4455 $$$

This beautifully decorated Center City townhouse offers seasonal outdoor dining in the garden and several stylish indoor dining rooms. The American menu features grilled fish, steaks, lobster, homemade desserts, and an outstanding wine list.

✗ **Jake's.** 4365 Main St., Manayunk; 215-483-0444 $$-$$$

Owner-chef Bruce Cooper (his wife is Jake) has garnered a reputation for food that is innovative but somehow classic rather than quirky. The place displays the hottest in contemporary crafts, many from local art galleries that punctuate trendy Manayunk. The chef has a particularly fine touch with seafoods and salads; desserts are a must.

✗ **Jim's Steaks.** 400 South St.; 215-928-1911 $

To try an authentic Philly cheesesteak, go to one of Jim's three locations. The Center City eatery has a tin ceiling, black-and-white tiled floor, and art-deco fixtures. The line moves fast, so be ready to order your choice of the traditional Cheez Whiz or provolone, onions, and other condiments served on a bun made by the Amorosa Baking Co. There are many cheesesteak restaurants in Philly, but this one uses beef ribeye. Jim's been cooking them 60 years.

✗ **La Famiglia.** 8 S. Front St.; 215-922-2803. $$$

For more than 20 years, this handsome restaurant has been serving fine Italian cuisine in elegant surroundings that include marble floors, fine furnishings, damask tablecloths, and Old Masters on the walls. Specialties include crostone, penne la Famiglia (with onions and prosciutto), agnoletti filled with ricotta, and semifreddo. 11,000-bottle wine cellar.

✗ **Le Bec-Fin.** 1523 Walnut St.; 215-567-1000 $$$

The Grande Dame of Philadelphia's long-standing, top-of-the-line restaurants, dining here is the centerpiece of an evening out. This outpost of Parisian and Lyonnais food with inspired touches from owner-chef Georges Perrier is considered one of the best—if not *the* best—in the city, though it has seen some stiff competition from several Center City upstarts. The French haute cuisine is served in a luxurious setting of Louis XV furniture, apricot silk walls, and crystal chandeliers. Le Bec-Fin translates as "Tip of the Beak" but is actually slang for the most sensitive part of the palate, a fitting name for a restaurant catering to people who appreciate exquisite food and surroundings. The prix-fixe $100 dinner includes a choice of appetizer, fish course, entree, cheese or salad, and an extravaganza of a dessert cart. The three-course lunch costs a relatively modest $36. Le Bar Lyonnais, just downstairs from the main dining room, has smallish portions of some specialty dishes (such as lobster bisque) for affordable prices. Reservations essential, usually far in advance. Lunch and dinner; closed Sunday. Jacket and tie required.

✕ **Le Bus Main.** 4266 Main St., Manayunk; 215-487-2663 $-$$
Affordable fresh, homestyle American foods feature homemade breads and pastries. Sunday brunch is especially varied and good; children's menus and vegetarian main dishes are always available. Outdoor dining in season. Open for lunch and dinner daily.

✕ **London Grill.** 2301 Fairmount Ave.; 215-978-4545 $$
In the art museum area, this restaurant is an excellent place for a casual bite or full meal. The decor is reminiscent of a bar with lots of brass railings and wood. The menu is creative American. Open for lunch and dinner daily; Sunday brunch.

✕ **Melrose Diner.** 1501 Snyder Ave., (South Philly); 215-467-6644 $
Included on a PBS show about historic Pennsylvania diners, this 24-hour institution does breakfast best. The waitresses call everyone "Hon."

✕ **Ocean Harbor.** 1023 Race St., Chinatown; 215-574-1398 $$
Dim sum is the lunchtime specialty here: multiple carts flying through the dining room with a dizzying selection. There are the usual pork and shrimp dumplings, but also vegetables, different kinds of seafood, and other specifically Chinese ingredients.

✕ **Old Original Bookbinder's.** 125 Walnut St.; 215-925-7027 $$$
One of America's most popular seafood restaurants, this eatery—operated continuously since 1865—is located a few blocks from the Delaware River in the historic area. Somewhat overpriced as a result of its popularity, the chowders, seafood, and fresh-baked desserts are nonetheless dependable and delicious.

✕ **Opus 251.** 251 S. 18th St.; 215-735-6787
Housed in the 82-year-old mansion that is now the Philadelphia Art Alliance, this elegant, European-style eatery melds "rustic" American cuisine with Mediterranean and Eurasian influences to arrive

Food & Lodging map, page 276; index of listings by region/chapter, page 277.

at dishes such as pepper-crusted cervena venison sirloin and potato-crusted ahi tuna. Excellent service.

✗ **Pamplona.** 225 S. 12th St.; 215-627-9059 $$
The classic Spanish tapas bar, updated for a young professional crowd that feeds on atmosphere. It's all here with the floor to ceiling windows that allow diners to see and be seen on popular 12th Street. There is a faux Picasso mural that overlooks the bustling dining room. Individual food items are tasty but expensive unless shared. This is a place to bring a group for food bites and sound bites (the acoustics are terrible).

✗ **Panorama.** In Penn's View Inn, 14 N. Front St.; 215-922-7800 $$
This award-winning Northern Italian restaurant offers great pasta dishes and exotic antipasto choices at reasonable prices. The name refers to an inside view— a wine-themed mural painted by an artist from the New Hope area. The artwork celebrates the restaurant's other unique feature: a specially designed wine storage system (the cruvinet system) that allows serving of 120 wines by the glass at "il Bar." Panoramic Flights include a 1.5-ounce tasting each of five wines. The pasta mista (house selected trio of pastas) offers a chance to taste a variety on one plate. The seafood and veal dishes are the restaurant's forte. Open weekdays for lunch; daily for dinner.

✗ **Reading Terminal Market.** 12th and Arch Sts.; 215-922-2317 $
A Philadelphia treasure, the Reading Terminal Market contains a profusion of more than 80 stalls, shops, lunch counters, and food emporiums in a huge, indoor farmers' market with 23 restaurants. Choose from numerous ingredients and prepared foods—Chinese, Greek, Mexican, Japanese, Thai, Middle Eastern, Italian, soul food, vegetarian, and Pennsylvania Dutch. Try a Philadelphia soft pretzel fresh from the oven. Get there early to beat the daily lunch rush. Open daily 8-6, closed Sundays.

✗ **The Restaurant School.** 4207 Walnut St. (University City); 215-222-4200 $$
The decor of separate dining rooms includes Tuscan farmhouse, Midwestern American home, and Great Chefs of Philadelphia in this restaurant that also has an open courtyard and a small pastry shop. Open for lunch and dinner daily.

✗ **Striped Bass.** 1500 Walnut St.; 215-732-4444 $$$
This seafood restaurant is housed in a stunning room with 28-foot ceilings and soaring marble pillars. Pan-roasted wild striped bass with ruby chard, porcini, and sage, and kasu-marinated Chilean sea bass are typical dishes with Pacific Rim overtones. There is an extensive raw bar and a chef's table adjacent to the open-to-the-dining-room kitchen which offers a grand feast. One of the city's best; reservations are essential.

✗ **Susanna Foo Chinese Cuisine.** 1512 Walnut St.; 215-545-2666 $$$
French and Chinese fusion is the inspiration of this award-winning, upscale restaurant with elegant decor. A few spe-

cialties include Hundred-Corner Crab Cakes and spicy Mongolian lamb. The Sunday brunch is ethereal dim sum. There is a full bar and a thoughtfully chosen, somewhat pricey wine list as well as imported beers, and an array of French and Asian desserts. Reservations essential. Jacket required.

✗ **White Dog Cafe.** 3420 Sansom St.; 215-386-9224 $$-$$$
This homey antique-filled eatery in the University City section emphasizes farm-fresh organic ingredients. The cafe serves contemporary American cuisine in three adjacent Victorian brownstones. Warm, charming, and informal.

✗ **Zocalo.** 3600 Lancaster Ave. at 36th St.; 215-895-0139 $$
At this University City contemporary Mexican restaurant, the kitchen makes its own corn tortillas and guacamole. Specialties are Oaxacan roasted duck with mole, and swordfish tacos.

⊞ **Abigail's Corby Carriage House.** 1935 Manning St.; 215-790-9062 $-$$
This historic 1850s brick carriage house with a sundeck sits one-half block from Rittenhouse Square in Center City. The recently renovated rooms have private baths, cable TV, free movies, telephone, washer/dryer, and a kitchen. Full breakfast included.

⊞ **Alexander Inn.** Spruce at 12th; 215-923-3535 $-$$
Located in the downtown historic district, this little luxury hotel has 48 designer guest rooms. A deluxe continental breakfast is included, and a fully equipped fitness center is available.

ALEXANDER INN

⊞ **Antique Row Bed & Breakfast.** 341 S. 12th St.; 215-592-7802 $
A European-style B&B in a 180-year-old townhouse on a tree-lined street just off historic Antique Row and one of the liveliest restaurant, shopping, and bar districts in the city. The spacious, comfortable, attractive rooms offer cable TV and full breakfast. Fully furnished flats are available for longer stays.

⊞ **The Bed and Breakfast Man.** 218 Fitzwater St.; 215-829-8951 $-$$
This B&B is in Queen Village, a short walk to most historic and entertainment attractions and only a very short taxi ride to Center City attractions. Comfortable, interesting rooms echo 19th-century Italy, England, France, and Philadelphia. All rooms have private baths, TV, and lovely views of the city.

⊞ **Four Seasons.** One Logan Sq. (19th St. and Benjamin Franklin Pkwy.); 215-963-1500 or 800-332-3442 $$$
Philadelphia's most expensive hotel

overlooks the fountains in Logan Circle and the Benjamin Franklin Parkway. The eight-story, U-shape hotel has the most attractive public areas, best service, and finest hotel dining in the city. Furniture in the 371 guest rooms is Federal style, dark and stately. Some rooms have private verandas. There's a library in each room plus the expected amenities of a luxury hotel. The Fountain Restaurant is one of the best in town. Complimentary town car service within the city limits.

FOUR SEASONS

⚏ **Independence Park Best Western.** 235 Chestnut St.; 215-922-4443 or 800-624-2988 $$
A great little historic Victorian hotel with 36 designer-decorated rooms and a Federal-style lobby set in the heart of Independence National Historical Park. Centrally located to Penn's Landing, the Liberty Bell, and Independence Hall. Complimentary Continental breakfast and afternoon tea are included.

⚏ **Korman Suites.** 20th St. (just off the Benjamin Franklin Pkwy.); 215-569-7000 $$

Affordability, luxury, and privacy come together here. The business-oriented, 100-suite facility offers panoramic city views from most of the spacious rooms, as well as fully equipped kitchens, dining/meeting areas, and washer/dryers in all accommodations. The Franklin Institute and Art Museum are within walking distance. Complimentary parking and free city-wide shuttle.

⚏ **Latham Hotel.** 135 S. 17th St.; 215-563-7474 or 800-LATHAM-1 $$-$$$
This historic hotel located in the heart of Center City has a beautiful lobby with hardwood floors, Oriental rugs, and crystal chandeliers. The 138 guest rooms have Louis XV furnishings and minibars. Nightly turn-down service and imported chocolates, and a newspaper in the morning.

⚏ **Omni Hotel at Independence Park.** 401 Chestnut St.; 215-925-0000 or 800-THE OMNI $$-$$$
All 150 rooms in this modern luxury hotel have a dramatic view of Independence National Historical Park. Rooms have a minibar, two telephones with computer/fax capabilities, marble bathrooms, hair dryers and bathrobes. The hotel has a health club with pool, jacuzzi, sauna, and exercise room. 24-hour room service, concierge, valet parking, twice-daily maid service, and overnight shoe shine. In the hotel are the Azalea Restaurant and a lobby bar with nightly entertainment.

FOOD & LODGING

☎ **Park Hyatt Philadelphia at the Bellevue.** 1415 Chancellor Court; 215-893-1234 or 800-233-1234 $$$
The magnificently restored historic French Renaissance hotel occupies the top seven floors of the 19-story Bellevue Building. With 170 luxurious guest rooms; unlimited use of the adjacent 93,000-square-foot Sporting Club, which houses an indoor pool, saunas, whirlpools, racketball and squash courts. Founder's, an excellent formal restaurant, is in the hotel; in addition, the hotel offers afternoon tea, a cocktail lounge, and 24-hour room service. Complimentary newspaper.

☎ **Penn's View Inn.** Front and Market Sts.; 215-922-7600 or 800-331-763 $$-$$$
Overlooking the Delaware River, this historic, European-style hotel offers 27 well-appointed rooms, some with fireplaces and jacuzzis. Room service, concierge, complimentary European breakfast, and discounted parking. Voted best small hotel by *Philadelphia* magazine. Panorama is off the lobby.

☎ **Rittenhouse B & B.** 1715 Rittenhouse Square; 215-545-1755 $$$
A handsomely decorated townhome with 10 plushly furnished rooms and the ambiance of a small luxury hotel. Full breakfast, afternoon tea included.

☎ **The Rittenhouse Hotel.** 210 W. Rittenhouse Square; 215-546-9000 or 800-635-1042 $$$
One of Philadelphia's best addresses, this property has 98 spacious and handsomely appointed guest rooms with rich mahogany furnishings and lush fabrics. Oversized marble bathrooms have both a bathtub and separate shower. All rooms have large windows that overlook Rittenhouse Square or the city. Con-cierge; courtesy town car transportation; five dining venues; 24-hour room service; indoor pool; fitness center; spa.

☎ **The Ritz-Carlton.** 17th and Chestnut Sts., 215-563-1600 or 800-222-8733 $$$$
For an upscale, chain hotel, few others meet the stature of the Ritz. Rises 15 stories above a suburban-style shopping mall plunked in the middle of Downtown. Close to Rittenhouse Square and the restaurant-club district. Superior service and all the amenities.

☎ **Rodeway Inn.** 1208 Walnut St.; 215-546-7000 or 800-887-1776 $-$$
This family-operated 1902 Victorian is within walking distance of the Pennsylvania Convention Center and historic sites, and features 32 spacious rooms or suites with cherrywood furnishings and cable TV. A full breakfast is included.

☎ **Sheraton Rittenhouse Square Hotel.** 18th and Locust Sts.; 215-546-9400 or 800-325-3535 $$-$$$
This prestigious building re-opened in December 1998 after a total renovation, making it the first environmentally smart hotel in the continental U.S. The 193-room hotel's environmental features include fresh filtered air in all guest rooms; an atrium with a 40-foot high bamboo garden; and non-toxic modern furnishings with 100% organic cotton.

Shippen Way Inn. 416-418 Bainbridge St.; 215-627-7266 $-$$
Charmingly restored, circa 1750 bed and breakfast inn is family-owned and operated. Nine rooms with private bath, Colonial gardens and reception room with fireplace. Near historic sites and Penn's Landing. Rates include breakfast, afternoon tea, or wine and cheese.

Society Hill Hotel. 301 Chestnut St.; 215-925-1919 $-$$
Built in 1832, this eclectic, 12 room "urban inn" was the city's first B&B. The rooms are small but cozy with brass beds and flowers. The property is in the heart of Independence National Historical Park. Continental breakfast is served in the rooms. Walk-up facility; no elevator. The hotel's European pub has nightly jazz piano and sidewalk dining when weather permits.

Ten Eleven Clinton Inn. 1011 Clinton St.; 215-923-8144 $$-$$$
The inn is two adjacent 1836 Federal townhouses located on a beautiful historic residential street in the heart of the city's business and cultural districts, and a five-minute walk to the Pennsylvania Convention Center. The seven luxury bed-and-breakfast apartments feature private baths, kitchens, fireplace, telephone, TV and VCR, hair dryers, laundry facilities, and outside courtyard.

Thomas Bond House. 129 S. Second St.; 215-923-8523 or 800-845-BOND $-$$$
This restored 1769 redbrick Georgian revival guesthouse is owned by the Na-

tional Park Service and located within Independence National Historical Park. With 12 period-furnished rooms, each with private bath, TV, and telephone; two have working fireplaces; three have whirlpool tubs. Continental breakfast on weekdays; full breakfast on weekends.

The Warwick Philadelphia. 1701 Locust St.; 215-735-6000 or 800-523-4210 $$$
One of Philadelphia's finest old hotels, located downtown just off Rittenhouse Square. The European-style building on the National Register of Hotels has an elegant lobby and more than 500 guest rooms furnished in traditional decor with beautiful marble bathrooms.

THE WARWICK PHILADELPHIA

Pittsburgh *map 3-A*

Baum Vivant. 5102 Baum Blvd.; 412-682-2620 $$$
Small, narrow, New York–style restaurant with superb fusion of Portuguese, Northern Italian, and French food. Some entrees—venison, boar, saddle of rabbit—require an adventurous palate. Veal chops, rack of lamb, roast pork, too.

✗ **Casbah.** 229 S. Highland Ave.; 412-661-5656 **$$-$$$.**
There is a lot of attention to detail at this restaurant, both in the Mediterranean menu and the atmosphere—soft lighting from copper sconces on textured, straw-colored walls. The chef features specials from Italian, African, Spanish, and French cuisine.

✗ **The Colony.** Greentree and Cochran Rds., Scott Township; 412-561-2060 **$$$**
Long before Ruth's Chris and Morton's of Chicago, Pittsburgh had The Colony. Upscale steakhouse with clubby interior, waiters in tuxedos, Pennsylvania-grown beef. Good veal and fish; complimentary fresh fruit as a finale. Good wine list.

✗ **Franco's Ristorante.** 1101 Freeport Rd., Fox Chapel; 412-782-5155 **$$**
A Pittsburgh classic. Fried zucchini, veal chops, and osso bucco are the specialties of Franco D'Amico, one of the city's favorite chefs. Popular with the Jaguar and Mercedes crowd from this ritzy suburb.

✗ **Grand Concourse.** One Station Square; 412-261-1717 **$$**
A beautifully restored old P&LE railroad station housing a seafood restaurant and the Gandy Dancer bar. Monongahela Room overlooks downtown. Locals take out-of-town guests here. Sunday brunch is Pittsburgh's biggest and most popular.

✗ **La Cucina Flegrea.** 2114 Murray Ave., Squirrel Hill; 412-521-2082 **$$**
Small, cramped restaurant with simply wonderful Italian and Mediterranean dishes. The chef-owner hails from Campi Flegrei, outside Naples, and she bakes her own bread, makes her own stocks, desserts, just about everything. Even persnickety reviewers from the *New York Times* like it.

✗ **Laforet.** 5701 Bryant St.; 412-665-9000 **$$$**
Classic French cuisine with contemporary touches. Good wine list, excellent for parties. Dinner only, Wednesday through Saturday.

✗ **Le Mont.** 1114 Grandview Ave., Mount Washington; 412-431-3100 **$$$**
New owners completely remodeled this landmark restaurant, and hired Donald Trump's personal chef. Entrees like raspberry duck, veal piccata with grilled shrimp. Tableside cooking, flaming desserts, and excellent view of Downtown Pittsburgh. Go at dusk and watch the city lights come on.

✗ **Le Pommier.** 2104 E. Carson St., South Side; 412-431-1901 **$$$**
Fine country French restaurant in two story-building that once housed the first woman barber in Pittsburgh. Emphasis on lighter foods, fish and vegetables, and menus that change seasonally. The wine list has won many *Wine Spectator* awards.

✗ **Lucca.** 317 S. Craig St., Oakland District; 412-682-3310 **$-$$**
Traditional Italian cuisine by Gino Croce, long-time popular Pittsburgh chef. Specialties include osso buco, Vir-

Food & Lodging map, page 276; index of listings by region/chapter, page 277.

ginia spots, crab cakes, veal dishes. Covered patio overlooking street. Close to Carnegie Museum.

✗ **LuLu's Noodle Shop and Yum Wok Pan Asian Diner.** 400 S. Craig St., Oakland District; 412-687-7777 $
Pan-Asian approach to noodle and rice dishes, all freshly made. Casual, trendy, noisy, and fun.

✗ **Mallorca.** 2228 E. Carson St.; 412-488-1818 $$-$$$.
Good Spanish and Portuguese food served by Spanish speaking waiters. The paella is the best dish on the menu but the suckling pig is the most interesting.

✗ **Monterey Bay Fish Grotto.** 1411 Grandview Ave., Mount Washington; 412-481-4414 $$$- $$$$
Many varieties of fresh fish, flown in daily— 16 to 18 varieties of fresh fish offered daily—plus crabcakes that many say are the best in Pittsburgh. Breathtaking skyline-and-water view meshes nicely with the coastal cuisine.

✗ **Pittsburgh Fish Market.** Doubletree Hotel, Downtown; 412-227-3657 $$$
Sushi, fish sandwiches, and a long menu of fresh fish prepared every imaginable way. Fine wine list. Visiting sports celebrities often hang out here; dinner is served until 1 A.M.

✗ **Primanti's on the Strip.** 18th and Smallman Sts., Downtown; 412-263-2142 $
Home of the original sandwich with fries inside. Hillary Rodham Clinton ate here; there is some debate on whether or not she swallowed. Open 24 hours.

✗ **Road to Karakesh.** 320 Atwood St., 412-687-0533
Moroccan fare like beef and lamb tagine and interesting couscous. B.Y.O.B.

✗ **Spice Island Tea House.** 253 Atwood St.; 412-687-8821 $
Wonderfully prepared Indonesian and Asian foods. Intimate, candle-lit dining room. B.Y.O.B.

✗ **Steelhead Grill.** Marriott City Center, Downtown; 412-394-3474 $$$
Excellent fish and seafood restaurant created by Drew Nieporent (of New York's Montrachet and Nobu, and San Francisco's Rubicon) and made famous by *Esquire* writer John Mariani who called it the "best Pittsburgh restaurant...ever."

✗ **Sunnyledge Restaurant.** 5124 Fifth Ave., Shadyside; 412-683-5014 $$-$$$
Small (35 seat) dining room and separate club room on first floor of hotel. Ambitious menu and dramatic, formal service. (Servers lift silver plate covers for everyone at a table simultaneously, butter is shaped like a rose.)

✗ **Tessaro's.** 4601 Liberty Ave., Bloomfield; 412-682-6809 $$
The definitive neighborhood restaurant-bar rich in local flavor, including characters from this Italian enclave and savvy out-of-towners who've been clued in. Also rich in the flavors of simple comfort fare. Specializes in burgers, chicken, fish and mesquite barbecue.

THE PRIORY

SUNNYLEDGE HOTEL

⊞ **Priory.** 614 Pressley St., North Side; 412-231-3338 $$$$
Restored 19th-century monastery with 24 rooms, concierge, antique furnishings, and European-style service. Free shuttle to downtown Pittsburgh. Garden courtyard, where guests may eat their full (included) breakfast on nice days.

⊞ **Sheraton Station Square.** 7 Station Sq. Dr.; 412-261-2000 $$$$
Overlooking Monongahela River on the city's South Side. Close to Freight House Shops and restaurants, incline to Mount Washington and Downtown.

⊞ **Sunnyledge Hotel.** 5124 Fifth Ave., Shadyside; 412-683-5014 $$$$
Restored Victorian home of Andrew Carnegie's personal physician, Dr. William McClelland. Eight rooms and suites, each decorated in old English style; private baths with jacuzzis.

⊞ **Victoria House B&B.** 939 Western Ave.; 412-231-4948 $$$
This three-story, redbrick inn is a showcase of the Victorian splendor that used to be the norm in one of the city's oldest residential neighborhoods. Painstakingly restored, the inn has lavishly decorated guest rooms and an impressive first floor of hardwood floors and high ceilings. Breakfast is served on a patio.

⊞ **Westin William Penn.** 530 William Penn Place; 412-281-7100 $$$$
The grand dame of Pittsburgh hotels. Lovely big lobby, where tea is served in afternoon. 595 rooms. Downtown, near courts and government offices.

Punxsutawney *map 2-B*

✕ **Coach Room.** In the Pantall Hotel; 135 E. Mahoning St.; 814-938-6600 $
Three meals a day. Known for haddock on Fridays, homemade pies anytime.

Food & Lodging map, page 276; index of listings by region/chapter, page 277.

Pantall Hotel. 135 E. Mahoning St.; 814-938-6600 $-$$
The Groundhog Capital's restored historic hotel, built in 1888. In the early 1900s diamonds were rolled out on the Victorian bar as local and New York City merchants bought and sold. Bill Murray stayed here when he made the movie *Groundhog Day.* 75 rooms, full facilities.

PANTALL HOTEL

Reading Area *map D-3*

Crab Barn. 2613 Hampden Blvd.; 610-921-8922 $-$$
A turn-of-the-19th-century barn was converted into this restaurant that looks like an Eastern shore crab house. Casual, family dining features seafood, steaks, chicken, and ribs. In good weather, you can dine on the outdoor deck.

Peanut Bar & Restaurant. 332 Penn St.; 610-376-8500 $-$$
The atmosphere here is still that of an old time bar room serving old favorites to innovative cuisine. The menu offers appetizers, salads with homemade dressings, chowders, vegetarian fare, grilled meats, swordfish, crab cakes, deli-style sandwiches and homemade desserts.

Stokesay Castle. Hill Rd. and Spook Lane; 610-375-4588 $$-$$$
Built as a honeymoon "cottage" for a new wife, the property is a close duplicate of the original Stokesay Castle in Shropshire, England, built in 1240. Unfortunately, it wasn't to the wife's liking, and was sold in 1956 for use as a restaurant. House specialties include chicken Tuscany, frog legs provençal, and veal de Gaulle (topped with asparagus, lobster, and Hollandaise).

House on the Canal Bed and Breakfast. 4020 River Rd.; 610-921-3015 $$
Built in the late 1700s, this lovely pillared farm house sits overlooking the Schuylkill River, a canal, and wooded countryside. For those who love the outdoors, fishing, bike paths, and walking trails are adjacent. A view of the falls of Felix dam and meandering wild Canada geese can be enjoyed from the spacious front porch. Rooms are done in Victorian decor with antiques.

Hunter House Bed and Breakfast. 118 S. Fifth St.; 610-374-6608 $
The Callowhill Historic District is home to this 1840s restored townhouse just one block from center square. Rooms are decorated with antiques, but have modern conveniences. From here it's a short walk to restaurants, shops and galleries, or a short drive to the Reading outlets. *See photo next page.*

FOOD & LODGING

HUNTER HOUSE

⊞ **Inn at Reading.** 1040 Park Rd. and Route 422 West, Wyomissing; 610-372-7811 or 800-383-9713 $$-$$$$
This modern inn with a traditional Colonial look offers 245 guest rooms including four suites. Executive level accommodations have a private lounge and free full buffet breakfast. The spacious rooms are decorated with English manor furnishing. All have in-room coffee makers, extensive cable TV channels, and complimentary daily *USA Today*. Courtesy limousine service to the airport is available upon request.

⊞ **Lincoln Plaza & Conference Center.** 100 N. Fifth St.; 610-372-3700 $-$$
Of the 104 rooms in this historic 18-story hotel, 32 are suites and seven have whirlpools. The public areas are elegantly decorated, and the attractive guest rooms have hair dryers, irons, and ironing boards. This downtown hotel offers area transportation.

Ronks *map D-3*

⊞ **Candlelight Inn Bed & Breakfast.** 2574 Lincoln Hwy. East; 717-299-6005 or 800-772-2635 $-$$
The driveway of this large county home is directly off Hwy. 30. The inn is surrounded by farmland and countryside. Each of the seven guest rooms is decorated with Victorian antiques. A full, elegant breakfast is included.

Scenery Hill *map A-3*

✕ **Century Inn.** Rte. 40; 724-945-6600 $$
Dining room offers lunch and dinner, with costumed waitresses serving classics like roast turkey and pork; cakes, pies, and rolls made in-house. A mixed grill of three sausages made on the premises is a lunch feature. The inn claims that General Lafayette and President Jackson ate there (at different times, of course).

⊞ **Century Inn.** Rte. 40; 724-945-6600 $$-$$$
Built in 1794, it's the oldest continuously operating inn on what became the National Road. The Whiskey Rebellion flag still hangs over the bar. Furnished entirely with antiques. Nine rooms, each with private bath and fireplace. Breakfast included; 35 miles south of Pittsburg.

Scranton *map D-2*

✕ **Carmen's.** 700 Lackawanna Ave.; 570-342-8300 $-$$$
This fine-dining restaurant is situated in

Food & Lodging map, page 276; index of listings by region/chapter, page 277.

the lobby of the restored Radisson Lack-awanna Station Hotel, and it features plush upholstered chairs, an old Italian marble floor, and an authentic vaulted Tiffany glass ceiling above. Reservations are imperative to enjoy the extremely popular Sunday buffet brunch with its multitude of stations. Innovative menu.

✕ **Farley's.** 300 Adams Ave. on Courthouse Square; 570-346-3000 $-$$.

This sharp-looking sports bar and restaurant is decorated in forest green with lots of brass railings. Open continuously from lunch through late night, it offers beef, seafood, ribs, chicken, and chops with an extensive beer selection.

✕ **Ryah House.** 1011 Northern Blvd., Clarks Summit; 570-587-1135 or 800-642-2215 $$-$$$

This Scandinavian-furnished restaurant is named for the fibers used to make the Nordic wall hangings. But the menu isn't Scandinavian. Mainstays include escargot, French onion soup, prime rib, scallops, horseradish-crusted grilled salmon, and the local favorite, Wiener schnitzel with spaetzle and red cabbage. Generous portions typify the all-inclusive dinners. Dinner only; closed Sunday.

✕ **Terrace Garden Cafe in Greystone Gardens.** 829 Old State Rd., Clarks Summit; 570-586-3215 $

Lunch and afternoon tea are served in this English garden center. Salads, pasta, soups, sandwiches, and seasonal specialties are served between 11 A.M. and 4 P.M. In summer, you can dine outdoors.

⊞ **The Inn at Nichols Village.** 1101 Northern Blvd. (Rtes. 6 and 11), Clarks Summit; 570-587-1135 or 800-642-2215 $$-$$$

About 10 minutes northwest of Wilkes-Barre is this modern hotel located in the foothills of the Endless Mountains. Indoor patios, courtyards, and a waterfall lend a relaxing aura to the property. The guest rooms are outfitted in well-maintained modern furnishings. There's a heated indoor pool and sauna. Two restaurants are in the hotel and the related Ryah House is across the street.

RADISSON LACKAWANNA STATION

⊞ **Radisson Lackawanna Station Hotel.** 700 Lackawanna Ave.; 570-342-8300 or 800-333-3333 $-$$

This fabulous hotel was resurrected from the abandoned Lackawanna Railroad Station. Many original fixtures from the station have been retained. Around the lobby ceiling are vistas from the railroad's route depicted in mosaic tile. The 145 guest rooms perimeter the six-story central atrium and are decorated in Federal reproductions. Carmen's and a sports bar are inside. Free parking.

SHADOWBROOK INN AND RESORT

⌂ **Shadowbrook Inn and Resort.** 615 S.R. 6E, Tunkhannock; 570-836-2151 or 800-955-0295. $$-$$$ **Photo coming** About 20 minutes northwest of Scranton is this all-inclusive resort dressed in Federal decor. The inn offers lots of sports facilities: racketball, swimming, golf, miniature golf, and bowling. Set on hundreds of acres of rolling forested land, it's also a relaxing getaway for the non-athletic.

Slippery Rock *map A-2*

⌂ **Applebutter Inn.** 666 Centreville Pike; 724-794-1844 $$$
1844 farm house converted to attractive 11-room inn, next door to—but not connected with—Wolf Creek School Cafe. All rooms have private baths, some have gas fireplaces. Massage and hot tub room. Full breakfast included.

⌂ **Wolf Creek School Cafe.** 664 Centreville Pike, Route 173; 724-794-1899 $-$$
Go for lunch in this one-room schoolhouse turned restaurant and have an ABC sandwich—apple, bacon, and cheddar on raisin bread. Dinner might be ham loaf, Yankee pot roast, hand-cut steak, stuffed seafood.

Somerset *map B-3*

⌂ **The Inn at Georgian Place.** 800 Georgian Place; 814-443-1043 $$$
Big red Georgian Revival mansion perched atop a hill featuring 11 guest rooms with private baths and breakfast included. Dinner served in the dining room on Friday and Saturday nights. $$ Lunch served on weekdays.

THE INN AT GEORGIAN PLACE

South Sterling *map D-2*

✕ **The French Manor.** Huckleberry Rd. off Rte. 191; 570-676-3244 or 800-523-8200 $$$
The 40-foot-high Great Room, with its vaulted cherry-wood ceiling and a mam-

moth plastered-stone fireplace at each end, makes a spectacular restaurant. French doors with leaded glass open onto a slate terrace that has a sweeping view of the countryside. The largely French menu changes seasonally. A recent selection included beef tenderloin on a roasted garlic and tomato sauce, and fresh salmon baked in champagne, white peppercorn, and asparagus. Open daily for breakfast and dinner

☷ **The French Manor.** Huckleberry Rd. off Rte. 191; 717-676-3244 or 800-523-8200 $$-$$$
Enjoy panoramic views as you take a peaceful walk, or go cross-country skiing on this 40-acre estate built circa 1935 as a summer residence for mining tycoon and art collector Joseph Hirschhorn. Modeled after his chateau in southern France, the fieldstone manor house has a slate roof, copper-mullioned windows, and arched oak door. The guest rooms have extensive woodwork and are decorated in a mix of contemporary style and French antique reproductions. The carriage-house has two suites with fireplace and jacuzzi. Golf and horseback riding nearby. Full breakfast included.

☷ **The Sterling Inn.** Rte. 191; 570-676-3311 or 800-523-8200 $$-$$$
This white and green frame hotel has a wide front porch with plenty of chairs to pass the time in. The varied rooms include traditional ones in the main inn, lodge and guest house; cottages; "Victorian fireplace suites;" and new trailside suites with jacuzzis and fireplaces. Full country breakfast; MAP available.

Speers *map A-3*

✗ **The Back Porch.** 114 Speer St., Lower Speers; 724-483-4500 $$
The Speers family, who built this big house in 1806, ran a ferry across the Monongahela River. In 1975, after two years of careful restoration, the home became a restaurant. Fans drive an hour or more from Pittsburgh for the signature rack of ribs, baked trout with crab cake stuffing, and quaint ambiance. Light fare is served in the **Side Door**, downstairs. Don't leave without having a bowl of the flavor-of-the-day ice cream, made in the family's shop right across the street.

Spring Mills *map A-3*

✗ **Hummingbird Room.** Route 45, 1 mile east of town; 814-422-9025 $$$
After working as sous chef at Le Bec Fin in Philadelphia, Eric Sarnow and wife Claudia moved to this little town near State College and opened the 85-seat restaurant in an 1847 building. Varied menu that changes four times a year. Fixed price and a la carte entrees also. Don't even try to get a reservation when Penn State's Nittany Lions are at home. Dinner only, Wednesday to Sunday.

State College *map B-2*

✗ **Dining Room at Nittany Lion Inn.** 200 W. Park Ave.; 814-863-5000 or 800-233-7505 $$
Varied menu is served in large, relaxing room. Popular with Penn State faculty

members. Breakfast, lunch and dinner.

X **Spats Cafe & Speakeasy.** 142 E. College Ave.; 814-238-7010 $$
Cajun-Creole cuisine and really good seafood. Not a student kind of place, even though it's close to campus, so not as hectic as many other restaurants.

X **The Tavern Restaurant.** 220 E.College Ave.; 814-238-6116 $
Penn State alumni come back for the lasagna and Toll House Pie they remember. On football weekends, it's not uncommon to wait two hours for a table (no reservations). Penn State basketball teams eat their pre-game meals here. Crowded, tables close together, and lots of fun. Dinner only.

X **Ye Olde College Diner.** 126 W. College Ave.; 814-238-5590 $
The best grilled stickies anywhere, also hamburgers, etc.. Silver chrome outside, tasteful paintings on the walls now that it's been spruced up. Open 24 hours.

Nittany Lion Inn. 200 W. Park Ave.; 814-863-5000 or 800-233-7505 $$$
Beautiful setting and 237 rooms under the trees on the edge of Penn State campus. Ask for a room in the new addition (they're more spacious.) Large conference rooms available.

Toftrees Golf Resort. One Country Club Lane; 800-252-3551 or 814-234-8000 $$$
Golf, swimming, tennis, hiking, and lots of conferences.

Stevensville *map C-1*

X **Apple Tree Bakery.** R.R. 1, S.R. 1012; 570-746-3942 $
If you like the taste and texture of old world baked goods, you'll love the products of the wood-fired brick oven—the largest in northeast Pennsylvania. Naturally leavened and most made with organic flours, the selection of breads includes German sourdough, Polish rye, and black Russian, as well as Italian and French breads. Snacks include pierogies, local cheeses, cookies. Sit outdoors by the pond and enjoy your selections.

Strasburg *map D-3*

Fulton Steamboat Inn. Rts. 30 & 896; 717-299-9999 or 800-922-2229 $-$$
No, it's not a mirage. It's a "steamboat" on dry land. Kids of all ages will get a kick out of sleeping on this new replica. Indoor pool, spa, and exercise room. Guest rooms—all different—have king, queen, and/or bunk beds.

Historic Strasburg Inn. One Historic Dr. (Rte. 896); 717-687-7691 or 800-872-0201 $-$$
This prestigious, large country inn is surrounded by 58 acres of Amish farmland. The 101 guest rooms are decorated in colonial furnishings with handmade floral wreaths, doilies, and a rocking chair. Heated pool, jacuzzi, fitness center, carriage rides, and bicycles.

Limestone Inn. 33 E. Main St.; 717-687-8392 or 800-278-8392 $-$$

On the National Register of Historic Places, this 200-year-old fieldstone home was the town's first post office, then a boardinghouse for a boys academy, and, after the Civil War, an orphanage. The inn was fully restored in 1986; Amish quilts grace the six antique-furnished rooms. Hearty, full breakfast is included.

LIMESTONE INN

☶ **Red Caboose Motel.** 312 Paradise Ln., Strasburg; 717-687-5000 $-$$
Train buffs will enjoy sleeping in one of the 43 renovated cabooses or coaches with modern motel furnishings. Two 80-ton P-70 Victorian coaches serve as the dining "cars" serving old-fashioned, locally fresh foods three times a day. The Strasburg steam train passes by on nearby tracks, and the Toy Train Museum is on adjacent property.

Stroudsburg *map D-2*

☶ **Beaver House.** 1001 N. Ninth St.; 570-424-1020 $$
A stone and log building resembling a hunting lodge is the location of this local favorite serving traditional fare. The dark-wood decor has a men's club feel. .

Tionesta *map A-2*

✕ **Five Forks Restaurant.** Rte. 62; 814-755-2455 $
Country restaurant named for the five forks of the Allegheny River. Eat on the covered deck (which is over an old roadbed once used by Seneca Indians and early settlers) and watch for bald eagles. All-time favorites like liver and onions, meatloaf, and fried chicken.

Titusville *map A-1*

✕ **Fayrway Room.** Rte. 8, four miles south of town; 800-461-3173 or 814-827-9611$
Salads, seafood. Three meals daily April to October. Sunday brunch year-round.

✕ **Molly's Mill.** 221 S. Monroe St.; 814-827-6597 $
Part of the same complex as Casey's Caboose Stop, this restaurant is in an 1890s renovated grain mill .It's where the local Kiwanis, Lions, and Rotary clubs meet. Create-your-own pasta, Grandma's chicken and biscuits, and sandwiches.

☶ **Casey's Caboose Stop.** 221 S. Monroe St.; 814-827-6597 $
Real cabooses, from 21 different trains, have been converted into unique, comfortable overnight units with modern amenities.

☶ **Cross Creek Resort.** Rte. 8, 4 miles south of Titusville; 800-461-3173 or 814-827-9611 $$$
Hiking, biking, cross country skiing, and, especially, golf, are the attractions.

27-hole course. Modern lodge with 94 rooms. Postcard setting, especially in October.

Troy map C-1

GOLDEN OAK INN

☒ **Golden Oak Inn Bed and Breakfast.** 196 Canton St.; 570-297-4315 or 800-326-9834 $$
The Queen Anne home, circa 1901, has charming oak woodwork, Victorian decor, and antiques. The inn is 24 miles from the New York border, making it close to the Corning Glass Center and several universities. In Pennsylvania, it's close to the Bradford Heritage Museum. Full breakfast included.

Union Dale map D-1

✗ **Stonebridge Inn & Restaurant.** R.R. 3; 570-679-9200 $$
Although built in 1979, this complex has the look of a small European village—a quaint, Bavarian hideaway. Situated atop nearly 200 acres traversed by a small trout stream, the inn is

minutes from Elk Mountain, a fine ski resort. The 13 rooms are handsomely decorated; continental breakfast is included. The restaurant serves formal cuisine; dinner Wednesday to Sunday.

Uniontown map A-3

☒ **B&B Inn of the Princess.** 181 W. Main St., or Rte. 40; 724-425-0120 $$$
Named after the former owner, Princess Lida of Thurn und Taxis, this inn has five rooms with large private bathrooms, Mission-style furnishings, and Porthault linens. Associated with Chez Gerard restaurant in nearby Hopwood. Includes breakfast and tea.

Volant map A-2

✗ **Dumplin Haus.** Route 208, 4 miles east of New Wilmington; 724-533-3732 $
Quaint eatery with home-style cooking in an old-fashioned Main Street setting in Amish country. Surrounded by gift shops. Appease your appetite for apple dumplings and cinnamon rolls here.

Washington map A-3

✗ **Angelo's.** 955 W. Chestnut St.; 724-222-7120 $-$$
Popular landmark, started in 1939 by Passalacqua family. Third generation of family serves "inventive regional Italian cuisine," including terrific flatbread appetizers and Pasta Lacqua, a simple, flavorful vegetarian topping on green and white fettuccine.

Washington Crossing *map D-3*

✗ **Washington Crossing Inn.** River Rd. (Rtes. 32 and 532), 215-493-3634 $-$$
Enjoy colonial charm at this distinctively picturesque inn, adjacent to Washington Crossing Historic Park. Fine casual dining on traditional cuisine. Candlelit intimate dining rooms with fireplaces. Martha's lounge offers cocktails and live music. Lunch, dinner; closed Monday.

Wilkes-Barre *map D-2*

✗ **Martini Ristorante & Bar.** Union and N. Main Sts.; 570-829-0000 $-$$$
A wood-fired oven and grill gives a great taste to the fresh fish, steak, and pizza at this downtown restaurant known also for its one-pound veal chop (featured in *Bon Appetit)*. The bar features martinis; the non-smoking dining area has a separately ventilated humidor area for cigar smoking in big overstuffed chairs. Lunch and dinner; closed Sunday.

⌂ **East Mountain Inn Best Western.** 2400 East End Blvd. (Exit 47-A off I-81), 570-822-1011; $-$$
Rooms in this slate-and-terra-cotta highrise hostelry have an expansive view of the valley. The hotel is atop a foothill to the Poconos. The lobby and guest rooms have a modern decor, and there are two restaurants in the hotel open daily. Large indoor pool, whirlpool, and sauna.

✗ **Bischwind Bed & Breakfast.** One Coach Rd., Box 7, Bear Creek; 570-472-3820 $$$

This 1890s English Tudor manor has an English garden, rooms with fireplaces, and a swimming pool. History buffs will love eating in the Presidential Dining Room, which has hosted Theodore Roosevelt, William Howard Taft, and helicopter tycoon Igor Sikorsky. Four-course breakfast included. Trails lead amid tall pines around a hundred-acre lake.

Wyalusing *map C-1*

⌂ **Browning Farms Bed and Breakfast.** Rte. 706, Wyalusing; 888-200-0423 or 570-746-1243 $
"Family Farm Fun" is the premise behind a stay at this working farm. There are small farm animals to feed and play with and other outdoor diversions such as hayrides, gardens, fishing, boating, and hiking. The six guest rooms are decorated in flowered chintz.

WYALUSING HOTEL

⌂ **Wyalusing Hotel.** 111 Main St.; 570-746-1204 $$
This historic property has been a hotel since 1860 when it was named the Brown Hotel for its architect. Brown is

FOOD & LODGING

known as the "Gingerbread Man" for his talent with delicately cut wood and decorative facades. The hotel's porches look like a Mississippi riverboat. Two eateries: a dining room and a barroom offering casual fare.

York *map C-3*

✗ **Central Market House.** 34 W. Philadelphia St; 717-848-2243 $
For more than 111 years, this large, high-ceiling brick edifice has housed stalls offering produce, meat, seafood, flowers, and handicrafts. Today there are 70 vendors, some offering deli foods, hand-rolled pretzels, bakery items, and hot sandwiches. Open Tuesday to Saturday, 6 A.M. to 3 P.M.

✗ **Isaac's Restaurant & Deli Inc.**
The Village at Meadowbrook, 2960 Whiteford Rd.; 717-751-0515 $
This spiffy eatery is decorated in forest green, light wood, and brass. Sandwiches, pita pizzas, and a variety of healthful foods are offered at reasonable prices.

✗ **Old Country Buffet.** 905 Loucks Rd.; 717-846-6330 $
This family-style all-you-can-eat buffet has a higher quality of food than most. The food is all made from scratch in small batches; offerings change daily.

✗ **Roosevelt Tavern.** 400 W. Philadelphia St.; 717-854-7725 $$
For more than 60 years, a tavern or tap room has existed in this 1860s historic building. It was a speakeasy fronting as a cigar store during Prohibition. Today's menu includes flounder, crab cakes, and other seafood; and meats including steaks, chicken, and veal.

✗ **Commonwealth Room.** In the Yorktowne Hotel, 48 E. Market St.; 717-848-1111 $-$$$
The Yorktowne Hotel's fanciest restaurant, the Commonwealth Room, has the best food in York. Brass chandeliers, ceiling-high mirrors, and upholstered chairs surround the tables. Sophisticated American cuisine is offered a la carte and prix fixe (lunch and dinner). Less expensive, more casual dining for breakfast, lunch, and dinner is available in the hotel's second dining room, **Autographs**.

🏠 **Past Purr-fect Bed & Breakfast.**
216 N. Main St., Jacobus; 717-428-1634 $$
This late 1800s Victorian-style home is actually a lovely bed-and-breakfast with large flower gardens, a pond, and majestic trees. Other attractive features are a screened porch, handcrafted oak floors, and, of course, copious cat motifs.

🏠 **Yorktowne Hotel.** 48 E. Market St.; 717-848-1111 $-$$
This beautifully restored hotel, built in 1925 and now a National Historic Landmark, has 161 rooms—seven with whirlpool tubs—furnished with period reproductions. There's also a fitness center and two restaurants that also deliver room service.

Food & Lodging map, page 276; index of listings by region/chapter, page 277.

TRAVEL INFORMATION

PENNSYLVANIA CLIMATE CHART

CITY	*Temperature (degrees F)*					*Precipitation (inches)*				
	JAN.	APR.	JUL.	OCT.	H/L	JAN.	APR.	JUL.	OCT.	R/S
Philadelphia	39/24	63/42	86/67	68/48	106/-11	3.2	3.5	4.1	2.7	41/22
Lancaster	37/22	61/38	87/65	68/44	107/-27	3.2	3.4	4.7	3.0	41/28
Scranton	32/19	59/39	81/60	61/41	101/-21	2.3	3.3	3.8	2.8	37/44
Harrisburg	37/21	61/41	85/65	65/45	107/-22	2.8	3.2	3.5	2.8	39/35
State College	34/19	58/37	82/61	62/40	102/-20	3.1	3.6	3.9	2.4	37/51
Bradford	28/17	52/35	77/59	59/38	100/-24	3.4	3.6	3.8	3.4	42/95
Pittsburgh	35/20	60/40	82/61	63/43	103/-22	2.8	3.3	3.8	2.4	37/43
Erie	32/20	53/38	79/60	60/45	100/-18	2.4	3.3	3.4	3.6	41/81

METRIC CONVERSIONS

To convert feet (ft) to meters (m), multiply feet by .305. To convert meters to feet, multiply meters by 3.28.

1 ft = .30 m	1 m = 3.3 ft
2 ft = .61 m	2 m = 6.6 ft
3 ft = .91 m	3 m = 9.8 ft
4 ft = 1.2 m	4 m = 13.1 ft
5 ft = 1.5 m	5 m = 16.4 ft

To convert miles (mi) to kilometers (km), multiply miles by .62. To convert kilometers to miles, multiply kilometers by 1.61.

1 mi = 1.6 km	1 km = .62 mi
2 mi = 3.2 km	2 km = 1.2 mi
3 mi = 4.8 km	3 km = 1.9 mi
4 mi = 6.4 km	4 km = 2.5 mi
5 mi = 8.1 km	5 km = 3.1 mi

To convert pounds (lb) to kilograms (kg), multiply pounds by .46. To convert kilograms to pounds, multiply pounds by 2.2.

1 lb = .45 kg	1 kg = 2.2 lbs
2 lbs = .91 kg	2 kg = 4.4 lbs
3 lbs = 1.4 kg	3 kg = 6.6 lbs
4 lbs = 1.8 kg	4 kg = 8.8 lbs

To convert degrees Fahrenheit (°F) to Celsius (°C), subtract 32 from degrees F and multiply by .56. To convert degrees C to degrees F, multiply degrees C by 1.8 and add 32.

0°F = -17.8°C	60°F = 15.5°C
10°F = -12.2°C	70°F = 21.1°C
32°F = 0°C	80°F = 26.7°C
40°F = +4.4°C	90°F = 32.2°C
50°F = +10.0°C	98.6°F = 37.0°C

■ VISITOR INFORMATION

Brandywine Valley/Chester County:
800-228-9933;
www.brandywinevalley.com

Bucks County:
800-222-4757; www.bctc.org

Delaware Water Gap:
800-995-0969; www.visithhc.com

Gettysburg:
717-334-6274; www.gettysburg.com

Harrisburg/Hershey:
800-995-0969; www.visithhc.com

Lancaster County:
717-299-8901; www.800padutch.com

Laurel Highlands:
800-925-7669; www.laurelhighlands.org

Lehigh Valley:
800-747-0561; www.lehighvalleypa.org

Philadelphia:
800-537-7676; www.libertynet.org/phila

Pittsburgh:
800-821-1888; www.pittsburgh-cvb.org

Poconos:
800-762-6667; www.poconos.org

Reading Area/Berks County:
800-443-6610; www.readingberkspa.com

■ PENNSYLVANIA OUTDOORS

For a detailed overview on outdoor recreation throughout the state, including links to numerous excellent outdoor websites, check out the Pennsylvania Department of Conservation and Natural Resources online at **www.dcnr.state.pa.us.**

◆ HIKING AND BACKPACKING

One of the best places to get information on hiking is the **Keystone Trails Association** (800-876-3455; www.pennaweb.com) a hiking club which can provide maps and suggestions for hikes throughout the state. The *50 Hikes in Pennsylvania* guidebook series, with three different volumes—Eastern, Central, and Western—is also a good source, and the books can be ordered by credit card through The Countryman Press at 800-245-4151.

◆ RAILS TO TRAILS

The Washington, D.C.-based Rails-to-Trails Conservancy is a non-profit, nationwide organization dedicated to creating a network of multi-use, public trails out of abandoned and reclaimed railroad beds. Pennsylvania boasts more than 150 official Rails-to-Trails pathways, totaling more than 850 miles of hiking, biking, and cross-country skiing trails throughout the state. For more information, call the Conservancy's Pennsylvania field office in Harrisburg at 717-238-1717.

I N D E X

COMPASS AMERICAN GUIDES

Ordering Information: COMPASS AMERICAN GUIDES are available in general and travel bookstores, or may be ordered directly by calling (800) 733-3000. Please use the ISBN numbers below when ordering to expedite your purchase.

Alaska (2nd edition)	$19.95 ($27.95 Can)	0-679-00230-8
Arizona (5th edition)	$19.95 ($29.95 Can)	0-679-00432-7
Boston (2nd edition)	$19.95 ($27.95 Can)	0-679-00284-7
Chicago (2nd edition)	$18.95 ($26.50 Can)	1-878-86780-6
Coastal California (1st ed)	$19.95 ($27.95 Can)	0-679-03598-2
Colorado (4th edition)	$18.95 ($26.50 Can)	0-679-00027-5
Florida (1st edition)	$19.95 ($27.95 Can)	0-679-93392-0
Georgia (1st edition)	$19.95 ($29.95 Can)	0-679-00245-6
Hawaii (4th edition)	$19.95 ($27.95 Can)	0-679-00226-X
Idaho (1st edition)	$18.95 ($26.50 Can)	1-878-86778-4
Las Vegas (6th edition)	$19.95 ($29.95 Can)	0-679-00370-3
Maine (2nd edition)	$18.95 ($26.50 Can)	1-878-86796-2
Manhattan (3rd ed)	$19.95 ($29.95 Can)	0-679-00228-6
Minnesota (1st edition)	$18.95 ($26.50 Can)	1-878-86748-2
Montana (4th edition)	$19.95 ($29.95 Can)	0-679-00281-2
New Mexico (3rd ed)	$18.95 ($26.50 Can)	0-679-00031-3
New Orleans (3rd ed)	$18.95 ($26.50 Can)	0-679-03597-4
North Carolina (2nd ed)	$19.95 ($26.50 Can)	0-679-00508-0
Oregon (3rd edition)	$19.95 ($27.95 Can)	0-679-00033-X
Pacific Northwest (2nd ed)	$19.95 ($27.95 Can)	0-679-00283-9
San Francisco (5th ed)	$19.95 ($29.95 Can)	0-679-00229-4
Santa Fe (2nd edition)	$19.95 ($26.50 Can)	0-679-00286-3
South Carolina (2nd ed)	$18.95 ($26.50 Can)	0-679-03599-0
South Dakota (2nd ed)	$18.95 ($26.50 Can)	1-878-86747-4
Southern New England (1st ed)	$19.95 ($27.95 Can)	0-679-00184-0
Southwest (2nd ed)	$18.95 ($26.50 Can)	0-679-00035-6
Texas (2nd edition)	$18.95 ($26.50 Can)	1-878-86798-9
Underwater Wonders of Nat'l Parks	$19.95 ($27.95 Can)	0-679-03386-6
Utah (4th edition)	$18.95 ($26.50 Can)	0-679-00030-5
Virginia (3rd edition)	$19.95 ($29.95 Can)	0-679-00282-0
Washington (2nd ed)	$19.95 ($27.95 Can)	1-878-86799-7
Wine Country (2nd ed)	$19.95 ($27.95 Can)	0-679-00032-1
Wisconsin (2nd ed)	$18.95 ($26.50 Can)	1-878-86749-0
Wyoming (3rd edition)	$19.95 ($27.95 Can)	0-679-00034-8

COMPASS AMERICAN GUIDES

Critics, booksellers, and travelers all agree: you're lost without a Compass.

"This splendid series provides exactly the sort of historical and cultural detail about North American destinations that curious-minded travelers need."
—*Washington Post*

"This is a series that constantly stuns us; our whole past book reviewer experience says no guide with photos this good should have writing this good. But it does."
—*New York Daily News*

"Of the many guidebooks on the market, few are as visually stimulating, as thoroughly researched, or as lively written as the Compass American Guides series."
—*Chicago Tribune*

"Good to read ahead of time, then take along so you don't miss anything."
—*San Diego Magazine*

NEW FROM COMPASS:

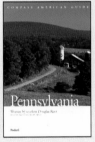

Vermont	Southern New England	Georgia	Pennsylvania
$19.95 ($27.95 Can)	$19.95 ($29.95 Can)	$19.95 ($29.95 Can)	$19.95 ($29.95 Can)
0-679-00183-2	0-679-00184-0	0-679-00245-6	0-679-00182-4

Compass American Guides are available in general and travel bookstores, or may be ordered directly by calling (800) 733-3000. Please provide title and ISBN when ordering.

■ ABOUT THE AUTHOR

A graduate of Pennsylvania State University, Douglas Root has written for several newspapers including *The Pittsburgh Press,* where he was an award-winning writer for the Sunday magazine. He received an Alicia Patterson Foundation fellowship for documentary journalism, and he has written for *TIME, The Washington Post, Washingtonian, The Philadelphia Inquirer,* and *Mother Jones.* A resident of Pittsburgh for the past 20 years, Root is now director of communications and intergovernmental relations for the city.

CONTRIBUTORS

Cici Williamson, a food columnist who has published articles in dozens of newspapers and travel magazines, provided the food and lodging recommendations in this book for eastern and central Pennsylvania, and added insights on the Poconos and on the towns of the lower Delaware River and of the Brandywine Valley. **Woodene Merriman,** longtime food editor of the *Pittsburgh Gazette,* contributed food and lodging information for western Pennsylvania. Attorney **Walter Cohen** of Harrisburg, at one time acting attorney general of Pennsylvania, reviewed this book and contributed his insights.

■ ABOUT THE PHOTOGRAPHER

A Lancaster County resident, Jerry Irwin is a nationally recognized photographer known especially for his images of the Amish. His photo-articles have appeared in *National Geographic, LIFE, Country Journal,* German and French *GEO,* and numerous other publications. A former locomotive engineer with the old Pennsylvania Railroad, Irwin has also been an active skydiver for 30 years.